C. C. WANG

LINES OF ABSTRACTION

C. C. WANG

LINES OF ABSTRACTION

Edited by Wen-shing Chou and Daniel M. Greenberg

HUNTER COLLEGE
ART GALLERIES

HIRMER

WAM
UNIVERSITY OF MINNESOTA

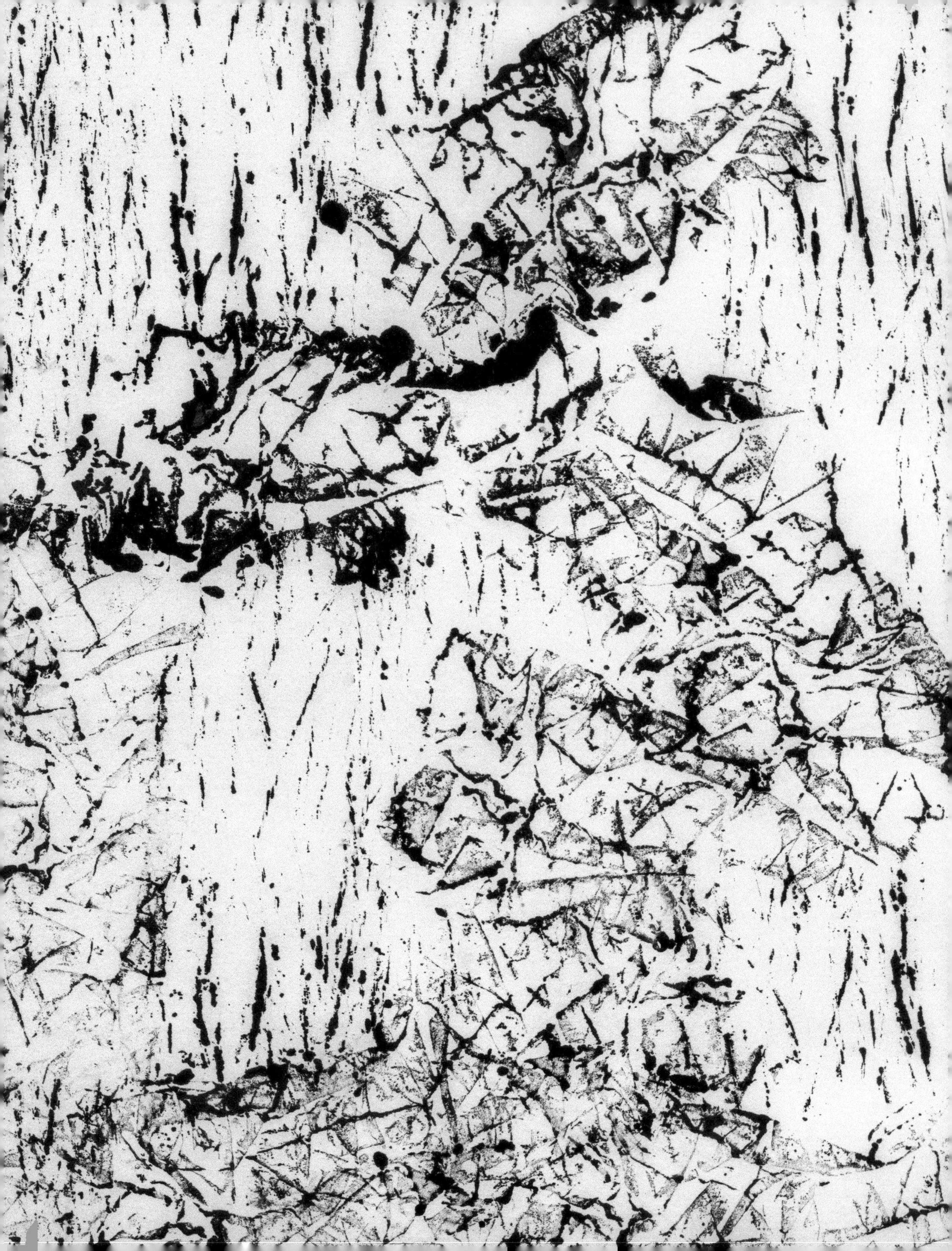

CONTENTS

Detail of no title (Landscape No. 970-B), 1987, pl. 9.

FOREWORD

This publication, *C. C. Wang: Lines of Abstraction*, and the exhibition it accompanies (presented at the Hunter College Art Galleries' Bertha and Karl Leubsdorf Gallery, February 2–April 29, 2023) are exemplary products of Hunter's Advanced Certificate in Curatorial Studies. Established in 2015, the graduate Certificate in Curatorial Studies formalized the curatorial training already taking place in the Department of Art and Art History, acknowledging the curatorial ambitions of our students, faculty, and curatorial staff of the Hunter College Art Galleries. In 2022 the college received a generous grant from the Wolf Kahn Foundation and Emily Mason and Alice Trumbull Mason Foundation on behalf of artists Emily Mason and Wolf Kahn in support of our curatorial certificate publications. We are thrilled that *C. C. Wang: Lines of Abstraction* is the first publication of many to come that will benefit from this incredible gift. The books that the Hunter College Art Galleries produce in association with Hirmer Publishers provide the opportunity for our MA Art History and MFA Studio Art students to contribute well-researched, timely texts to scholarly publications, positioning them in dialogue with leading scholars in the field.

Centered on the artistic experimentations of C. C. Wang 王己千 (Wang Chi-ch'ien, 1907–2003), *Lines of Abstraction* is the culmination of an exciting collaboration between Hunter College Professor Wen-shing Chou and her graduate curatorial practicum students and University of Minnesota Professor Daniel M. Greenberg and his undergraduate students. Edited by Professors Chou and Greenberg, the publication features essays by Arnold Chang, artist, scholar, and former student of C. C. Wang; Joseph Scheier-Dolberg, Oscar Tang and Agnes Hsu-Tang Associate Curator of Chinese Painting and Calligraphy at the Metropolitan Museum of Art; Margaret Liu Clinton, Hunter College MA Art History candidate and Hofmann Graduate Curatorial Fellow; and University of Minnesota undergraduate student Jordan Homstad. The book also includes contributions by Hunter MA Art History students Thais Bignardi-Engstrom, Carolyn Bishop, Jeremy Gloster, Lindsey Poremba, and Mia Ye. We are deeply appreciative to the Weisman Art Museum at the University of Minnesota for their support of this publication and for the opportunity to highlight the important scholarship of our faculty and students.

At Hunter we are committed to developing publications that engage critical conversations and contemporary creative practice, and to developing exhibitions as a crucial mode of art historical research and recovery. Seen as the last in a centuries-old line of Chinese scholar-artists, C. C. Wang was long recognized as a preeminent twentieth-century connoisseur and collector of pre-modern Chinese art. He developed a lifelong relationship with the Metropolitan Museum of Art, serving as an appraiser and consultant. The Met arranged to purchase masterpieces from the C. C. Wang Family collection, which helped to create the museum's world-class collection of Chinese art. While he was less well known as an artist, C. C. Wang never stopped exploring with brush and ink, honing his technique and pushing his materials. Held twenty years after the artist's passing, *C. C. Wang: Lines of Abstraction* recenters Wang's extraordinary career on his own artistic practice, highlighting his profound and critical engagement with Chinese ink painting and his eagerness to experiment with tradition. While the exhibition's framework focuses on the study of a Chinese, and subsequently Chinese American, artist in postwar New York, we believe this exhibition presents an excellent opportunity for conversations about artistic exchange and the conditions of diaspora across cultures.

Our students benefited greatly from the opportunity to study C. C. Wang's work in person, meeting and learning from experts. We extend our deep appreciation to Arnold Chang, Freda Murck, Kathleen Yang, Fu Qiumeng, Joseph Scheier-Dolberg, and Benjamin Weiss for their participation in the pedagogical process of creating an exhibition and publication through a graduate seminar. This project would not have been possible without the generosity of the exhibition lenders, C. C. Wang's family, and the Estate of C. C. Wang. We also recognize the extraordinary work that Professors Chou and Greenberg and their students have put into realizing *C. C. Wang: Lines of Abstraction*, and the work of the Hunter College Art Galleries' staff.

Additional support for *C. C. Wang: Lines of Abstraction* is made possible by the James Howell Foundation, the Leubsdorf Fund, and the Renate, Hans, and Maria Hofmann Trust, and we extend our gratitude for their commitment to Hunter. Lastly, we acknowledge Hunter College President Jennifer J. Raab, Bershad Professor of Art History and Director of the Hunter College Art Galleries Joachim Pissarro, and Director of the Advanced Certificate in Curatorial Studies Professor Harper Montgomery for their unwavering championing of the curatorial work of our students and faculty.

Howard Singerman

Phyllis and Joseph Caroff Chair, Department of Art and Art History, Hunter College
Executive Director, Hunter College Art Galleries

Sarah Watson

Chief Curator & Director of Administration, Hunter College Art Galleries

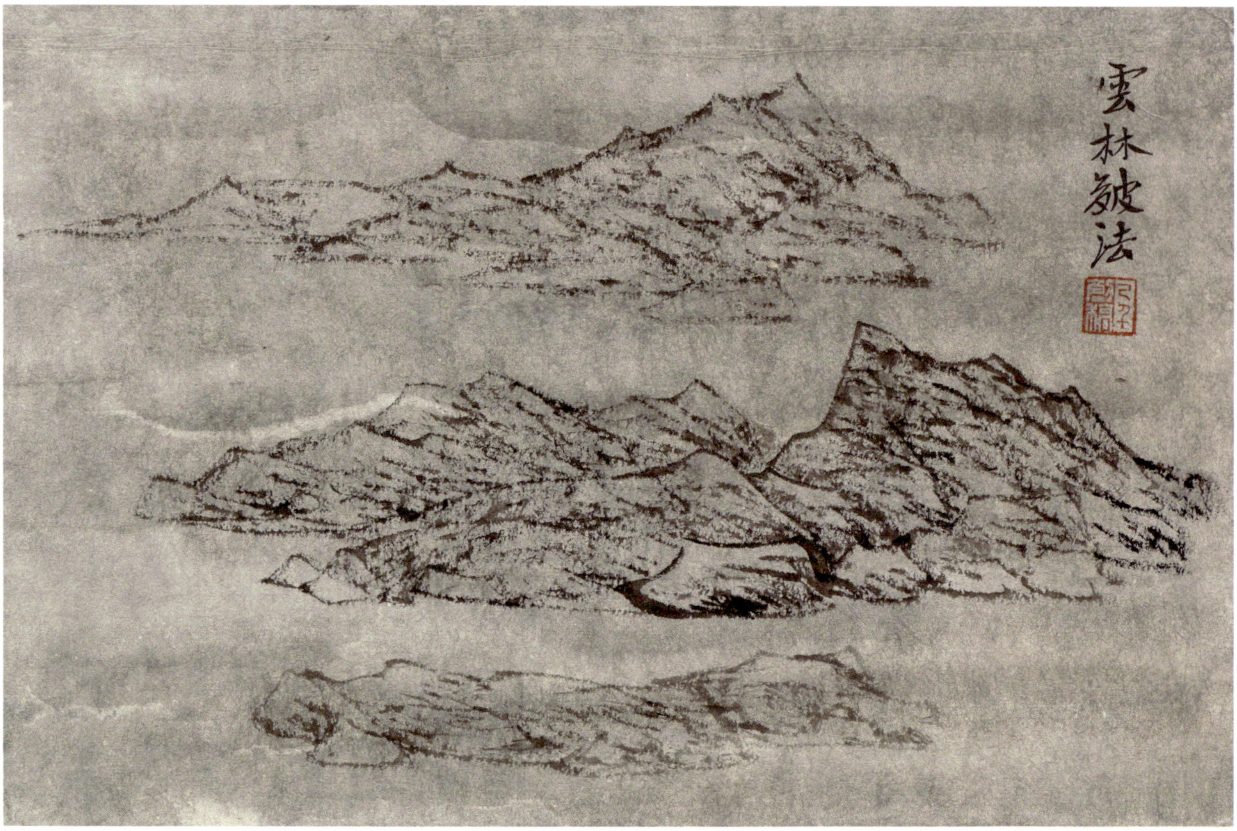

Fig. 1. Demonstration of Ni Zan's textured brush in *C. C. Wang's Instructional Manual of Brushwork*, undated (ca. 2000–2002). Album of 17 painted leaves; ink on paper, 9 ¼ × 13 ¾ inches (23.5 × 34.9 cm). Courtesy Private Collection. Inscription: 雲林皴法 "Texture strokes in the style of Yunlin (Ni Zan, 1301–1374)." Seal: 己千創稿 "Sketches created by Jiqian."

C. C. Wang's Art of Kinesthetic Knowing

WEN-SHING CHOU

> "If you really want to grasp the true essence of brushwork (*bimo*), you must experiment with the brush yourself. Why is it that I can discern a work by Ni Zan by seeing only one corner of a painting by him? Because I have already immersed myself in his works and have practiced with my own hand many hundreds of times; I am familiar with every twist and turn of his wrist, and the rhythm and motion of its increasing or decreasing pressure."—C. C. Wang[1]

The unity between connoisseurship and art practice emerges as one of the central themes in a book of conversations between C. C. Wang 王己千 (Wang Chi-ch'ien, Wang Jiqian, 1907–2003) and the art historian Joan Stanley-Baker (Xu Xiaohu 徐小虎).[2] In the selection above, Wang explains that his familiarity with Ni Zan 倪瓚 (1301–1374), one of the most revered literati painters (the scholar-artists of dynastic China), comes from wielding the brush just as the fourteenth-century painter did, hundreds of times (fig. 1). When Stanley-Baker presses, "Isn't this sort of exercise basically for creating forgery?," Wang's reply clarifies his purpose: "No. Perhaps traditional books and Western scholars all insist that Chinese painting is merely 'copying ancients' or 'always repeating what someone else has done.' But in fact, what we hold to be most precious are the fresh elements and the contributions of the individual. These fresh elements should not be simply fashionable or without any basis. Instead, they should contain within them experience of the past."[3]

So vast and wide-ranging are the past experiences encompassed by Wang's own artistic repertoire that his art over the span of seven decades becomes a unique portal for discerning layers of embodied knowledge. The exhibition

C. C. Wang: Lines of Abstraction, on view at the Hunter College Art Galleries' Leubsdorf Gallery from February 2 to April 29, 2023, showcases Wang's lifelong search for the past and future of the ink painting tradition through a deeply personal art practice. Featuring works from six private collections, the retrospective presents many of the artist's lesser-known works that exemplify his continued dialogue with numerous traditions across the span of seven decades, from Republican-era Shanghai (1911–49) to postwar New York, where he arrived in 1949 and where he would spend the majority of his time during the rest of his life. Wang's own fame as a connoisseur, collector, and tastemaker have often overshadowed his reputation as an artist. *Lines of Abstraction* sets out to recenter Wang's painting practice as an unparalleled quest for "kinesthetic knowing," which formed the basis of his artistic and art historical contributions.

I introduce kinesthetic knowing as an overarching framework for understanding the trajectory of Wang's long career.[4] Denoting a way of possessing and processing knowledge through embodied practice, kinesthetic knowing can be seen as a throughline across his diverse and versatile experimentations: beginning with the practice of copying old paintings and emulating the style of prior masters in his formative years in Shanghai; continuing through sensitive explorations of medium and materiality; then a recovery of order partly through chance methods of mark making; and, finally, the distillation and abstraction of painterly and calligraphic lines and dots that retain the movement and rhythm—the kinesthetic memory—of a lifelong practice of the brush. Viewed together, works in the exhibition display Wang's quest for an individual and modern expression through his deepening study of traditions via tactile, physical, and experiential means. This trajectory of Wang's practice also makes clear that issues of surface, materiality, chance, and abstraction, which guided his exploration, were in every way as central to the artistic language of postwar abstraction as they were to developments in Chinese literati art, even if the latter had not been previously defined by those same terms and categories. To reconsider Wang's work at the intersection of these movements and traditions is therefore to recover a story of postwar New York as a cosmopolitan junction where abstraction flourished and where Chinese literati art and theories first gained their critical recognition in the West.

Wang's substantial engagement with Chinese painting history and his breakthrough transformation have been the subject of numerous insightful studies.[5] But neither the narrative of Wang as the last literati artist nor that of him as an émigré who bridged traditional Chinese painting with Western modernism sufficiently accounts for the evolving definitions of literati art, modernism, and abstraction. What has yet to be unpacked is the entanglement of literati art, modernism, and abstraction in the twentieth century—a history in which Wang's artistic, connoisseurial, and collecting endeavors played no small part.[6] Subsequent essays in this volume explore Wang's diverse oeuvre through the lens of the shifting paradigms of the global twentieth century. Each chapter presents a different facet of the artist's multidimensional career that has yet to be considered in depth: Daniel M. Greenberg meditates on Wang's "deconstruction" of traditional Chinese painting and calligraphy through his use of line; Margaret Liu Clinton dismantles the narrative of Wang's connection to abstract expressionism to recover his distinct contribution to the artistic landscape of postwar New York; Jordan Homstad approaches a later phase in Wang's career through his engagement with New York City's urban street art; Joseph Scheier-Dolberg reevaluates Wang's impact on the field of Chinese painting history; and, finally, Arnold Chang recollects Wang's transformative mentorship as a contemporary ink painter.

Copying and Emulation

Wang's unique upbringing as a member of the last generation educated in the classical tradition of scholar-officials of dynastic China and his formative years in Republican Shanghai under the tutelage of the painter and collector Wu Hufan 吳湖帆 (1894–1968) have been well chronicled.[7] Having come of age before museums and photographic reproductions became viable options for the study of paintings, Wang was first exposed to painters of the so-called Orthodox Painting School of the Qing dynasty and their lineage of painters through his teachers and their circles of artists, collectors, and dealers.[8] Then, by serving on the selection committee of the 1935 Burlington House exhibition of Chinese art in London, the first exhibition abroad of art from the former imperial collection, Wang learned about the masterpieces of the Song and Yuan dynasties. Wang's collaboration with the German art historian Victoria Contag on the innovative and monumental seal dictionary further widened his knowledge of Ming and Qing art.[9] These experiences led the art historian Jerome Silbergeld to conclude that, "by 1940, while still in his thirties and before seeing any Western collections, C. C. Wang had probably seen as much of China's best painting as any man in history."[10]

If Wang rarely published studies on paintings, it is because his knowledge was principally tactile and experiential.[11] The tremendous impact of those early

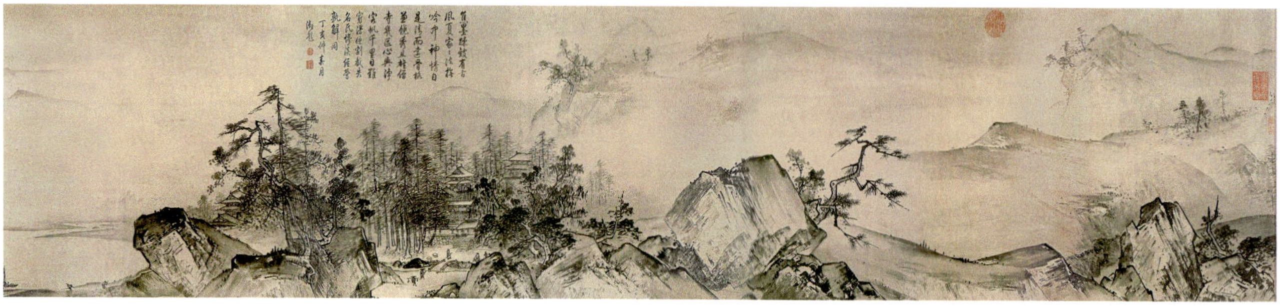

and close encounters with Chinese painting is therefore best reflected in Wang's own paintings from the period (figs. 3, 4; pls. 1a–c, 2). His formidable knowledge and subsequent collection of paintings were amassed to service his own painting practice, and later, those of his students.[12] Throughout his time in Shanghai, both as a student and later as a teacher, this kinesthetic form of knowledge was strictly expressed through the act of copying and emulation. In 1934, at the studio of his teacher Wu Hufan, Wang copied a scroll by the late-Ming artist, theorist, collector, and politician Dong Qichang 董其昌 (1555–1636) (pl. 1c), whose art, theories, principles of brushwork, and study of old masters were embraced as orthodoxy by the eponymous Orthodox School.[13] As the original inscription by Dong Qichang—which Wang faithfully copied—indicates, that painting was itself an emulation of works by the painters Zhao Gan 趙幹 (fl. mid-10th century) and Li Tang 李唐 (ca. 1066–1150). By copying Dong Qichang's original work (now lost along with many others in Wu's collection), Wang was fulfilling a time-honored tradition for generations of artists in dynastic China that was as foundational as it was exclusive, accessible only to the privileged few who had the social connections to see original works in private hands.

Yet technological changes also brought about new possibilities during the same period. Mounted to the same handscroll as Wang's copy of Dong Qichang's painting are two other works: an undated copy of a second painting attributed to Dong Qichang (pl. 1b) and a 1937 copy of *Pure and Remote View of Streams and Mountains* by the Song dynasty painter Xia Gui 夏圭 (fl. 1180–1224) in the National Palace Museum (pl. 1a; fig. 2). In his role as an advisor to the Burlington House exhibit, Wang would have seen Xia Gui's painting for the first time in 1935 while it was in temporary storage. But judging from the fact that Wang's copy was completed in his own studio and by how closely it nonetheless

Fig. 2 (above). Xia Gui. A section from *Pure and Remote View of Streams and Mountains*, ca. 1200. Handscroll; ink on paper, overall 18 ¼ × 137 ¾ inches (46.4 × 349.9 cm). National Palace Museum, Taipei.

Fig. 3 (right). C. C. Wang. *Western Stone Pillar Waterfall of the Yandang Mountains*, 1934. Folding fan; ink and color on paper mounted on wood, 18 ¼ × 12 ⅛ inches (46.4 × 30.8 cm). Collection of Mr. and Mrs. Arnold Chang. Inscription: 寫雁蕩西石梁瀑一角,甲戌五月,奉穀孫先生法正,莫釐王遷 "Painted a view of the West Shiliang Waterfall in Yandang [Mountain] in the fifth month of the *jiashu* year, presented to Master Gusun for correction, [by] Wang Qian from Moli." Seal: 王遷 Wang Qian.

follows the beginning section of the original in composition, Wang likely based his copy on a photographic facsimile, rather than relying on his memory of what would have been a brief viewing. Advancement in collotype prints had made reproductions of artworks such as *Pure and Remote View* more widely available and also made possible, for the first time, the close copy of a work from an imperial collection.[14] If works in any medium or materials are conducive to black-and-white collotype reproduction, foremost among them would be the monochromatic ink paintings on paper that were favored by generations of literati painters. The richly layered tonality, subtle texture, and cohesive composition were treasured aspects of *Pure and Remote View* that remained evident, if only partially, through monochromatically toned collotype reproduction.[15]

Wang also created works in the popular format of fan paintings and hanging scrolls that emulate the restrained brushwork and the tightly structured compositions of painters of the Qing Orthodox School (figs. 3, 4).[16] Compare,

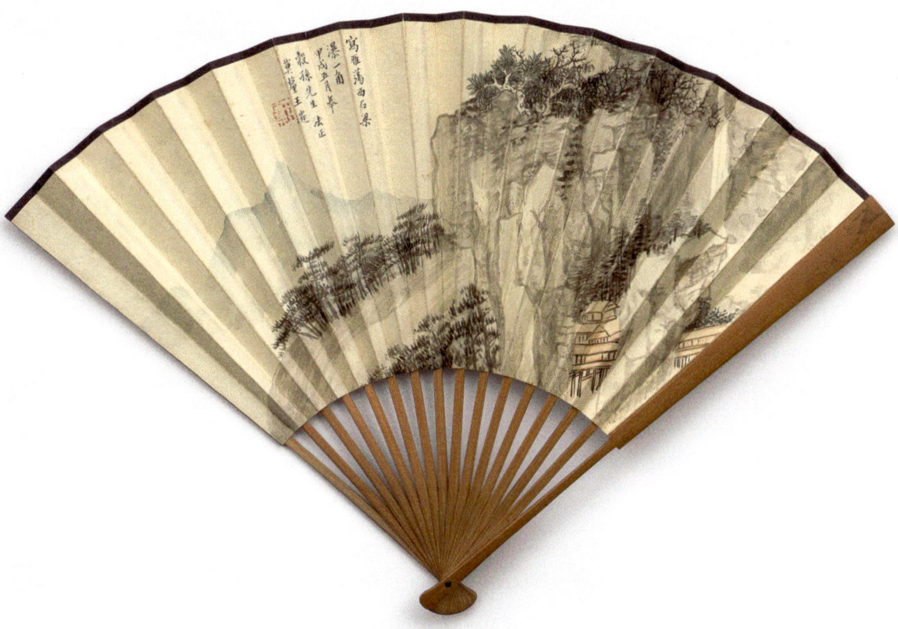

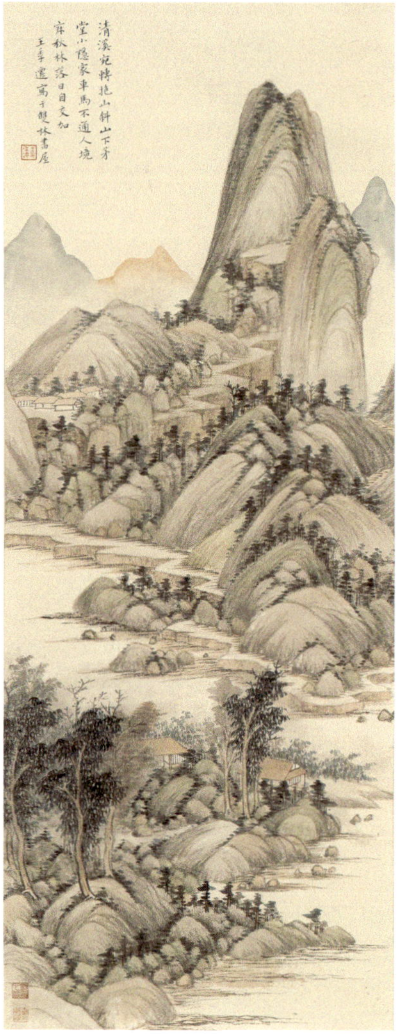

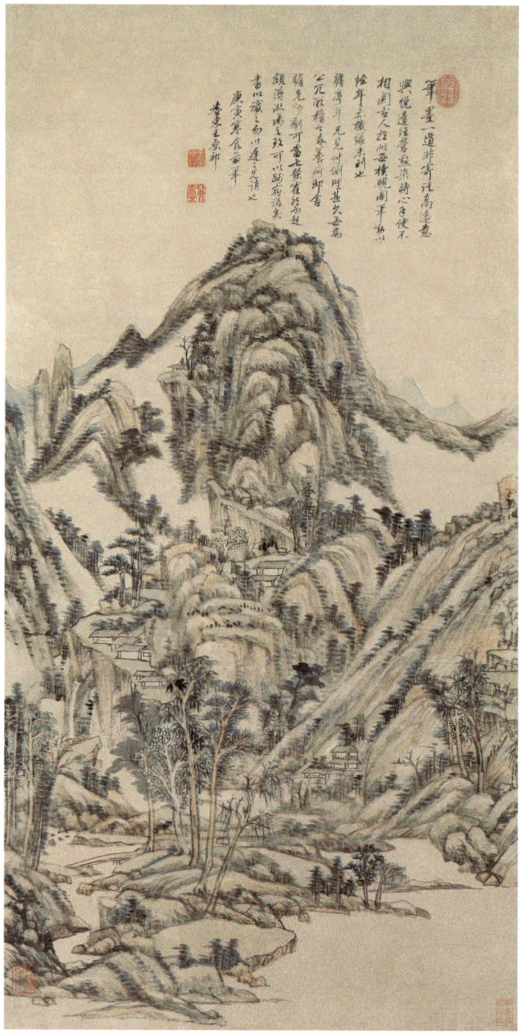

for example, a painting by C. C. Wang with one by Wang Yuanqi 王原祁 (1642–1715), a leading figure of the Orthodox School (fig. 5). Every brushstroke, every subtle use of color and texture, and every form rendered is tightly and sensitively woven with the others to create an ordered and cohesive world on the surface of the paper. The primary goal was to display the control, discipline, and fluency that is required to generate an original yet systematic variation in accordance with the strictures of the Orthodox School.

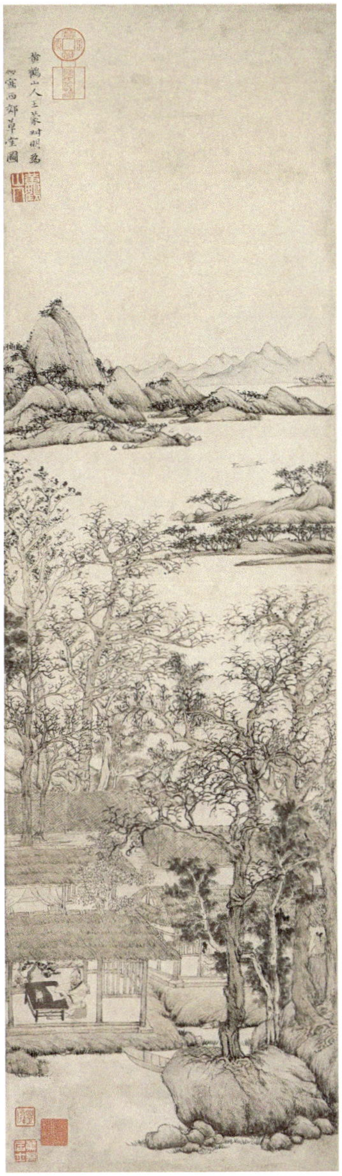

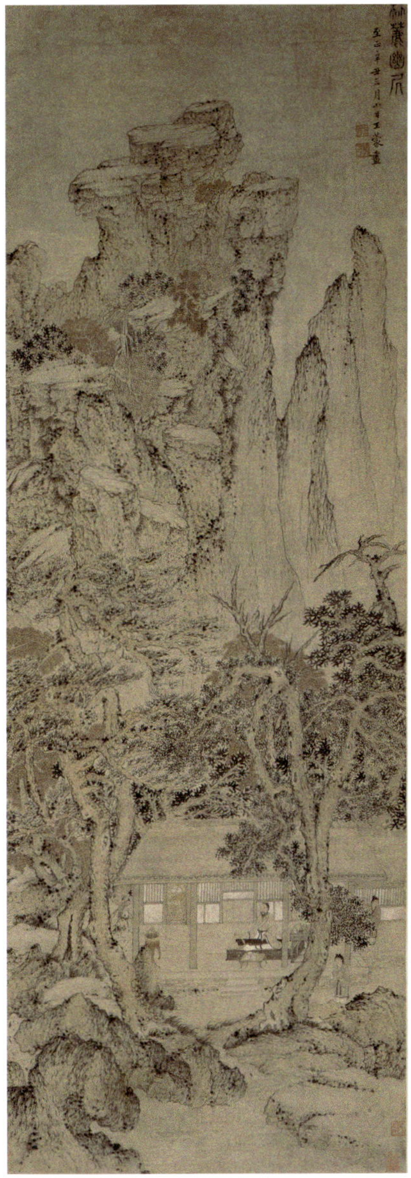

Fig. 4 (far left). C. C. Wang. no title (Landscape), undated (before 1949). Hanging scroll; ink and color on paper, 34 ⅜ × 12 ⅞ inches (87.3 × 32.7 cm). Collection of Mr. and Mrs. Arnold Chang. Inscription: 清溪宛轉抱山斜,山下茅堂小隱家. 車馬不通人境寂,秋林落日自交加. 王季遷寫于雙林書屋 "A clear creek meanders down the hill; at the foot of a mountain lies a small thatched cottage, hidden from view; a silent realm where no carts or horses can reach, where the autumn forest and setting sun accompany each other." Seal: 王季遷印 "Seal of Wang Jiqian."

Fig. 5 (left). Wang Yuanqi. *Landscape for Zhanting*, 1710. Hanging scroll; ink and color on paper, 37 ½ × 18 ½ inches (95.3 × 47 cm). The Metropolitan Museum of Art, New York, Gift of Marie-Hélène Weill and Guy A. Weill. 2011.574.

Fig. 6 (right). Wang Meng. *Thatched Hut in the Western Suburbs*, 14th century. Hanging scroll; ink and pigment on paper, 15 ⅛ × 10 ¾ inches (97.5 × 27.2 cm). The Palace Museum, Beijing.

Fig. 7 (far right). Wang Meng. *Quiet Life in a Wooded Glen*, dated 1361. Hanging scroll; ink and light colors on paper, 70 × 25 ¼ inches (177.8 × 64.2 cm). The Art Institute of Chicago, Kate S. Buckingham Endowment Fund, 1947.728.

In another work from the 1940s, C. C. Wang stated in the colophon that his painting combined the "brush manner" of two paintings by the Yuan-dynasty painter Wang Meng 王蒙 (ca. 1308–1385) (pl. 2). The resulting composition seems more disjointed than either of the two original paintings by Wang Meng (figs. 6, 7), but C. C. Wang's self-conscious play with recombining and recomposing the images, and his literal copy of Wang Meng's tense and agitated brushwork—significantly more difficult to reproduce than that of the

Orthodox School painters—demonstrate a dexterity that few have achieved. Both paintings by Wang Meng had been owned by C. C. Wang's friend Zhang Congyu 張蔥玉, and after acquiring at least one of them, Wang successfully sold it to the Art Institute of Chicago in 1947.[17]

Like painters before him, Wang adhered to the practice of the copy as a necessary foundation for developing one's own "singing voice"—his favorite analogy to the literati notion of expressive brushwork—and as a means of dialogue with a lineage of past painters.[18] When Wang became one of the only members of his circle to leave China in 1949, in part to escape the vicissitudes of the Chinese Civil War and in part to broaden his artistic training, his already encyclopedic knowledge of Chinese paintings found a new outlet in museums abroad.[19] Whereas such knowledge was never articulated—it was taken to be self-evident within the Chinese context—it demanded a new, systematic reformulation in the West. As one of the only classically trained connoisseurs of Chinese art living in the United States in the 1950s, Wang worked closely with museum curators and art historians to give language to the self-expressive brushwork (as opposed to likeness) of literati art for an American audience. In the second half of the twentieth century, their efforts transformed US collecting practices along with the study of Chinese painting, as detailed in Scheier-Dolberg's essay in this volume.[20] Ironically, while many intellectuals and art educators within the avant-garde modernist milieu of 1930s Shanghai considered the Orthodox School's emphasis on brushwork and lineage to have epitomized everything that was backward, repressive, and derivative in traditional Chinese culture,[21] a few decades later art historians in Wang's circle in the postwar United States reframed the same aesthetics and principles of the brush through the language of surface, materiality, and abstraction.[22] Ming and Qing literati art that was the target of an ideological critique and considered a major barrier for modernity in China now became repositioned as an early precursor to modernism in the West.

Beyond its impact on museum practices, collecting history, and art historiography, this paradigm shift—the reframing of the literati art of the brush as quintessentially modern—offers insights into Wang's own search for individuality. His was a modernist project that involved neither the negation of tradition nor the rejection of Western modernism. Long before moving abroad, he had expressed an admiration for Western art in 1930s Shanghai. When he saw photographic reproductions of works by European painters introduced by the artist and art educator Liu Haisu 劉海粟, he noted, "Van Gogh's vibrant coloration, Cézanne's self-possession, Gauguin's severe classicism . . . all share some methods and flavors of Chinese painting. . . . Chinese painting emphasizes brushwork, and Western painting color, each with its special aim. . . . If one day in the future, these can all be synthesized, that would be an outstanding achievement in the global art scene."[23] True to his aspiration, just as swiftly as museums in the United States tapped Wang for his connoisseurial expertise in Chinese painting, he embarked on a study of Western art by enrolling in classes at the Art Students League in New York. From 1949, the same year he moved to the city, until 1974, his studies were largely academic, most frequently focused on life drawing and anatomy (fig. 8). They reflect a pursuit of the "fundamentals" of the Western tradition from a mindset that was likely not so different from his pedagogical insistence that Chinese painting must be taught and studied through copying old masters, and that contemporary experimentations of artists like himself can only originate from oneself rather than be imitated.[24]

A still life from this period, painted with casein on canvas, shows Wang's synthesis of Georges Braque, Paul Cézanne, and Henri Matisse, European artists from half a century earlier (pl. 3). Decades later, Wang credited his courses at the Art Students League with teaching him about elements of design and

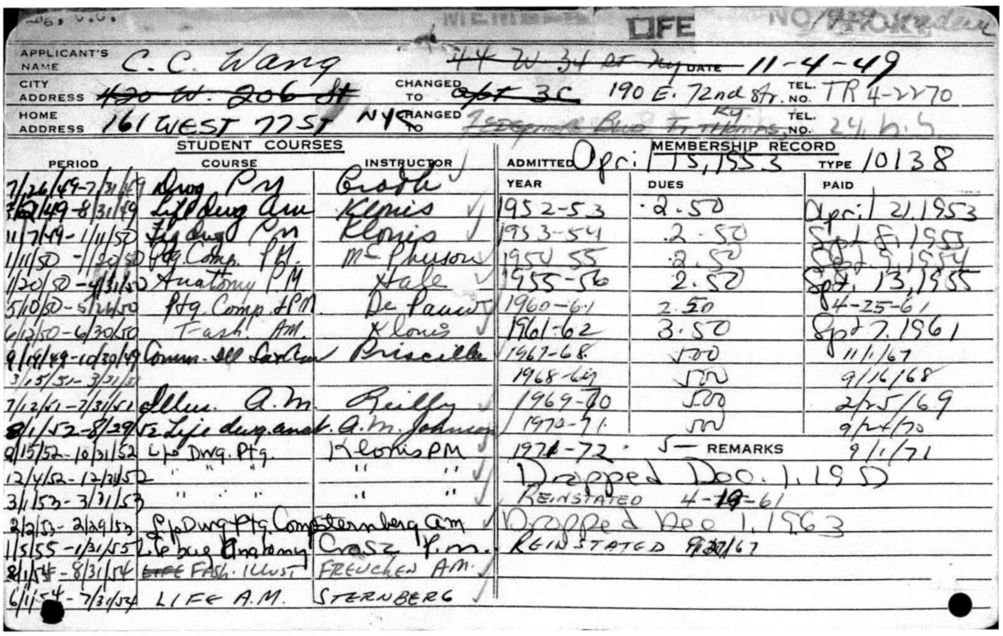
APPLICANT'S NAME C. C. Wang — DATE 11-4-49
CITY ADDRESS 420 W. 206 St — CHANGED TO Apt 3C 190 E. 72nd St. — TEL. NO. TR 4-2270
HOME ADDRESS 161 WEST 77 ST NY — CHANGED TO [illegible] — TEL. NO. [illegible]
STUDENT COURSES — PERIOD / COURSE / INSTRUCTOR
MEMBERSHIP RECORD — ADMITTED April 15, 1953 — TYPE 10138

YEAR	DUES	PAID
1952-53	2.50	April 21, 1953
1953-54	2.50	[illegible]
1954-55	2.50	[illegible]
1955-56	2.50	Sept. 13, 1955
1960-61	2.50	4-25-61
1961-62	3.50	Sept 7, 1961
1967-68	5.00	11/1/67
1968-69	5.00	9/16/68
1969-70	5.00	2/25/69
1970-71	5.00	9/24/70
1971-72	5	9/1/71

REMARKS
Dropped Dec. 1, 1955
Reinstated 4-19-61
Dropped Dec 1, 1963
Reinstated 9/27/67

Fig. 8. C. C. Wang's record of enrollment at the Art Students League of New York from 1949 to 1971.

composition that he had not acquired in his classical training that privileged brushwork.[25] Although Wang did not pursue the genre of still life or the media and materials of casein or oil on canvas, he drew from his studies of Western art with a similar spirit of emulation as he approached Chinese artists of each period and specialty to identify their distinct achievements. Throughout the 1950s, Wang largely continued to paint in the traditional genres of landscape and bird-and-flower paintings while searching for a path to invigorate his practice with new learning as well as a new audience in a foreign country (fig. 9).[26]

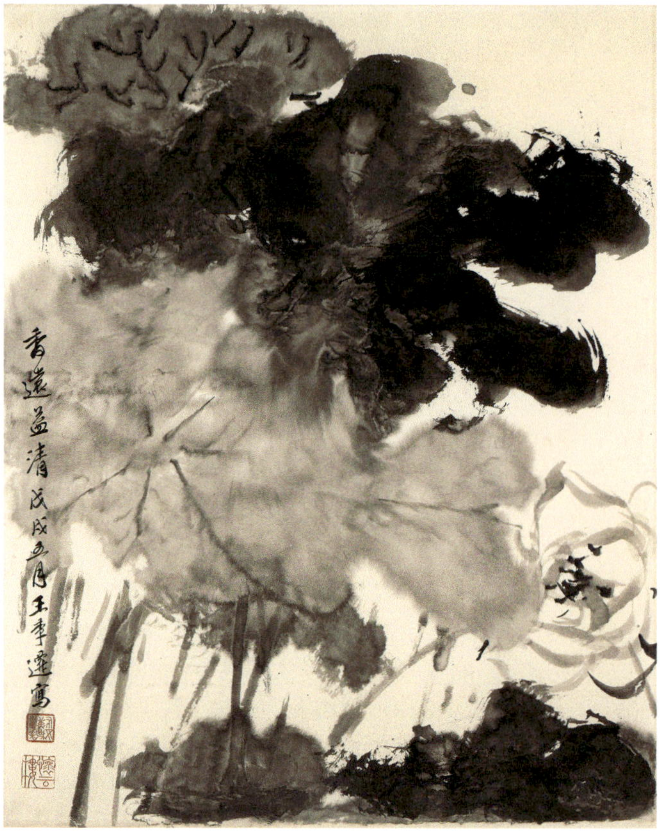

Fig. 9. C. C. Wang. *Lotus*, May 1958. Ink on paper, 25 3/16 × 19 9/16 inches (64 × 49.7 cm). Princeton University Art Museum, Gift of Mr. and Mrs. Frank F. Cho in memory of James T. C. Liu, Professor of East Asian Studies and History, Princeton University, 1965–88, 2009-17. Inscription: 香遠益清戊戌五月王季遷寫 "Distant fragrance is even more pure. 1958, 5th month. Inscribed by Wang Jiqian." Seals: (top left, impressed upside down) 季遷旅美之作 "Created by Jiqian while staying abroad in America." (bottom left) 懷雲樓 "Hall where Ni Zan is treasured."

Medium and Materials

Given the stimulation New York offered, Wang's embrace of abstraction and experimentation in the 1960s has been aptly characterized as only possible due to his move abroad and his direct exposure to contemporary artists working in postwar New York.[27] But what has not been emphasized is his abiding interest in exploring the interactive materiality of paper, ink, and brush. A deep understanding of the freedom and the means to experiment with materials and techniques—just as the artists he observed had done—also contributed to his breakthrough transformations. His new explorations arose as much from what he saw around him in New York's art world as from decades of hands-on study of paintings by old masters. Whether it was the observation that Xia Gui sometimes pre-sprayed paper with an adhesive to prepare a less absorbent surface that would engender a special texture for the brushstrokes in *Pure and Remote View*, or that a painting on silk by Ni Zan would have otherwise revealed the artist's *biqu* 筆趣 (flavor/play of the brush) had it been done on Yuan-dynasty paper, or that the Ming-dynasty painter Xu Wei 徐渭 (1521–1593) mixed thin adhesive in his ink to create a special effect,[28] or that the Song-dynasty painter

Fan Kuan's 范寬 (ca. 960–after 1023) textured stroke could only be rendered by a worn-out brush of a particular size, width, and length[29]—Wang's sensitivity to the precise conditions and qualities of ink, brush, and painting surface was closely related to his authentication of works (which required, for example, his knowledge of whether a paper was antiqued by dying or if the ink tone was pure). But the keen awareness also conveys how much he internalized process and materiality through not only looking but also by *doing*.

Wang's works from the 1960s onward exhibited a continued experimentation with available tools, techniques, and materials and likely stemmed from his observations on the manipulation of medium and materiality in old paintings. One of his earliest investigations was an untitled painting (*Ox Blood Experiment*), made in the Year of the Ox in 1961 (pl. 4). The painting is unusual for its elongated vertical format and its combination of pink, black, and white hues, prompting one to wonder which colors were made or mixed with ox blood, or if the title referenced the ox-blood glaze popular among New York collectors of Chinese ceramics at the time. Pigments of varied translucency allow brushstrokes of varying sizes and wetness to be visible. In this abstract work, the only decipherable forms are those made using the black-and-white brushstrokes reminiscent of Chinese talismanic writing.

Wang's works like *Ox Blood Experiment* went virtually unnoticed in New York while his paintings of flowers and genre subjects with gestural brushstrokes—produced under the financial pressure to sell—met the popular American taste for Chinese painting (see fig. 9).[30] However, once Wang was able to travel abroad (after obtaining US citizenship in 1957), his regular trips to Asia brought his ink experimentations into productive synergy with Chinese diasporic artists in Hong Kong and Taiwan who sought to combine abstract expressionism with traditional Chinese materials.[31] Wang was invited to teach in 1957 at the newly established art department of the New Asia College (now the Chinese University of Hong Kong), where he subsequently served as the department chair from 1962 to 1964 and returned to teach in 1974.[32] Among the artists he met in Hong Kong were a younger generation in what became known as the New Ink Art movement, who sought to combine abstract expressionism with traditional Chinese materials.[33] While Wang's art was grounded in his classical literati upbringing and connoisseurial training, artists of the New Ink Art movement only returned to the use of traditional Chinese materials after a primary training in modernist aesthetics and literature, along with Western artistic mediums.

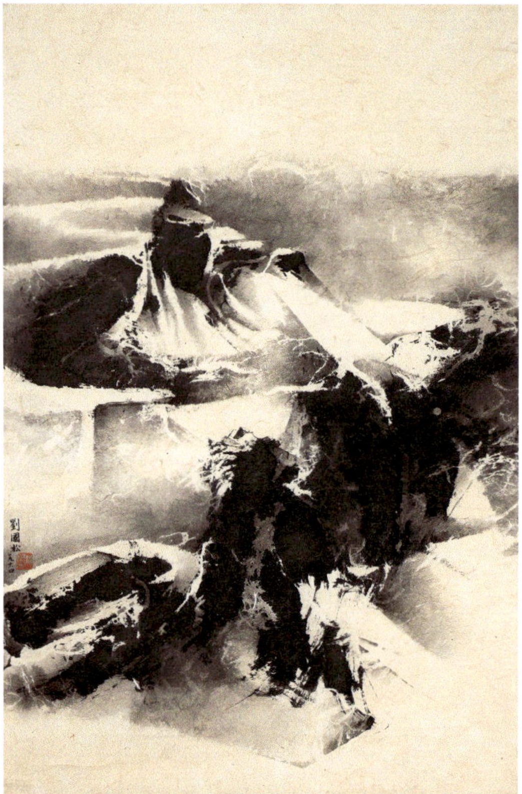

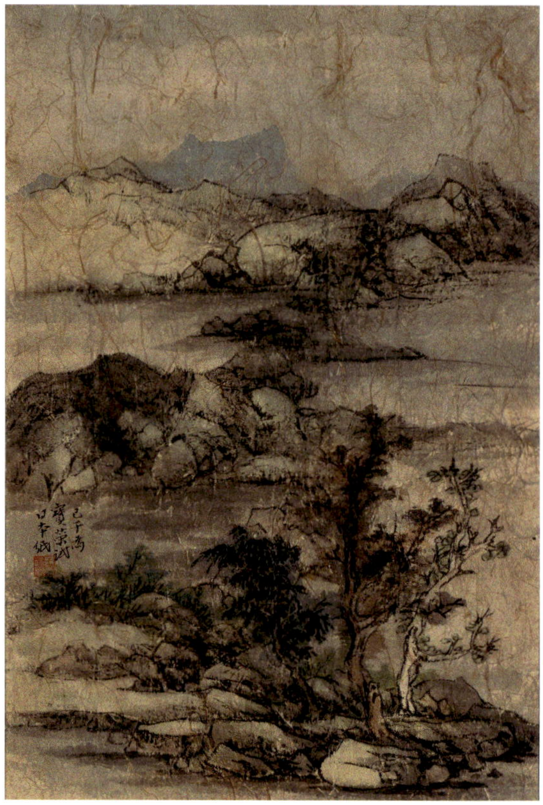

One artist who engaged in frequent exchanges with Wang over the next decades was Liu Kuo-sung 劉國松 (Liu Guosong). An early work by Liu, *Wintry Mountains Covered with Snow*, shows his favorite technique of first applying ink on a special mulberry paper he had designed and commissioned, and then removing coarse filaments to create a simultaneously abstract and representational surface (fig. 10). Wang also experimented with similar methods when Liu gifted him some of this paper.[34] The untitled work from 1989 (*Mountain Valley at Night*) shows a reliance on the coarseness of the paper to create a dramatic contrast of light and dark (pl. 11). But whereas the chiaroscuro of Liu's work is illusionistic in the play of light and shadow, Wang's vision focused on locating the geological texture and movement of mountains, and the layering of hills in the landscape painting tradition, as well as the art historical reference to brushwork through the fibrous patterns of the paper. In another example that Wang painted on Japanese paper given by another friend, the landscape was executed in a more traditional manner, with ink and color on top of a very fibrous surface (fig. 11). Yet in this work, too, there exists a dynamic competition for an affinity with nature, between the lines of brushwork and the streaks of filament.

Order and Chance

Much of Wang's preoccupation beginning in the 1960s lay in exploring the dialogic relationship between chance and control; brushwork and surface texture created without a brush; and abstraction and monumentality of landscape representation. Through these explorations Wang immersed himself in the physical act of mark making and deepened his creative engagement with the past. *Landscape No. 475* shows Wang's signature method of crumpling paper, dipping it in ink, impressing semi-random textural patterns on another sheet of paper, and then adding lines and wash to the impressed patterns to build out a recognizable landscape (pl. 6). Wang made use of opaque gouache colors, white casein, transparent watercolors, and ink to create a layered effect. In addition, he stained the back side of his paper with two different colors to create an effervescence through the layered treatments and accretions of ink from both sides of the paper.[35] The resulting dreamscape was produced during a period when Wang was suffering from health problems that led to two successive heart surgeries late in 1983.[36] The gentle, laborious, and unpredictable process of accruing ink and pigment on paper creates the appearance of a self-generated landscape,[37] with a contemplative mood that mirrored Wang's coming to terms with his own mortality.[38]

In something of a paradox, while the painters of the Qing Orthodox School practiced restraint through total order and control, Wang pursued the art of restraint through chance and spontaneity. His experiments with crumpled papers and other strategies to create marks without a brush used the element of chance as a way to limit the final outcome of his work. If expressive brushwork represents the single most-important aspect of literati painting, and indeed the overriding criteria for Wang's connoisseurship of old paintings, what happens when it is replaced with a form of mark making where the hand and the brush can no longer be engaged or visible? In experimenting with chance, Wang augmented the quest for good brushwork, defined in the Chinese literati context as mark making that has an affinity with nature and the natural world. In 1977 he wrote about the element of chance in his use of wrinkled and crumbled paper:

Fig. 10 (far left). Liu Kuo-sung. *Wintry Mountains Covered with Snow* 寒山雪霽, 1964. Hanging scroll; ink on fibrous paper, 33 ⅝ × 21 15/16 inches (85.4 × 55.8 cm). The Harvard Art Museums/Arthur M. Sackler Museum. The Chu-tsing Li Collection, Gift of B. U. K. Li in honor of Chu-tsing Li and in memory of Yao-wen Kwang Li and Teri Ho Li.

Fig. 11 (left). C. C. Wang. no title (Landscape), undated (ca. 1990s). Ink and color on paper, 23 ¼ × 15 ⅜ inches (59.1 × 83 cm). Collection of Pao Yung Chao. Inscription: 己千為寶榮試日本紙 "Jiqian experiments with Japanese paper for Pao Yung." Seal: 王季遷印 "Seal of Wang Jiqian."

> Those wrinkles help to inspire or push an image from my mind and determine the direction which my paintings will take. I think this is a good technique. Besides, it's very exciting. I never know beforehand exactly what the image will turn out to be. . . . My landscapes often create themselves in the wrinkle patterns which I achieve accidentally. The wrinkles are utterly free from logic, but I have been able to use them to form my compositions which, ultimately, are quite tightly controlled. . . . Too many words have been said and written about brushwork. Now, I think, we can go a little further beyond brushstrokes.[39]

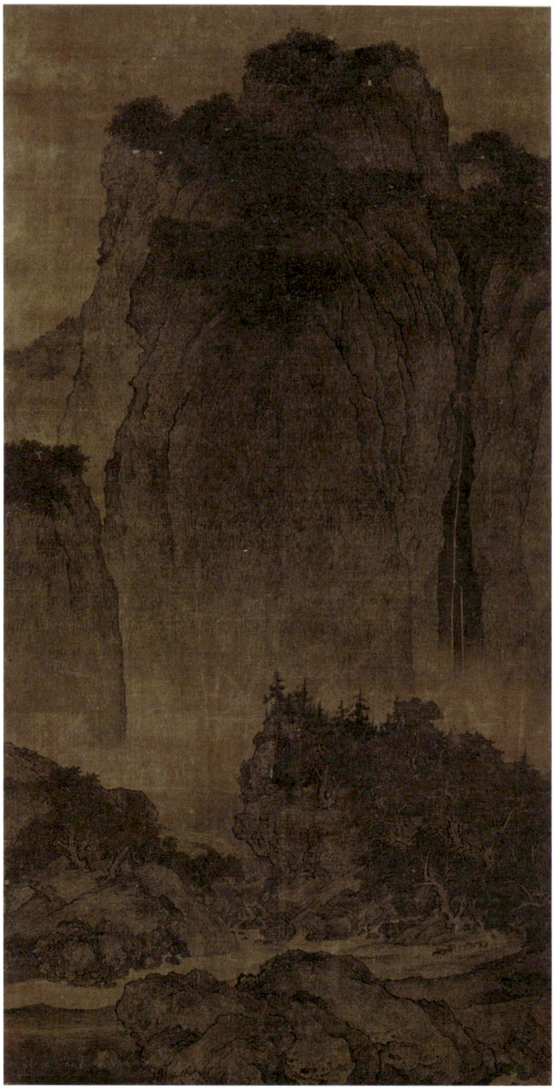

In the same text, Wang noted the inspiration he received from the wrinkles as no different from Jackson Pollock's process of being *in* his painting, the "single stroke" of the Qing-dynasty Shitao's 石濤 (1642–1707) sustained surge of creativity, and the Song-dynasty Guo Xi's 郭熙 (ca. 1020–ca. 1090) method of gazing at natural markings on his walls for inspiration.[40] While Wang's technique and visuality were new and uniquely his own, what he chose to emphasize in his statement above was a universal affinity with other acts of artistic inspiration. His attempt to push beyond brushstrokes was precisely to build on the past achievements of the brush.

Wang's quest for good brushwork without a brush is nowhere more evident than in his 1985 homage to Fan Kuan (pl. 7). Though not a direct copy, the towering mountain and waterfall in the distance and a set of hills in the

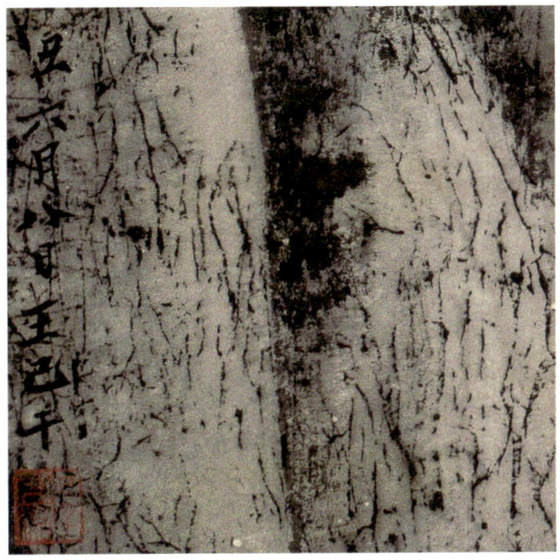

Fig. 12 (left). Fan Kuan. *Travelers among Mountains and Streams*, early 11th century. Hanging scroll; ink on silk, 61 ⅛ × 29 ¼ inches (155.3 × 74.4 cm). National Palace Museum, Taipei.

Fig. 13 (above left). Detail from Fan Kuan, *Travelers among Mountains and Streams* (fig. 12).

Fig. 14 (above right). Detail from C. C. Wang, no title (Landscape after Fan Kuan), 1985, pl. 7.

foreground visibly evoke Fan Kuan's *Travelers among Mountains and Streams* (fig. 12), the icon of the Northern Song monumental landscape painting tradition. Wang replaces Fan Kuan's signature brush method, or *cunfa* 皴法 (later known as the "raindrop" method), with ink impressions from a roller wrapped in crumpled, ink-dipped paper that are then layered with dry and wet lines and ink washes to bring out the contour, vegetation, and forms of the mountain (figs. 13, 14). In another gesture toward *Travelers among Mountains and Streams*, Wang hides his signature inside the textured hills, just as Fan Kuan did.

Wang's imitation of Fan Kuan's brush method, without the use of a brush, displays an ingenious nod to the ultimate accomplishment of *Travelers among Mountains and Streams*—a manifestation of *li* 理, or the fundamental order of nature according to Neo-Confucian metaphysics, through painting. Wang's impressions created by semi-accidental means follow Fan Kuan's meticulous labor of the brush—both are as natural as nature itself, creating not an artifice or illusion of reality, but an immersion in that world. Here, Wang's recognition of Fan Kuan's pursuit to break the boundary between artistic creation and natural order is entirely kinesthetic—Wang's interest is not in reproducing the work of the earlier artist, but in embodying and pushing further Fan Kuan's process of creation.

To situate his own positionality in conversation with Fan Kuan's, Wang employs one of his favorite seals, "Neither Northern nor Southern, both Ancient and Modern 非南非北, 亦古亦今," in the bottom right corner, declaring his freedom from the classifications of the Northern and Southern lineages of painters, from the dichotomy of ancient and modern between which he was so often caught. Another seal he frequently used—"Neither East nor West 不是東西"—carries the double meaning of being worthless. Together the two seals playfully reject the easy labels that have so often been forced upon Wang. They also gesture to the sense of synthesis and universal affinity of the various schools, traditions, and practices, both past and present, that shaped his art.

Abstraction

Toward the end of a twenty-five-year experiment with forms and techniques of chance that began in the late 1960s, Wang completed works that are without any trace of the brush, leaving the intentional and unpredictable impressions created by ink rollers and crumpled papers as the only marks on the surface. The monochromatic impressions in an untitled work from 1987 (Landscape No. 970-B) draw the viewer to the repetitions of the mark making, thus inviting them to imagine the movement of the roller on the page (pl. 9). The same impression of repetitive motion on the surface of the paper is seen on a tightly built sketch of an ink monochrome landscape (pl. 10), and on a radically new kind of landscape composition made up of calligraphic strokes of the standard script (*kaiti* 楷體) over a surface of pretreated ink washes (pl. 17). In the final decade of his life, the concern for lines and textured patterns returned Wang to his earliest beginnings, when he learned to write and practice calligraphy as a young boy.[41] The Chinese word for text/word is *wen* 文, which literally means pattern or striation. Written words are first of all patterns, and Wang turned them from their abstraction as linguistic symbols into his own abstract imagery (fig. 15; pls. 15, 16).

Fig. 15. C. C. Wang. no title (Abstract Brushwork), no date. Ink and color on paper, 12 ⅝ × 49 ⅛ inches (32.1 × 124.7 cm). Collection of Pao Yung Chao. Inscription: 己千 "Jiqian." Seal: Self-portrait of artist.

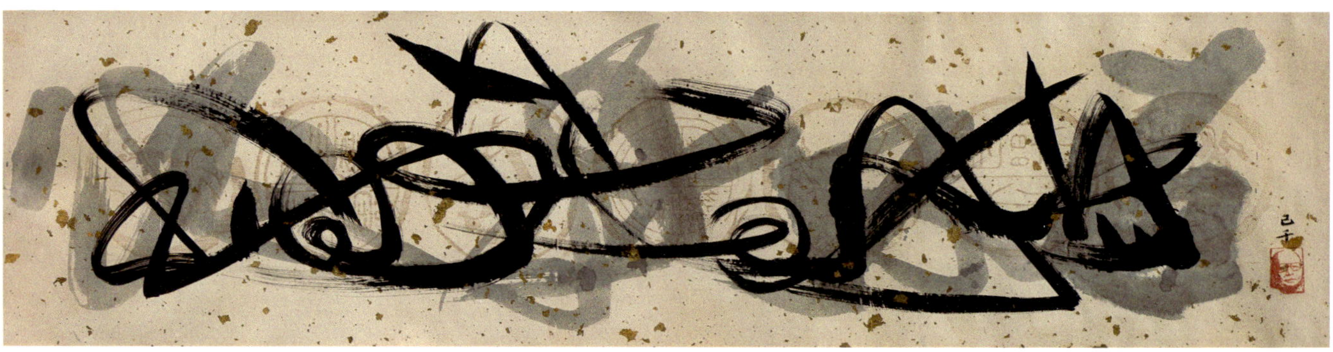

In these works, the object of Wang's kinesthetic engagement was no longer a particular master's expressive brushwork, treatment of materials, or artistic project, but the distillation of a life practice. Each line and each decipherable stroke still follow the same movement, speed, direction, and pressure of the wrist as those in Wang's calligraphy and painting practice, yet the strokes and lines no longer serve the purpose of forming characters, words, or conventional landscapes—thus producing a fresh visual experience. Wang's daily writing practice on New York City phone books captures this transformation in precise temporal terms, with pages of increasingly illegible and abstracted writing that turned into its own visual and rhythmic composition (fig. 16). He also played with lines of writing by using nontraditional writing implements, such as a sponge brush used for house painting (see p. 95, fig. 4),[42] to achieve the uniform lines of the seal-script calligraphy derived from stone and metal carvings, the sharp edges of graffiti art,[43] and the gestural marks of abstract expressionism (pls. 19, 20). In lines, the most basic component of both painting and calligraphy, Wang arrived at a final abstraction that retains his lifelong quest for kinesthetic knowledge.[44]

In the 1990s, while Wang was breaking new ground through experimentation with calligraphic gestures and forms, the octogenarian continued to work in the traditional idiom of landscape painting, as well as to employ similar brush techniques to depict the urban landscape outside the window of his 69th Street home on the Upper East Side of Manhattan (pl. 13). These "mind landscapes" are deeply referential, evoking and synthesizing the expressive brushwork of master painters. The versatility is on full display in an album of sixteen leaves titled *Splendid Views of Rivers and Mountains* (pls. 14b–q). The leaves variously invoke the brushwork of his favorite painters Shitao (pl. 14g), Mi Fu 米芾 (1051–1107) (pl. 14l), and Ni Zan (pl. 14q), but he injects the leaves with a sense of monumental landscape and vibrant coloration.

As a show of deference toward his tradition, Wang rarely discussed his art in personal or biographical terms. But Stanley-Baker drew out the emotional depth of Wang's commitment to the landscape tradition as an uprooted individual when she asked in a 1970s interview: "C. C., in these ten years you have painted nothing but grand rivers and mountains. You live in a city in a foreign country without grass and trees, and day after day, from your brush emerge vast and boundless rivers and mountains, majestic heaven and earth. Doesn't this clearly indicate you are suffering from homesickness?" And Wang replied, "I do miss my homeland very much."[45] This sense of nostalgia reveals itself very

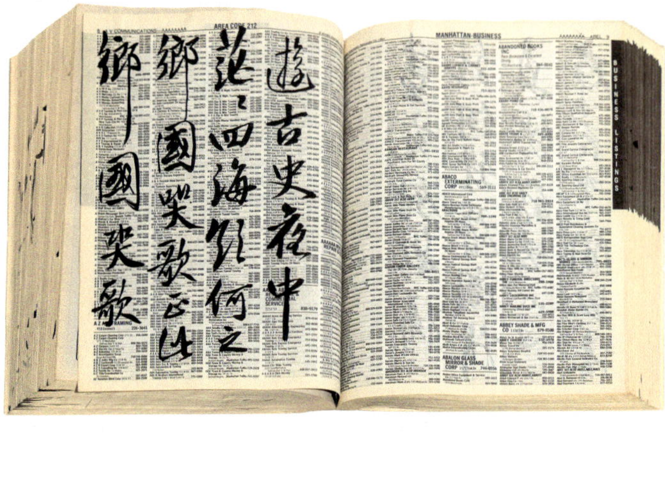
AREA CODE 212
MANHATTAN-BUSINESS
BUSINESS LISTINGS

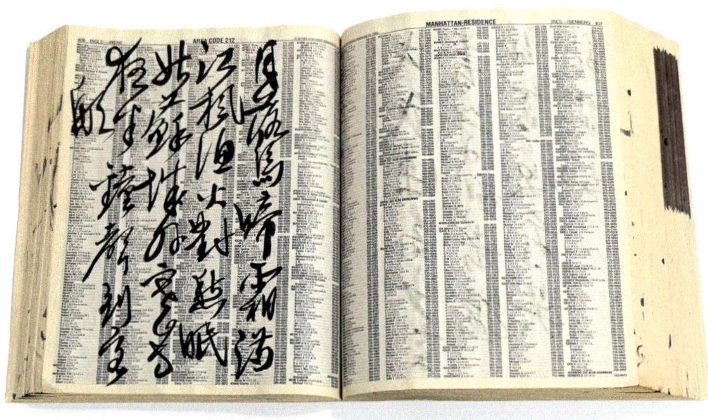
AREA CODE 212
MANHATTAN-RESIDENCE

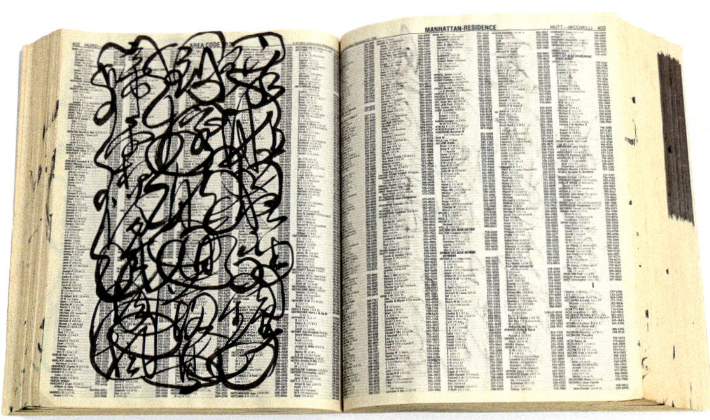
MANHATTAN-RESIDENCE

occasionally in colophons and only allusively through his choice of seals.[46] But it is through the act of painting landscapes—of embodying and enacting the tradition of landscape paintings by past artists that he collected and studied around the world—that he expressed the longing for an irretrievable homeland. His paintings of lofty mountains are rarely monumental in their physical dimension. Staying true to the conventions of literati painting, their relatively miniature size speaks of a faraway and pristine place, contained in memory rather than crossing over to the present world.

Conversely, his abstract works derived from calligraphy and still life—works of the here and now—are often larger and unbounded by conventional or defined scale. In the last two years of his life, when travel had become limited, Wang turned for inspiration to his collection of scholar's rocks—natural formations, sculpted by the processes of erosion, that have been collected and shown in China since the tenth century as accoutrements of the scholar's study or garden. By displaying the marvelous transformative forces of nature, the rocks are seen as microcosms of monumental mountains and rivers.[47] Wang first began collecting scholar's rocks in his twenties and continued to build a collection that became one of the finest in the United States.[48] He completed many paintings of rocks in the last year of his life, some at an astonishingly large scale considering his age and limited physical strength. Wang's hometown of Suzhou is famous for producing one of the most prized types of garden rocks, called the Taihu Rock 太湖石—the form that seems to inspire one untitled work (*Scholar's Rock*) (pl. 23). Signed "Jiqian in [his] 95th year," this work employs a type of ink-monochrome brushwork similar to that of a landscape painting in the idiom of Ni Zan that he completed in the same year (pl. 22). But instead of hills made up of gentle and lightly inked lines and washes that recede into the distance and into the paper itself, *Rock* renders the form and surface texture of an imposing, monolithic form with darker-toned ink and greater contrast, standing without the suggestion of a ground, on the pretreated surface of inky static that Wang often used late in life.

Wang's interest in painting scholar's rocks at the end of his life represents a fitting return to nature itself as the site of kinesthetic knowing. Just as human bodies are used as models in Western academic painting traditions, Wang noted, Chinese landscape painters prefer rocks as models to understand "the bones and frame" of nature. For rocks, he continued, "like paintings, are not restricted by years or given cultures, nor are they confined to the West or the East. They can serve as a bridge that transcends time, space, and culture."[49] Like the scholar's

Figure 16. C. C. Wang. no title (Phone Book with Artist's Calligraphy Practice), 1998, pl. 18.

rocks that inspired Wang, the painting supplies the texture and surface of a geological specificity at the same time as it renders an abstraction that was for him without temporal, spatial, and cultural bounds. In the toggle between representation and abstraction coalesces Wang's lifelong pursuit to embody past experiences and to bring to them something new.

NOTES

1. “你如果要真正抓住筆墨的真意, 你就需要自己試驗用筆. 為什麼我只看倪瓚所畫的一角, 就可以認出他的作品? 因為我已經沈迷于他的畫中, 並且親手練習了好幾百遍, 所以我對他手腕的每個轉折, 腕力增加或減少律動等, 都很熟悉.” Joan Stanley-Baker [Xu Xiaohu 徐小虎], *Hua yu lu: Wang Jiqian jiao ni kan dong Zhongguo shuhua* 畫語錄 : 王季遷教你看懂中國書畫 (C. C. Wang reflects on painting) (Taipei: Diancang yishu jiating gufen youxian gongsi, 2013), 41. The original interviews and conversations took place between 1971 and 1979 in New York and San Francisco.

2. C. C. Wang was given the name Jiquan 季銓 at birth; changed his name to Jiqian 季遷 in 1932; signed his works as Jiqian 紀千 from the early 1960s; and changed his name to Jiqian 己千 in 1970. C. C. stands for the initials of his various names “Chi-ch'üan” or “Chi-ch'ien” following the Wade-Giles romanization system. For more on the meaning and change of his names, see Jerome Silbergeld, *Mind Landscapes: The Paintings of C. C. Wang* (Seattle: Henry Art Gallery and University of Washington, 1987), 13, 37.

3. “徐: 這種練習不就是在制造贋品嗎? 王: 不是, 傳統的書本和西方的學者也許都堅持: 中國畫只是‘抄襲古人,’ 或者是 ‘不斷地重複某人所做過的’ 而已, 但事實上, 我們覺得珍貴的, 是畫中所加入的新鮮成分, 以及個人的貢獻, 而這種新鮮成分並非粗俗而沒有根據的, 而是一種包含了過去的經驗.” Stanley-Baker, *Hua yu lu*, 37.

4. In a fascinating study of modern design education from the 1850s to the 1940s, Zeynep Çelik Alexander uses “kinaesthetic knowing” to describe a form of cognition and intelligence without language. Here, I use “kinesthetic knowing” not to emphasize the form of knowing itself, but the kinesthetic process by which one gains the insight and understanding that have guided generations of scholar-artists. See Zeynep Çelik Alexander, *Kinaesthetic Knowing: Aesthetics, Epistemology, Modern Design* (Chicago: University of Chicago Press, 2017).

5. In addition to Silbergeld, *Mind Landscapes*, major publications include Meredith Weatherby, ed., *Mountains of the Mind: The Landscape Painting of Wang Chi-ch'ien* (New York: Weatherhill, 1970); James Cahill, *C. C. Wang: Landscape Paintings* (Seattle: Xi An Tang, 1986); Arnold Chang, “C. C. Wang at Ninety: A Kaikodo Celebration,” *Kaikodo Journal* 3 (Spring 1997): 10–17; and Ming Hua, “Bridging the Tradition to the Modern, the East to the West: C. C. Wang and His Life in Art” (PhD diss., Arizona State University, 2014).

6. Wang has been heralded as a modern embodiment of the millennium-old tradition of Chinese literati painting. Following his move to New York in 1949, he embraced the visual language of postwar abstraction, earning further accolades for the dexterity of his vision and practice. See Joan Stanley-Baker, “The Last Literatus,” *Asian Pacific Quarterly of Cultural and Social Affairs* 6 (1974): 1–15. These narratives are also attested to in large part by the artist himself. See *Mountains of the Mind: The Landscapes of C. C. Wang* (Washington, DC: A. M. Sackler Foundation, 1977).

7. The most detailed biography of Wang is found in Silbergeld, *Mind Landscapes*, 13–37. For a thorough study of Wu Hufan's connoisseurship, see Clarissa von Spee, *Wu Hufan: A Twentieth Century Art Connoisseur in Shanghai* (Berlin: Reimer, 2008).

8. The Orthodox School refers to a movement that began in the seventeenth century in which painters ardently followed the theories and innovations of the artist, theorist, and politician Dong Qichang 董其昌 (1555–1636) as they best understood them. See James Cahill, "The Orthodox Movement in Early Ch'ing Painting," in *Artists and Traditions: Uses of the Past in Chinese Culture*, ed. Christian F. Murck (Princeton, NJ: Princeton University Press, 1976), 169–81.

9. Chi-ch'ien Wang (C. C. Wang) and Victoria Contag, *Seals of Chinese Painters and Collectors of the Ming and Ch'ing Periods*, rev. ed. (1940; Hong Kong: Hong Kong University Press, 1966).

10. Silbergeld, *Mind Landscapes*, 21.

11. Wang wrote two seminal essays on Ni Zan. See Chi-ch'ien Wang "Ni Yunlin shengping ji shiwen 倪雲林生平及詩文 (The life and writing of Ni Tsan)," *Gugong jikan* 故宮季刊 1, no. 2 (1966): 29–42; and "Ni Yunlin zhi hua 倪雲林之畫" (Paintings of Ni Tsan), *Gugong jikan* 2, no. 1 (1967): 53–54.

12. See Arnold Chang's essay in this volume.

13. The colophon details that the copy was done "underneath the chrysanthemum blossoms of the garden and in front of the true brush trace of Old Dong" at the Plum Shadows Studio (Meiying shuwu 梅景書屋), Wu Hufan's studio.

14. See, for example, the serial *Gugong shuhua ji* 故宮書畫集 by Guoli beiping gugong bowuyuan 國立北平故宮博物院, published between 1930 and 1936. For more on early collotype reproductions, see Cheng-hua Wang, "New Printing Technology and Heritage Preservation: Collotype Reproduction of Antiquities in Modern China, circa 1908–1917," in *The Role of Japan in Modern Chinese Art*, ed. Joshua Fogel (Berkeley: University of California Press, 2013), 273–308, 363–72.

15. *Pure and Remote View* is a rare work of ink on paper by Xia Gui that Wang noted as the very best that he had seen. See Kathleen Yang, ed., 王季遷讀畫筆記 *Through a Chinese Connoisseur's Eye: Private Notes of C. C. Wang* (Beijing: Zhonghua shuju, 2010), 174.

16. The Four Wangs of the Orthodox School are Wang Shimin 王時敏 (1592–1680), Wang Jian 王鑒 (1598–1677), Wang Hui 王翬 (1632–1717), and Wang Yuanqi 王原祁 (1642–1715).

17. See the object description on the website of the Art Institute of Chicago, https://www.artic.edu/artworks/61483/quiet-life-in-a-wooded-glen-%E6%9E%97%E9%BA%93%E5%B9%BD%E5%B1%85%E5%9C%96, accessed October 13, 2022. Wang sold the work for $12,000. His address on the invoice is cited as the Hotel Salisbury, 123 W. 57th Street, New York. This transaction must have been carried out while he was on his visit abroad to Japan and then to the United States in 1947.

18. Wang said, "Brushwork is like a voice. The painting is like the story which provides the narrative, the message. Those who don't understand go to the opera in order to 'watch' the battles and the love scenes. But those who know, the aficionados, go with their eyes closed, to hear the singer and follow the voice. We go to 'listen' to Mei Lanfang, not to 'watch' acrobatics." Quoted in Joan Stanley-Baker, "Calligraphy in China," in *The Living Brush: Four Masters of Contemporary Chinese Calligraphy; C. C. Wang, Wang Fangyu, Tseng Yuho, Grace Tong*, exh. cat., Pacific Heritage Museum (San Francisco: American Asian Cultural Exchange Pacific, 1997), 19.

19. See Joseph Scheier-Dolberg's essay in this volume.

20. Until the 1950s, collecting practices in museums in the West, and the United States specifically, were still predominantly influenced by the earlier wave of collectors such as Charles Freer (1854–1919), who was in turn influenced by Japan-inflected art historians, including Ernest Fenollosa (1853–1908), who valued the realism of Song-dynasty and earlier paintings as the "apex" of Chinese painting. See Ingrid Larsen, "'Don't Send Ming or Later Pictures': Charles Lang Freer and the First Major Collection of Chinese Painting in an American Museum," *Ars Orientalis* 40 (2011): 6–38. When C. C. Wang arrived in the United States in the 1950s, he worked with a small cohort of art historians and museum curators to bring the art and theory of Dong Qichang to the forefront of the canonical tradition.

21. This coincided with the May Fourth Movement that blamed traditional Confucian values for China's weakness against the forces of Japanese and European

imperialism, and its adherents embraced Western art, learning, and ideals of democracy in search of a Chinese modernity. See David Der-wei Wang, "In the Name of the Real," in *Chinese Art: Modern Expressions*, ed. Maxwell K. Hearn (New York: Metropolitan Museum of Art, 2001), 28–59.

22. See, for example, Wai-kam Ho and Dawn Ho Delbanco, "Tung Ch'i-chang's Transcendence of History and Art," in *The Century of Tung Ch'i-ch'ang, 1555–1636*, ed. Wai-kam Ho (Kansas City: Nelson-Atkins Museum of Art, 1992), 3–41.

23. Wang Jiqian, *Wang Jiqian shu hua guo yan lu* 王季迁书画过眼录 (Works of painting and calligraphy seen by C. C. Wang) (Shanghai: Shanghai shuhua chubanshe, 2021), 106.

24. See Li Tung-keung 李東強, "Professor Wang Jiqian 王季遷老師," in Department of Fine Arts of the Chinese University of Hong Kong, *Department of Fine Arts at 50* (Hong Kong: Department of Fine Arts, Chinese University of Hong Kong, 2007), 33.

25. Silbergeld, *Mind Landscapes*, 29.

26. See Margaret Liu Clinton's essay in this volume.

27. Hua, "Bridging the Tradition to the Modern," 229.

28. Yang, *Wang Jiqian Duhua Biji*, 73, 108, 174.

29. Stanley-Baker, *Hua yu lu*, 54–55.

30. For more on the lack of visibility of Chinese or Chinese American artists in New York City, see Margaret Liu Clinton's essay in this volume. For more on the Mi Chou gallery, see Joseph Scheier-Dolberg's essay in this volume and Frank Fulai Cho, "Reminiscences of Mi Chou: The First Chinese Gallery in America," *Chinese American Forum* 1, no. 3 (May 1985): 4–8.

31. He taught traditional Chinese ink painting, keeping his own experiments separate and away from his students, yet his exhibits from as early as 1962 showed only works that represent a dramatic departure from tradition. Julia Andrews and Kuiyi Shen locate Wang's achievement within the chapter "Alternate Chinas: Hong Kong and Taiwan" in their authoritative survey, *The Art of Modern China* (Berkeley: University of California Press, 2012), 233–34.

32. Hong Kong reconnected Wang with the old world of painting and collecting he had left behind in Shanghai.

33. These include Lui Shou-Kwan 呂壽琨, Wucius Wong 王無邪, and Liu Kuo-sung 劉國松.

34. Silbergeld, *Mind Landscapes*, 110.

35. For Wang's process, see ibid., 108.

36. Hua, "Bridging the Tradition to the Modern," 280.

37. Joan Stanley-Baker, "C. C. Wang and the Rebirth of Painting and Calligraphy," in *The Exhibition of C. C. Wang*, ed. Lin Ping (Taipei: Taipei Fine Arts Museum, 1994), 8.

38. Hua, "Bridging the Tradition to the Modern," 280.

39. *Mountains of the Mind* (1977), n.p.

40. Ibid.

41. See ibid.

42. Wang referred to them as "painted or manufactured calligraphy." See Jan Stuart, "C. C. Wang: Singing Brush and Dancing Ink," *Arts of Asia* 32, no. 3 (May 2002): 44.

43. See Jordan Homstad's essay in this volume.

44. For a close analysis of C. C. Wang's lines, see Daniel M. Greenberg's essay in this volume.

45. "CC, 這十年間您除了畫 '大江山,' 就沒有畫別的, 您住在國外一個無草無樹的都市裡, 天天由畫筆中寫出浩然無盡的江山, 雄偉的天地, 這不就很明顯地說明您患了思鄉病嗎? 王: 是的, 我非常思念我的祖國." Stanley-Baker, *Hua yu lu*, 308–9.

46. Although he all but stopped the traditional literati practice of inscribing colophons on paintings, perhaps in tacit acknowledgment of the loss of an audience and a community for whom the practice was meaningful, Wang was moved to resume the practice in the company of like-minded friends when he chanced upon his own works from the 1930s that had resurfaced. On a still life of peonies that he painted in the 1930s in Shanghai, and that had appeared on the market and was purchased by a collector friend, he inscribed, "此余昔年寓上海時所寫, 前塵夢影, 已不復記憶為誰所作, 輾轉流傳, 近竟為張君鼎丞[臣]得於香港, 回憶此二三十年間, 戰亂頻仍迄無寧, 歲兒余以, 劫後餘生, 偷安余江海浪跡之中, 有家不能歸去, 撫卷悵然, 不能自己, 畫固不足觀, 而張君珍之重之, 倘亦有同感於斯耶? 爰誌數語歸之. 季遷時客九龍 (I painted this when I was living in Shanghai in the bygone days. [These are all] dreams and shadows of the past. I can no longer remember for whom I made it. After passing through multiple hands, the painting was recently obtained by Mr. Zhang Dingcheng [*sic*]

in Hong Kong. Remembering back to the last two to three decades, there has been constant war and chaos, and no peace still now. In my years so far, I have survived calamities and sought ease by roaming about in the waves, with a home I can't return to. In front of the scroll, I am moved to sadness, unable to contain myself. The painting is by itself nothing worthy to behold, but Mr. Zhang so treasured and valued it, perhaps because he also shares those similar sentiments? I therefore mark [the painting] with a few words and return it. Jiqian [C. C. Wang] while visiting Kowloon)." Though such inscribed reflections are rare, Wang often relied on personal seals to express similar sentiments when he could not do so via colophons. Among his wide repertoire of seals, many indicated that a work was created, copied, or collected by him (such as "王季遷海外所見名跡 *Wang Jiqian haiwai suojian mingji* [Overseas masterpieces seen by Wang Jiqian]"), but others evoked familiar phrases or poetic idioms. During this period of the 1950s and '60s, one of the seals he used was "季遷旅美之作 *Jiqian lümei zhizuo* (Created by Jiqian while staying abroad in America)," and throughout the following decades, he frequently used other seals that evoke his exile, political instabilities, and longing for home: "海外遺民 *Haiwai Yimin* (Leftover people living overseas)"; "家在姑蘇 *Jiazai Suzhou* (Home is Suzhou)"; "石橋邨裏人家 *Shiqiao cunli renjia* (Of the family of the Stone Bridge Village)." For compilations of his seals, see Silbergeld, *Mind Landscapes*, 123–26; *Mountains of the Mind* (1970), 123–26; Cahill, *C. C. Wang: Landscape Paintings*, 877–84; and http://www.sealbank.net/m3mainfind.asp?L1=7&L2=71&L3=540&SK=US771540 (accessed October 4, 2022)

47. John Hay, *Kernels of Energy, Bones of Earth: The Rock in Chinese Art* (New York: China House Gallery, 1985).

48. Jerome Silbergeld, "Art without Age: Being Old and Young and C. C. Wang," in *The Lyrical Brush of C. C. Wang* (New York: Plum Blossoms Gallery, 2001), 5–10. He also collected paintings of rocks, such as *Red Friend* by the seventeenth-century painter Lan Ying 藍瑛 (1585–ca. 1664), now at the Metropolitan Museum of Art. See the museum's online collection: https://www.metmuseum.org/art/collection/search/39713, accessed October 26, 2022.

49. C. C. Wang, "Rare Rocks Are God's Creations," in *The Spirit of Gongshi: Chinese Scholar's Rocks*, ed. Keming Hu (Newton, MA: L. H., 1999), 16.

PLATES

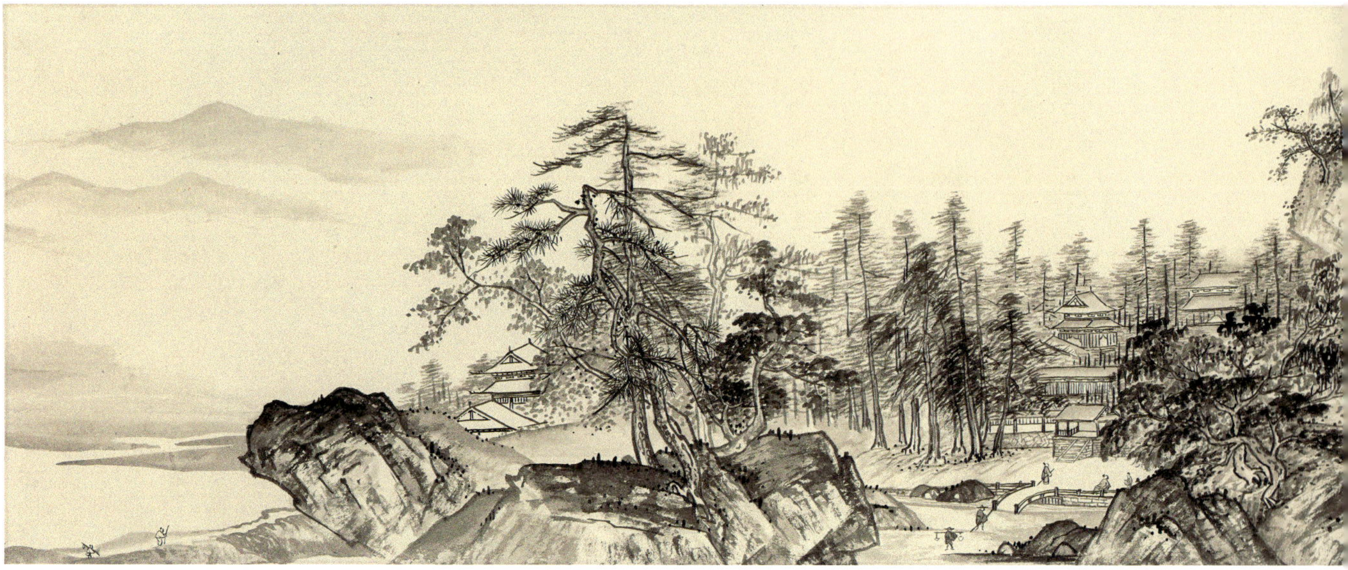

PLATE 1

no title (Collected Landscapes after the Old Masters), 1934–37
Handscroll in three parts, ink on paper
Collection of Mr. and Mrs. Arnold Chang

1a first painting (After Xia Gui), 1937
10 ¼ × 52 ⅞ inches (26 × 134.3 cm)

Inscription:

丁丑夏六月仿夏禹玉溪山清遠卷, 似仁淵譜兄正之, 洞庭王季銓寫於補拙山房.

"Copying the handscroll *Clear and Distant Views of Streams and Mountains* by Xia Yuyu (Xia Gui, fl. 1180–1224) in summer, the sixth month of the *dingchou* year, dedicated to my sworn elder brother Renyuan for correction, painted by Wang Jiquan from Dongting in Buzhuo Shanfang (Mountain Adobe of Compensating for Incompetence)."

Seal: 王選青 "Wang Xuanqing"

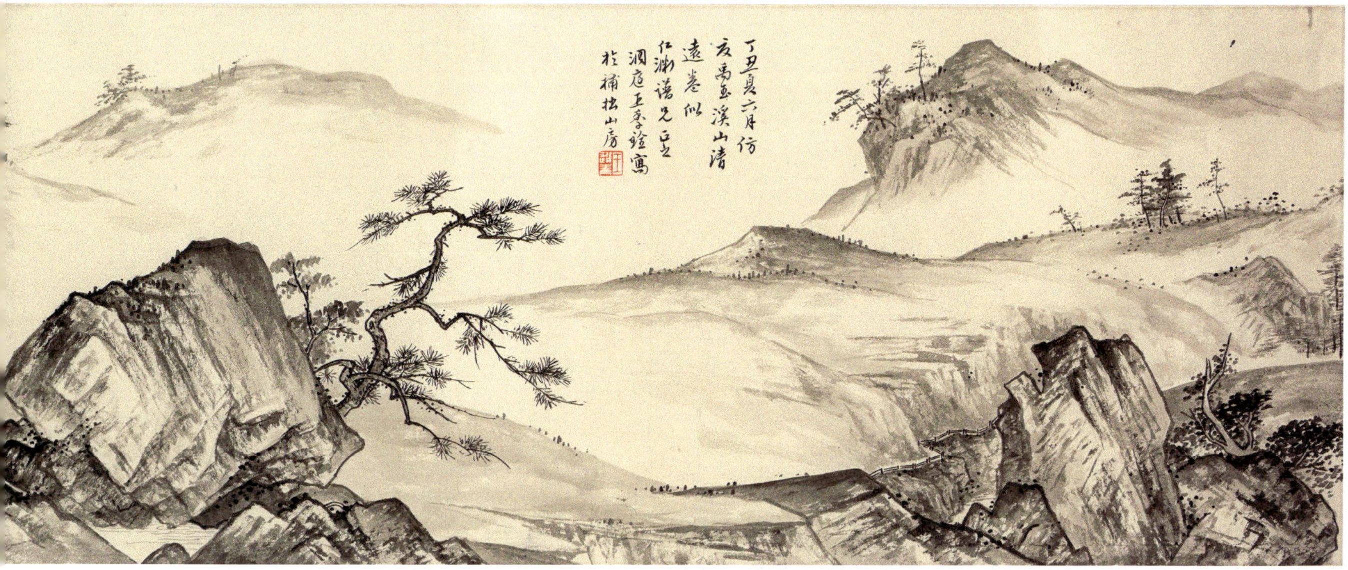
丁丑夏六月仿
夏禹玉溪山清
遠卷似
仁淵諸兄正之
洞庭王季銓寫
於補拙山房

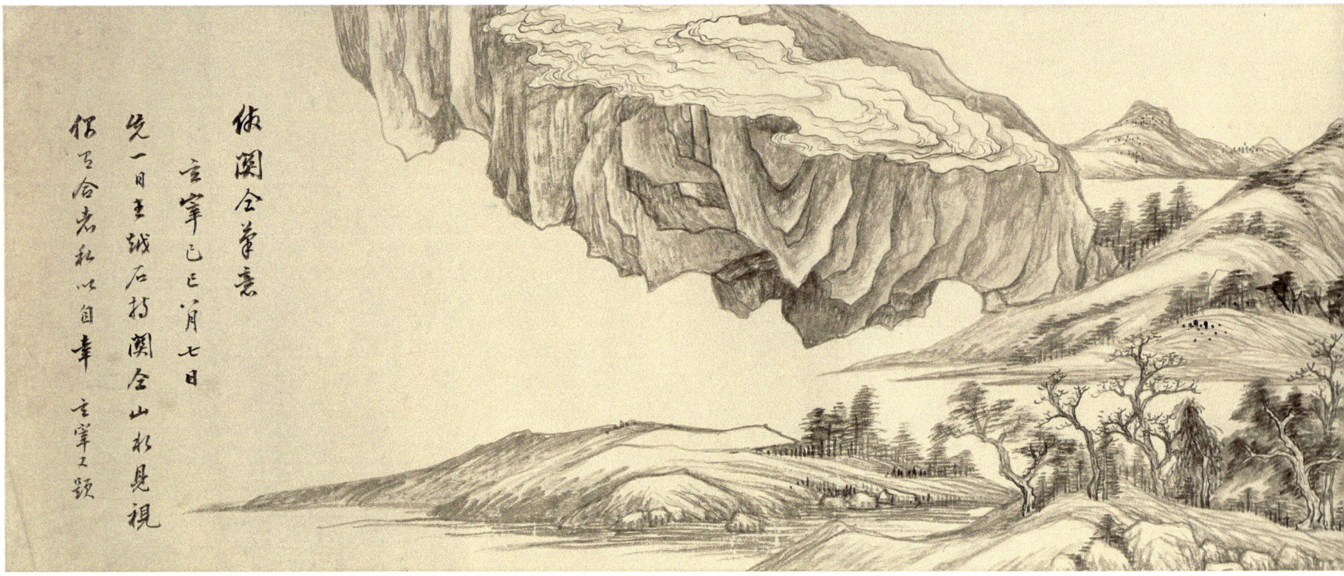

PLATE 1

no title (Collected Landscapes after the Old Masters), 1934–37
Handscroll in three parts, ink on paper
Collection of Mr. and Mrs. Arnold Chang

1b second painting (After Dong Qichang), undated (ca. 1930s)
10 ⅝ × 53 inches (27 × 134.6 cm)

Inscription:

仿關仝筆意, 玄宰己巳八月七日. 先一日, 王越石持關仝山水見視, 偶有合者, 私以自幸, 玄宰又題.

"After Guantong's *Brush Conception* [by] Xuanzai (Dong Qichang, 1555–1636), on the seventh day of the eighth month of the *jisi* year. The day before [the above date], Wang Yueshi brought me Guantong's landscape paintings for inspection. When I occasionally see one that I like, I feel grateful. Inscribed again by Xuanzai."

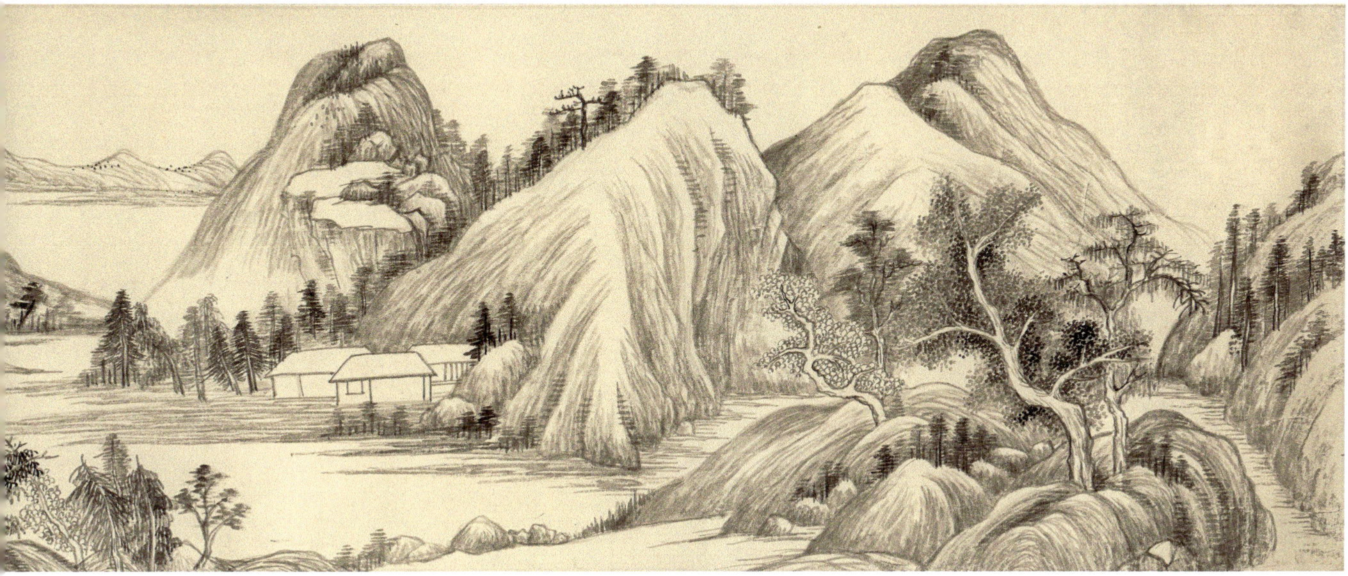

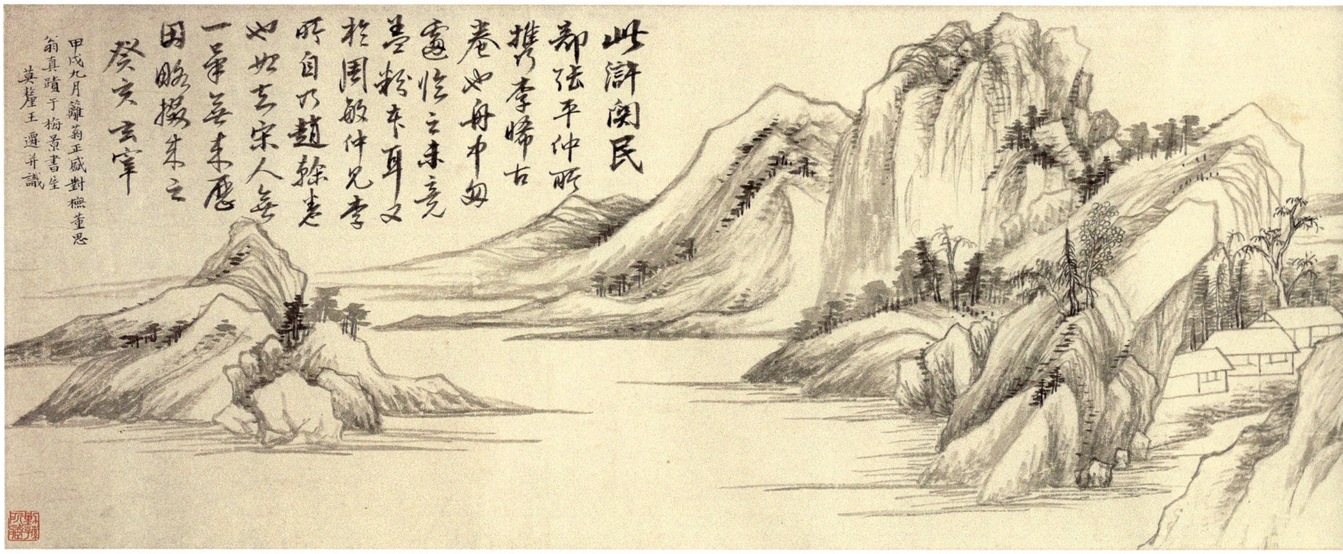

PLATE 1

no title (Collected Landscapes after the Old Masters), 1934–37
Handscroll in three parts, ink on paper
Collection of Mr. and Mrs. Arnold Chang

1c third painting (After Dong Qichang), 1934
10 ⅝ × 54 ¾ inches (27 × 139.1 cm)

Inscription:

此滸關民部張平仲所攜李晞古卷也, 舟中匆遽臨之未竟, 蓋粉本耳. 又于周敏仲見李所自, 乃趙幹卷也. 始知宋人無一筆無來歷, 因略掇成之, 癸亥玄宰.

甲戌九月籬菊正盛, 對橅董思翁真跡于梅景書屋, 莫釐王遷並識.

"This is [my copy of] the handscroll by Li Xigu (Li Tang, ca. 1066–1150) brought [to me] by Zhang Pingzhong, who is from Xuguan (Xushuguan Town in Jiangsu Province) and serves with the Ministry of Civil Affairs. My copy of the handscroll was hastily made in a boat, resulting in an unfinished draft. [Later], in Zhou Minzhong's place, I saw a scroll by Zhao Gan (fl. mid-10th century), which might have been the inspiration for Li Tang's work. In light of this, I learned that none of the brushstrokes by Song-dynasty artists were without foundation. [Based on Zhao Gan's painting], I completed [the draft]. [By] Xuanzai [Dong Qichang] in the *guihai* year.

In the ninth month of the *jiashu* year, the chrysanthemums on the fences are in full bloom. Facing the blossoms, I copied an authentic painting by Dong Siweng (Dong Qichang) in Meijing Shuwu (the Studio of Plum Scenery, owned by Wu Hufan [1894–1968]). Inscribed by Wang Qian from Moli."

Collector's Seal: 勤蓀所藏 "In the collection of Qinsun"

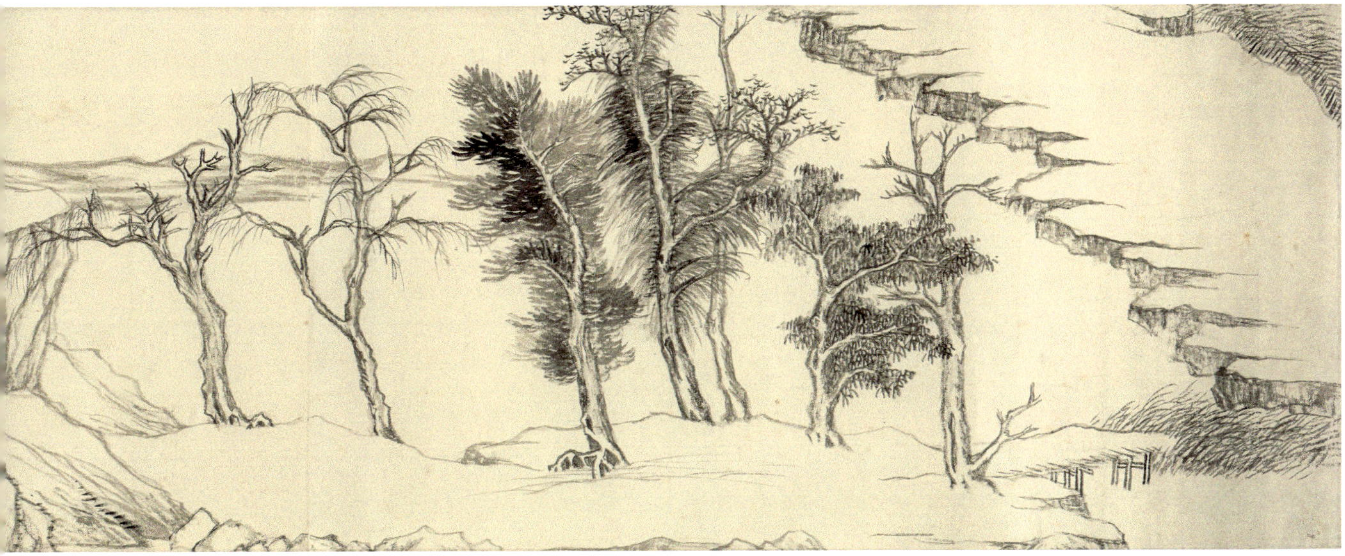

PLATE 2

Landscape after Wang Meng, undated (ca. 1940s)
Hanging scroll, ink and color on paper
Image: 42 × 19 ⅝ inches (106.7 × 49.8 cm)
Overall with mounting: 80 ¼ × 25 ⅛ inches (203.8 × 63.8 cm)
Collection of Mr. and Mrs. Arnold Chang

Inscription:

屋上青山屋下泉, 泉流直到竹廚邊.

客來何物供清坐, 露茗新抽穀雨前.

參用王叔明林麓幽居, 西郊草堂兩圖筆法, 王季遷寫.

"Above the hut are green mountains and below a stream, which flows to the scullery [surrounded by] bamboo groves. What should my guest sit on for refreshment when he arrives? Tea buds with dew that are newly sprouted before Grain Rain.

Inspired by the brushwork method of two paintings by Wang Shuming (Wang Meng, 1308–1385), *Quiet Life in a Wooded Glen* and *Thatched Cottage in Western Suburb*, painted by Wang Jiqian."

Seal: 王季遷印 "Seal of Wang Jiqian"

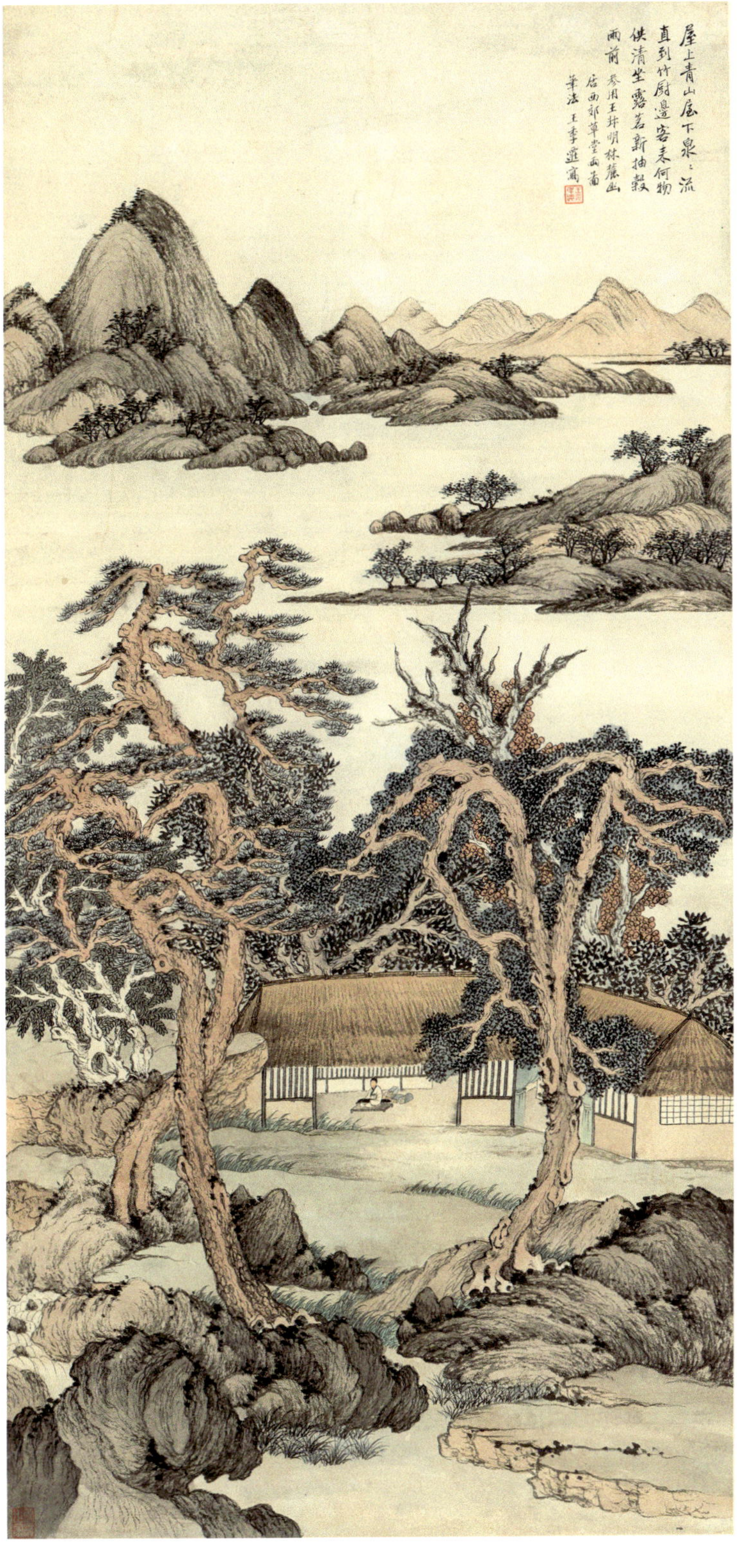
屋上青山屋下泉泉流直到竹廚邊客來何物供清坐露茗新抽穀雨前
參用王叔明林麓幽居西郊草堂畫筆法 王季遷寫

Painted seven years after he began taking classes at the Art Students League in New York, *Still Life* is the only surviving example of C. C. Wang's work from his time as a formal student of Western painting techniques. Emblematic still life themes—a lute, half a melon, paired fruits, a basket, a striped tapestry—are set in dynamic relationships and rendered across a range of hues. The loose brushwork, unlined forms, and layered painting application reveal Wang's deep admiration for Cézanne, Matisse, Braque, and other forebears of Western modernist painting, whom Wang began studying in Shanghai in the 1930s.[1] *Still Life* evidences the rigorous approach he took to learning new techniques and exemplifies early forays into compositional and textural strategies that Wang would later credit with transforming and expanding his traditional literati practice.

1. Jerome Silbergeld, *Mind Landscapes: The Paintings of C. C. Wang* (Seattle: Henry Art Gallery and University of Washington Press, 1987), 68.

PLATE 3

Still Life, 1956
Casein on canvas
26 × 40 inches (66 × 101.6 cm)
Courtesy Private Collection, New York

Inscription: 无言 "Wordless"

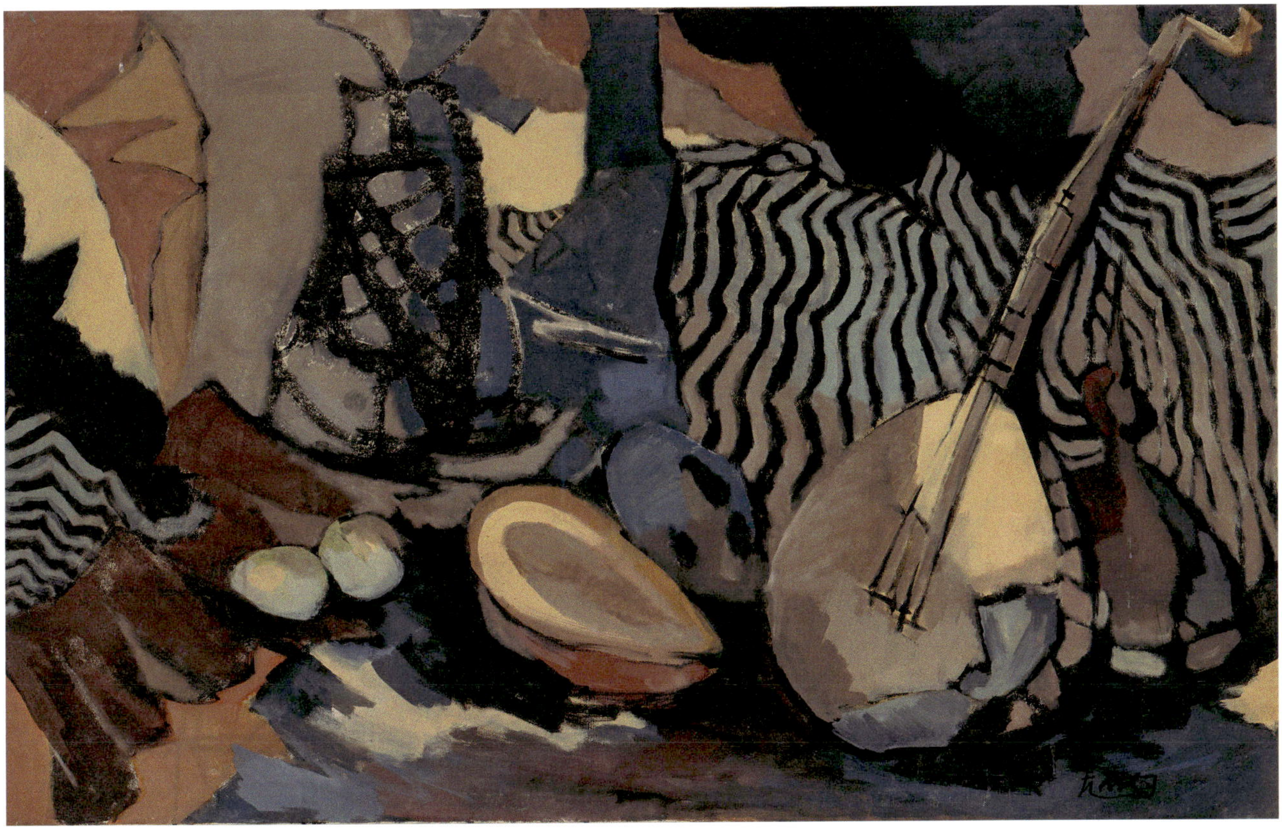

Painted eleven years after arriving in New York City, *Ox Blood Experiment* offers one of the earliest examples of the material and compositional investigations that Wang would continue for over five decades. Rather than working in the format of the standard horizontal, large-scale canvas of his Western contemporaries, Wang reoriented his composition vertically at an intimate scale. The use of ox blood alludes to the Chinese zodiac Year of the Ox, which recurred the year that the work was made. With time and environmental exposure, the red tones have slowly oxidized and transformed into copper. The resulting variations in tonality and texture emphasize the movement of the brush across the paper, while creating a sense of depth within each brushstroke. To a certain degree, Wang surrendered his skilled brushwork to the material tendencies of this sanguineous medium as he began to embrace uncontrolled outcomes. *Ox Blood Experiment* marks an adventurous turn in Wang's practice, perhaps the first moment he began mining the potential of abstraction in the service of individual expression.

PLATE 4

no title (Ox Blood Experiment), 1961
Ox blood and ink on paper
35 ½ × 6 ½ inches (90.2 × 16.5 cm)
Courtesy Private Collection, New York and Fu Qiumeng Fine Art, New York

Inscription: 辛丑紀千 "*Xinchou* [1961], Jiqian"

Seal: 王季遷印 "Seal of Wang Jiqian"

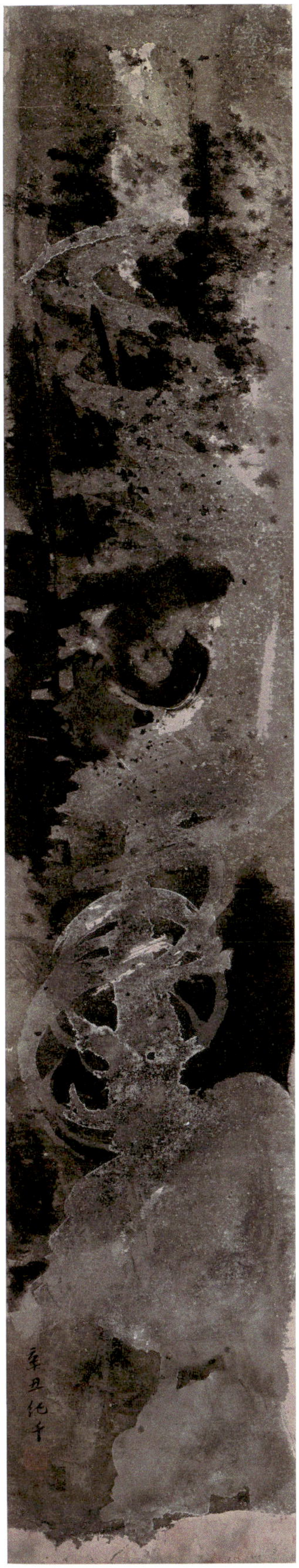
辛丑纪千

These bowls, the result of a fruitful familial collaboration, bring together Wang's painting with the ceramics of his daughter Yien-koo King. The vessels provide an alternate surface and medium for Wang to showcase the subtlety of his brushwork. Plum blossoms float atop a layer of smooth but dappled glaze, while earth tones remind us of the transformed clay's textural elements. The bowls are reminiscent of Cizhou wares from Northern China, in which bird-and-flower paintings are commonly applied in black or brown slips atop a layer of white slip. Throughout Wang's long career, King provided invaluable support to her father, overseeing responsibilities that ranged from studio assistant to manager. These elegantly thrown ceramic vessels remind us that she is an artist in her own right, and the quality of her craftsmanship provides a firm foundation for Wang's brushwork. This intimate partnership would later be shared as a gift to Wang's student Arnold Chang.

PLATE 5

5a C. C. Wang and Yien-koo King
no title (Ceramic Bowl with Plum Blossoms), undated (ca. 1970s)
Glazed earthenware
Height: 2 ¾ inches (7 cm)
Diameter: 9 ½ inches (24.1 cm)
Collection of Mr. and Mrs. Arnold Chang

Inscription: 己千 "Jiqian"

5b C. C. Wang and Yien-koo King
no title (Ceramic Bowl with Plum Blossoms), undated (ca. 1970s)
Glazed earthenware
Height: 2 ½ inches (6.4 cm)
Diameter: 11 inches (27.9 cm)
Collection of Mr. and Mrs. Arnold Chang

Inscription: 己千 "Jiqian"

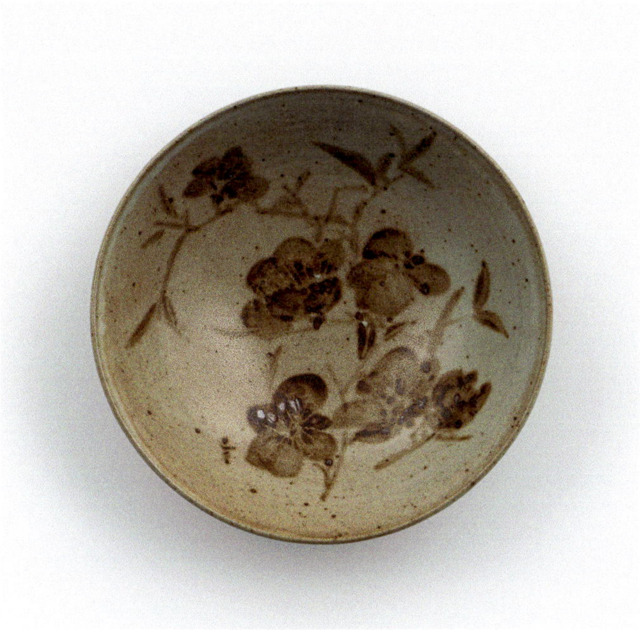

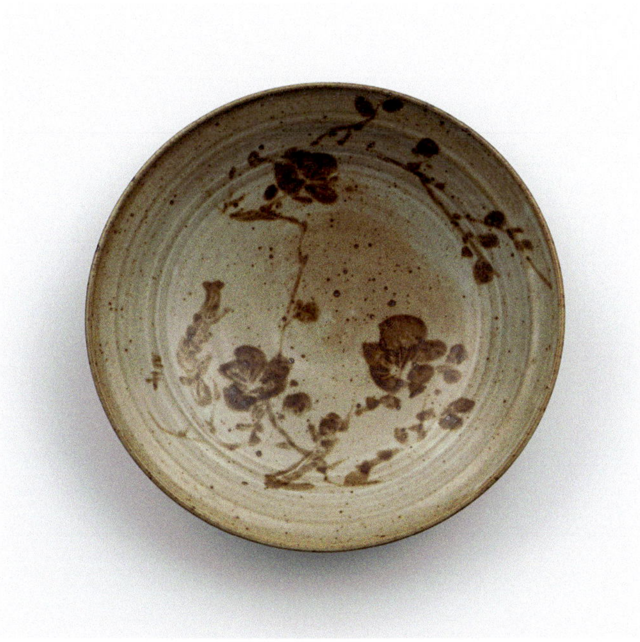

PLATE 6

Landscape No. 475, 1983
Hanging scroll, ink and color on paper
Image: 39 ⅞ × 20 inches (101.3 × 50.8 cm)
Overall with mounting: 75 ⅜ × 25 inches (191.5 × 63.5 cm)
Courtesy Private Collection, New York

Inscription: 癸亥五月七日, 己千 “*Guihai* [1983], May 7, Jiqian”

Seal: 肖形印: 羊 Square pictorial seal: Ram

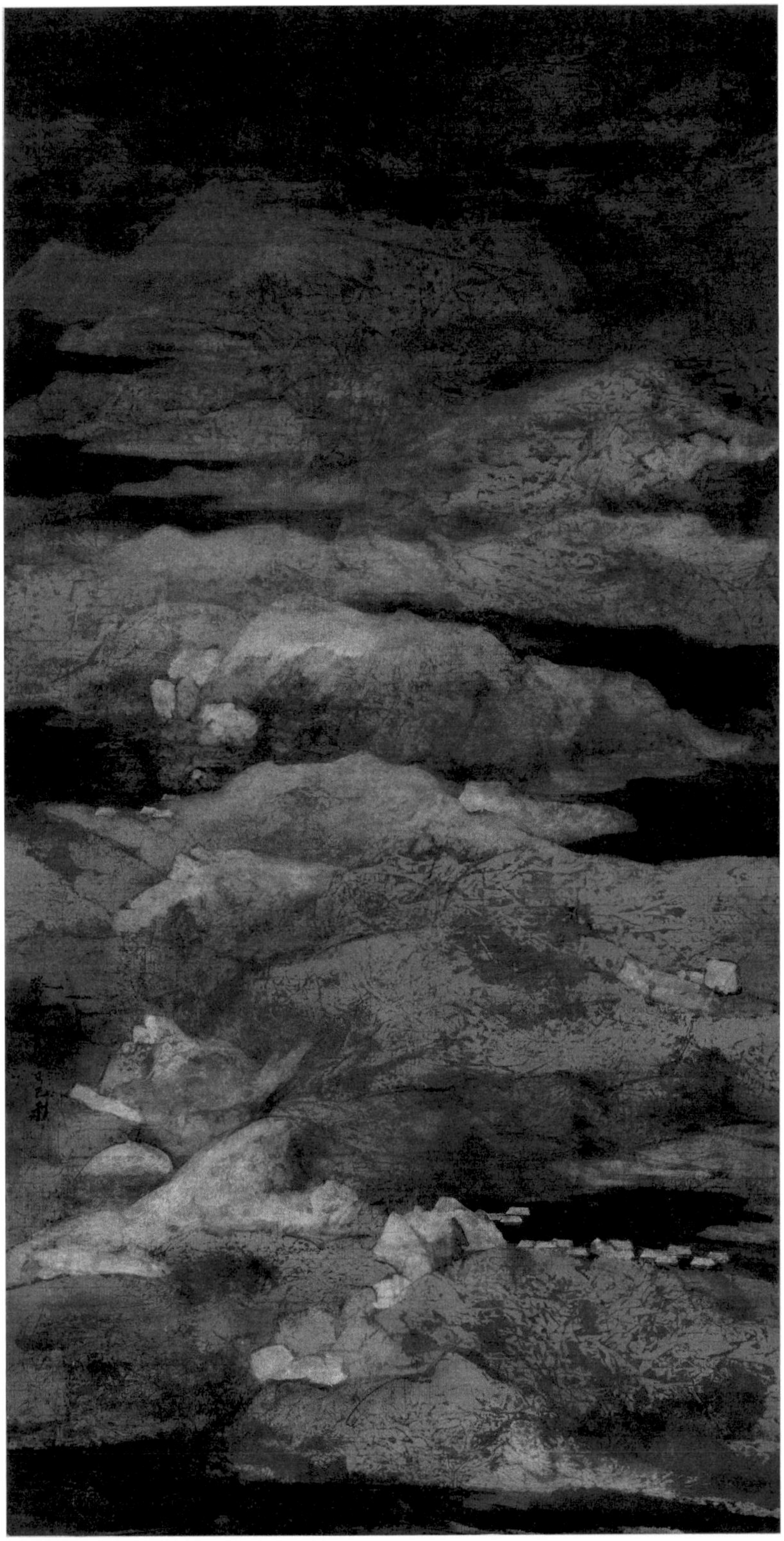

This towering landscape is a pointed homage to *Travelers among Mountains and Streams*, a landmark accomplishment in the history of Chinese painting by the reclusive Northern Song painter Fan Kuan (ca. 960–after 1023). In Wang's work, a formidable mountain rises from mists and streams, looming above a foregrounded ridge dotted with miniscule houses, echoing the scale and composition of Fan Kuan's painting of nearly a millennium earlier. To convey the roughness of the rocks, Wang replaced the master's signature "raindrop" method of brushwork with textures created by chance, applying a roller wrapped with crumpled paper that had been dipped in ink.

Fan Kuan sought to convey the essence of nature rather than strict likeness and once declared that it is "better to study nature, and, better still, to follow one's heart." Wang's experiments incorporating chance elements echo his predecessor and honor the monumental landscape painting tradition while forging visual innovations.

PLATE 7

no title (Landscape after Fan Kuan), 1985
Hanging scroll, ink on paper
Image: 49 × 26 inches (124.5 × 66 cm)
Overall with mounting: 89 × 31 inches (226.1 × 78.7 cm)
Courtesy Private Collection, New York

Inscription: 乙丑六月八日王己千 "*Yichou* [1985], June 8, Wang Jiqian"

Seal, below signature: 己千創稿 "Sketches created by Jiqian"

Seal, bottom right corner: 非南非北, 亦古亦今 "Neither the Northern nor the Southern [School]; both ancient and modern"

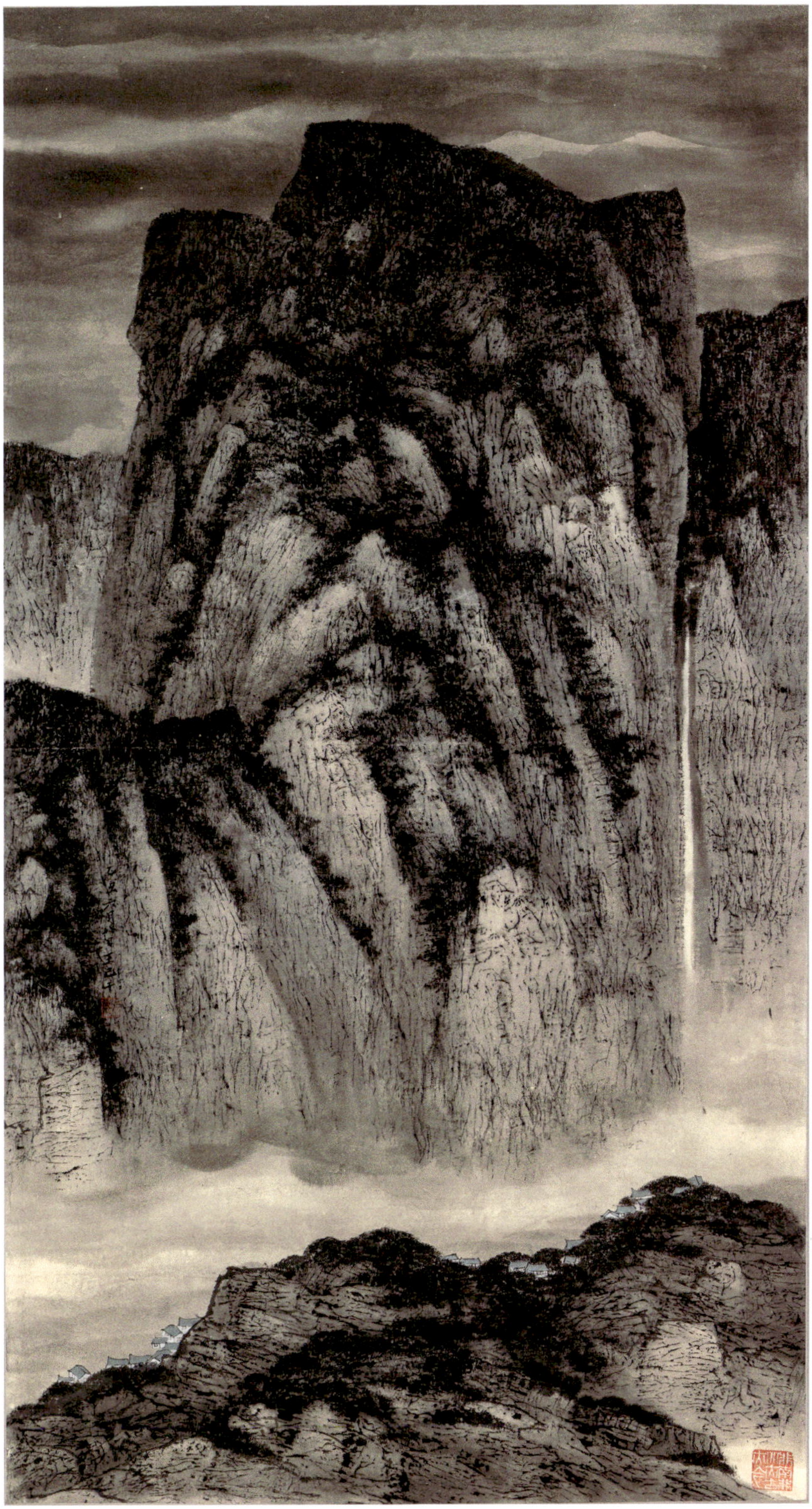

PLATE 8

no title (Dark Mountains), 1986
Hanging scroll, ink on paper
Image: 24 ⅜ × 26 ⅛ inches (61.9 × 66.4 cm)
Overall with mounting: 68 × 35 inches (172.7 × 88.9 cm)
Courtesy Private Collection

Inscription: 丙寅七月廿七日, 王己千 "*Binyin* [1986], July 27, Wang Jiqian"

Seal: 己千創稿 "Sketches created by Jiqian"

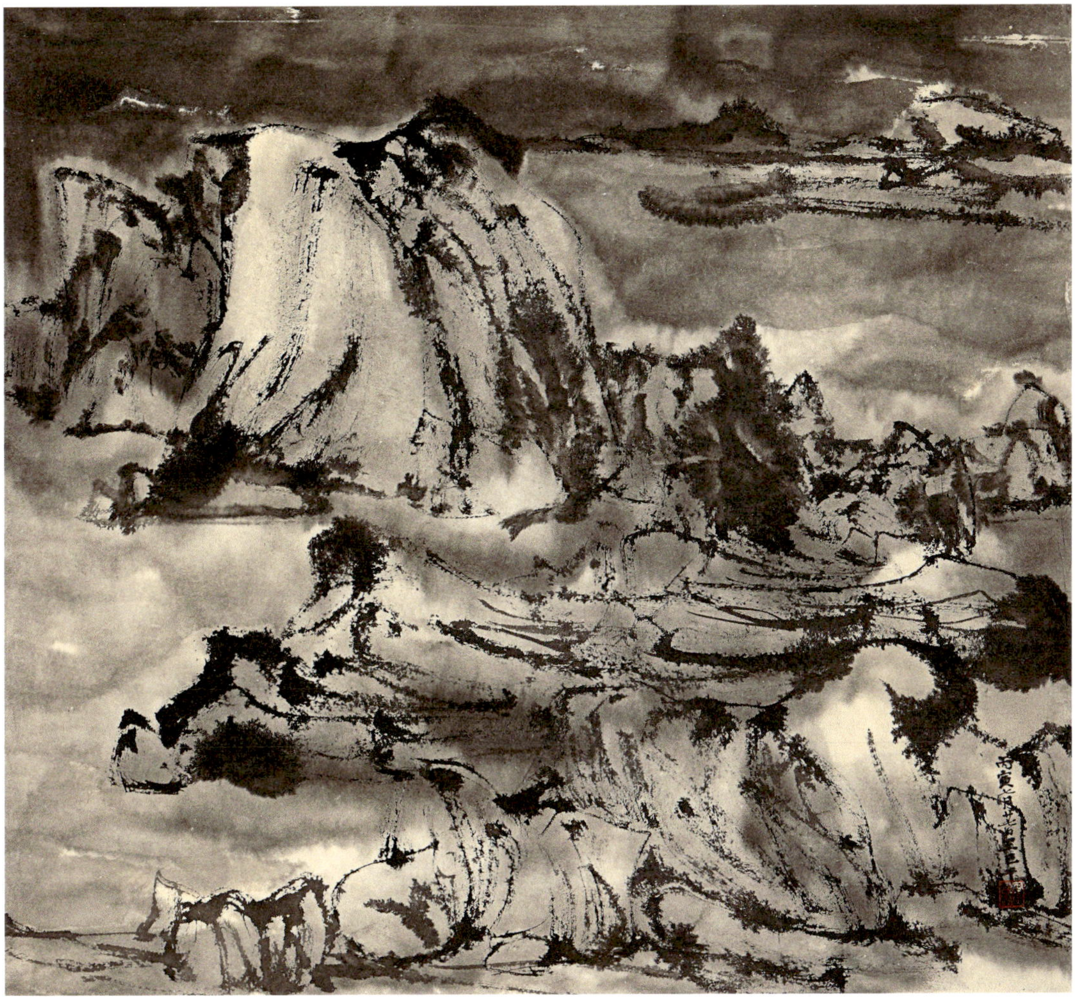

PLATE 9

no title (Landscape No. 970-B), 1987
Ink on paper
17 ¾ × 30 ⅞ inches (45.1 × 78.4 cm)
Courtesy Private Collection, New York and Fu Qiumeng Fine Art, New York

Inscription (identical on both vertical and horizontal axes):
丁卯二月十日，王己千心造 “*Dingmao* [1987], February 10, wholeheartedly made by Wang Jiqian”

Seal (vertical axis): 己千創稿 “Sketches created by Jiqian”

Seal (horizontal axis): 季遷心境 “Jiqian's realm of mind”

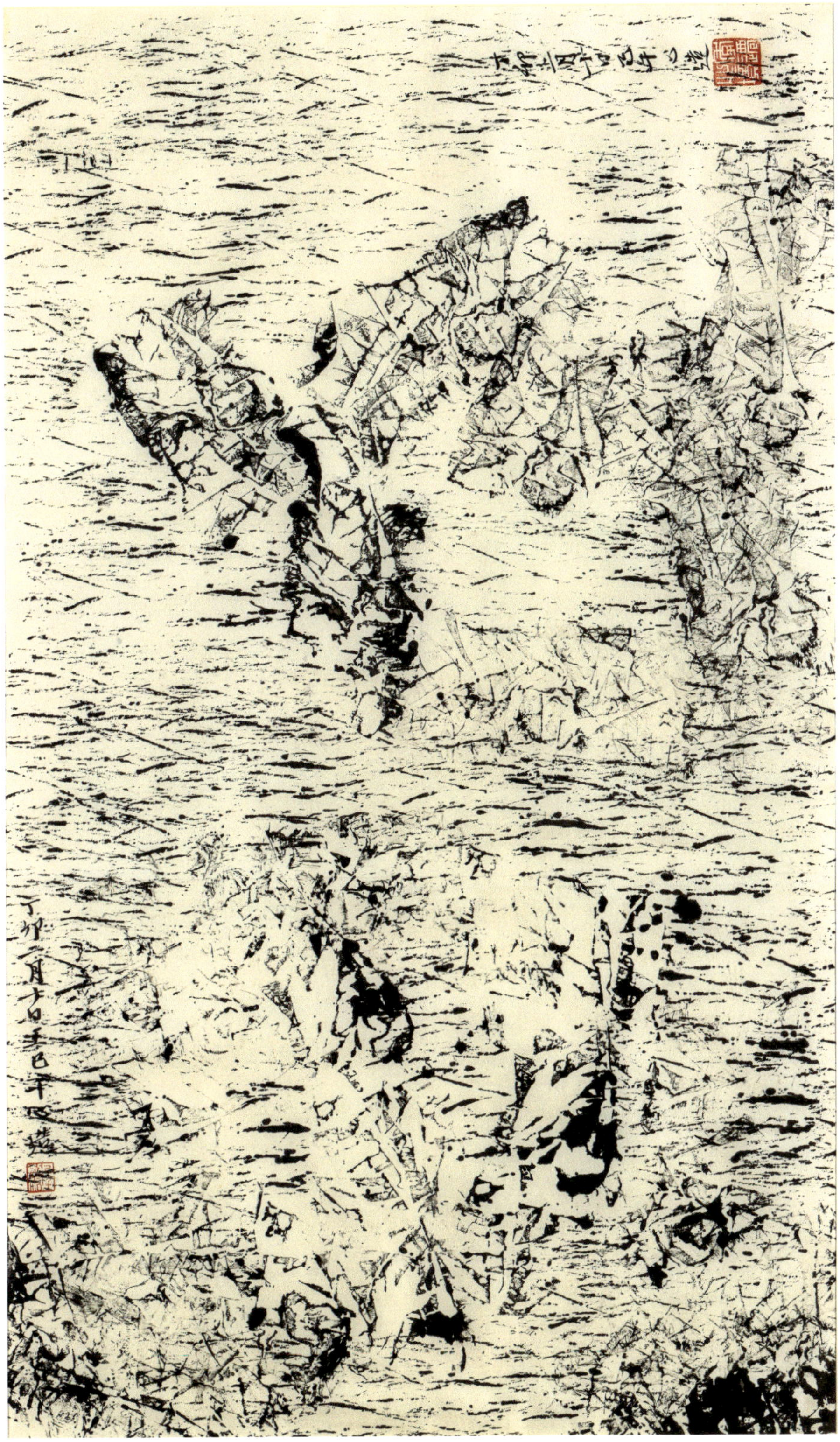

Linear Brushwork Experiment was likely developed from a technical demonstration performed by Wang for his students and offers insight into the artist's approach to creating landscape forms. This painting focuses on the brushwork necessary to create rocks and mountains, building a single, twisting form that stretches from the foreground into the distance. Trees, shrubs, and houses—important formal elements in many of Wang's paintings—are omitted, forcing a viewer to concentrate on the interplay of lines used to construct this stripped-down, almost skeletal landscape. Whether playing with wet or dry brushwork, ink tones, or textural gestures, here line alone efficiently expresses space and builds structural form. Whether in pursuit of abstraction or naturalist representation, this linear quality can be seen across Wang's body of work.

PLATE 10

no title (Linear Brushwork Experiment), 1989
Ink on paper
45 × 24 ¼ inches (114.3 × 61.6 cm)
Courtesy Private Collection, New York and Fu Qiumeng Fine Art, New York

Inscription: 己巳一月三日己千稿 "*Jisi* [1989], January 3, sketch by Jiqian"

Seal: 己千創稿 "Sketches created by Jiqian"

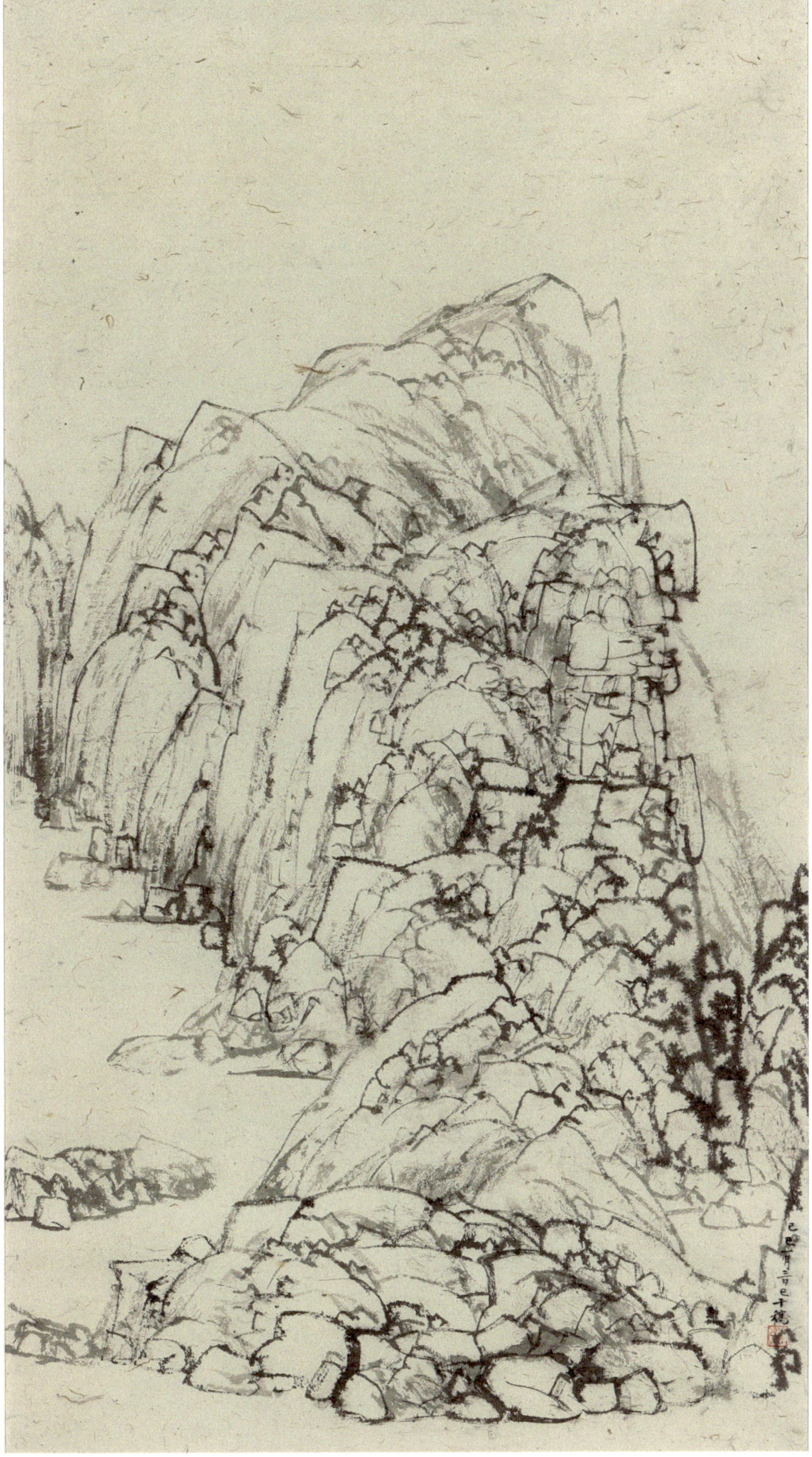

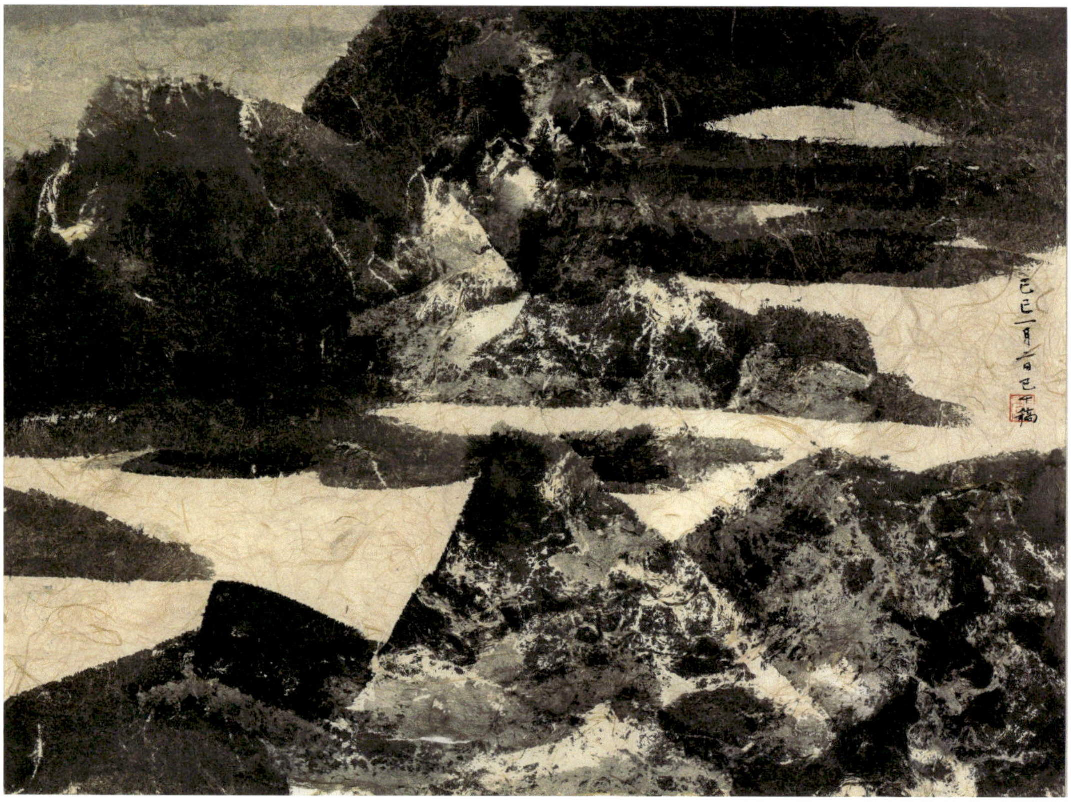

PLATE 11

no title (Mountain Valley at Night), 1989
Ink on paper
18 ¾ × 25 inches (47.6 × 63.5 cm)
Courtesy Private Collection, New York and Fu Qiumeng Fine Art, New York

Inscription: 己巳一月二日己千稿 "*Jisi* [1989], January 2, sketch by Jiqian"

Seal: 己千創稿 "Sketches created by Jiqian"

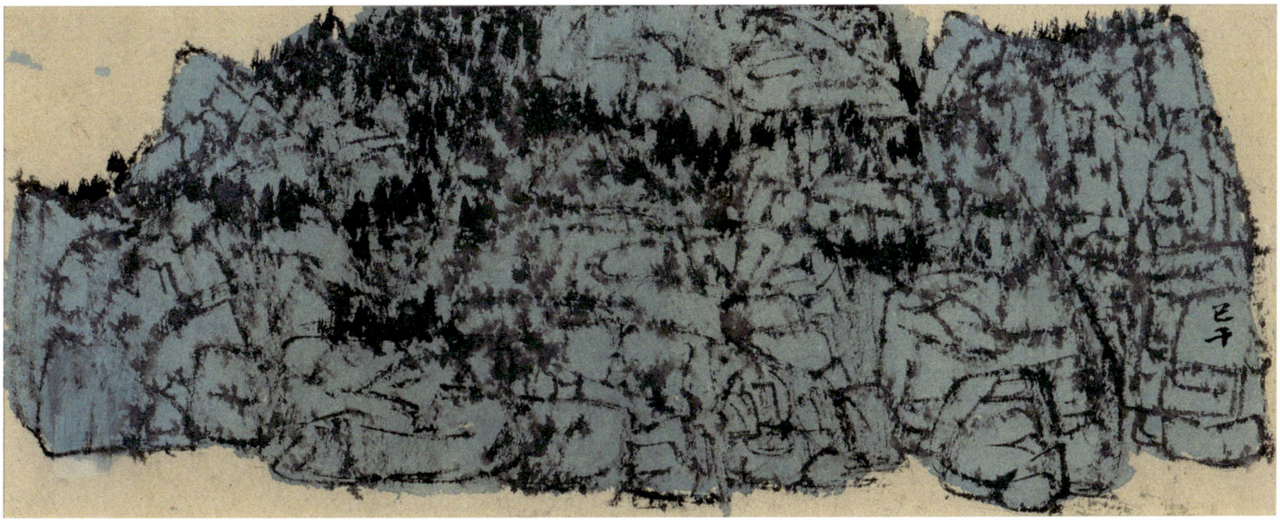

PLATE 12

no title (Blue Forest), undated
Ink and color on paper
5 ¾ × 13 ¾ inches (14.6 × 34.9 cm)
Courtesy Private Collection, New York and Fu Qiumeng Fine Art, New York

Inscription: 己千 "Jiqian"

This whimsical painting depicts a springtime street view from the window of Wang's ninth-floor studio, which was located half a block from the Leubsdorf Gallery at Hunter College. The center of the composition is a carriage house (now the Urasenke Chanoyu Center) on 69th Street that once served as the studio of the artist Mark Rothko. In this tight composition, Wang set buildings of varying heights, shapes, and sizes alongside one another with rooflines sloping at opposing angles. Unlike technical renderings of Manhattan that might depict glass, steel, brick, and stone in a straightforward fashion, Wang emphasized the spire and arched openings of the Romanesque Revival–style studio and imbues the urbanscape with gentle hues more common to natural landscapes than to built environments. His verdant palette recalls the artist's depictions of mountains, valleys, and buttes.

Wang's use of pastoral colors and complex brushstrokes suggests that this unconventional landscape was not only inspired by observation but also by the artist's imagination. Integrating a Western modernist cityscape with a "mind landscape" of the Chinese literati tradition, whereby artists expressed their interiority through the form of exterior scenes, this painting's swooning buildings and exaggerated features offer a charming example of the artist's enthusiasm for stretching tradition.

PLATE 13

no title (Mark Rothko's Carriage House), 1994
Hanging scroll, ink and color on paper
Image: 14 ½ × 18 ½ inches (36.8 × 47 cm)
Overall with mounting: 71 × 24 inches (180.3 × 61 cm)
Collection of Mr. and Mrs. Arnold Chang

Inscription: 甲戌三月廿九日，己千 "*Jiaxu* [1994], March 29, Jiqian"

Seal: 己千製 "Made by Jiqian"

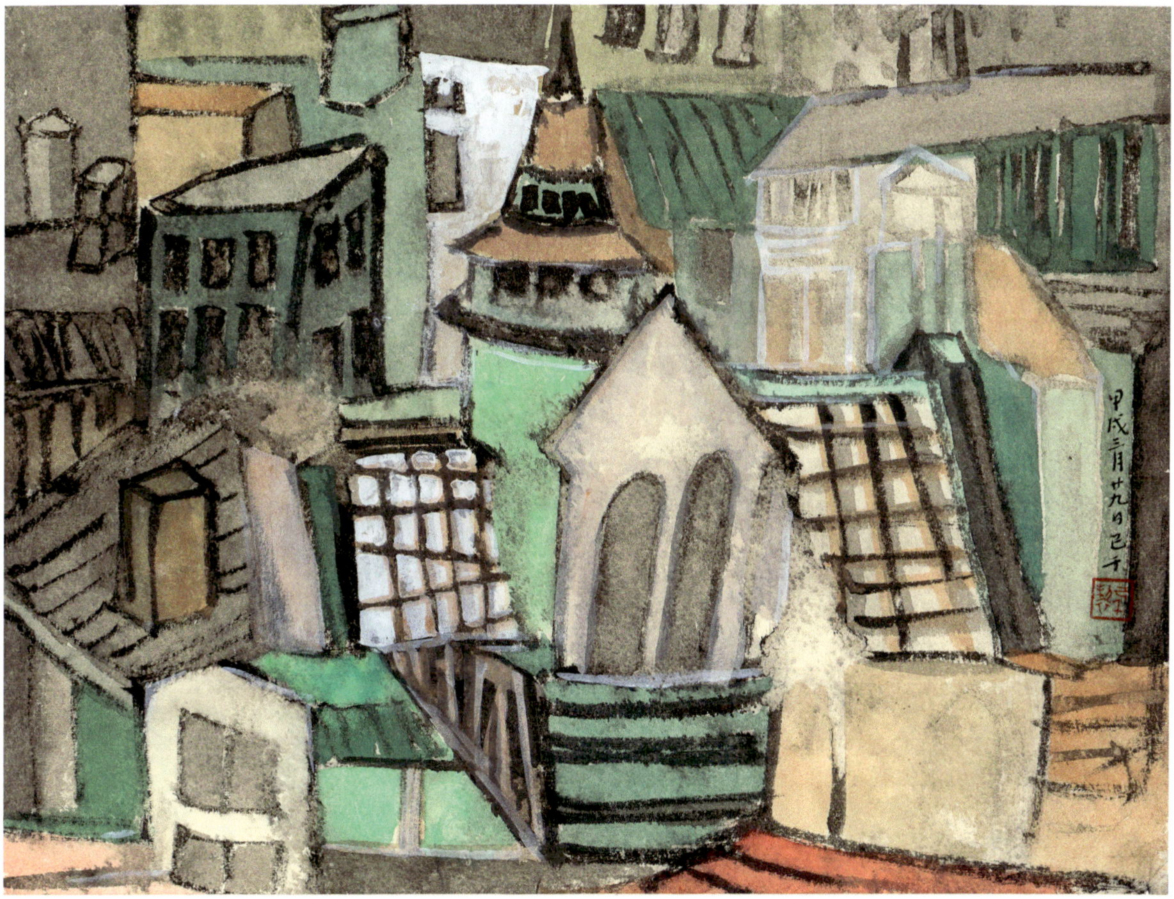
甲戌三月廿九日己千

Completed over the course of three years, this album is a virtuosic display of many painting styles and strategies that defined the artist's career. The multiplicity of the traditional album format allowed the artist to showcase a broad range of vistas, colorations, settings, and references to past masters. Wang masterfully captured the spirit of craggy rocks, misty mountain peaks, bare earth, defined foliage, floating evergreens, and eroding ranges by deploying all manner of wet and dry brushstrokes. Deliberate pigment choices evoke the archaic tradition (blue and green) and terrains of the American West (red earthen tones). Compositionally, he pushed views and perspective in a variety of directions—up close, far away, overhead, below.

Color is intentionally absent in one leaf to invoke the mode of artist Ni Zan (1301–1374) (leaf q). Another emulates the wet dots and splashed ink of Mi Fu (1051–1107) (leaf l). Dynamic rock formations in several other leaves recall the arterial lines of Shitao (1642–1707); one leaf in particular features a continuous rocky form across the center of the composition (leaf g), recalling an iconic painting from *Album for Daoist Yu* by Shitao, one of the most cherished paintings that Wang acquired from the collection of the German art historian Victoria Contag. A dedicatory colophon (Second End Colophon) by the artist's friend, the renowned calligrapher Zhang Longyan, notes Wang's works as "different in form and same in spirit" when compared to earlier masters, attributing his innovations to the daily perusal of Song and Yuan album paintings in his collection.

PLATE 14

Splendid Views of Rivers and Mountains, 1995–2001
16 painted leaves and 3 colophons
Ink and color on paper
Approximately 12 × 18 ½ inches (30.5 × 47 cm) each
Collection of Pao Yung Chao

Frontispiece a	Inscriptions: 江山勝覽 "Splendid Views of Rivers and Mountains" 寶榮伉儷囑, 王己千自署 "At the request of Pao Yung and his wife, self-inscribed by Wang Jiqian" Seal 1: 家在姑蘇 "Hometown in Suzhou" Seal 2: 谿岍草堂 "Thatched Cottage by Riverside"
Leaf b	Inscription: 乙亥,己千 "*Yihai* [1995], Jiqian"
Leaves c, d	Inscription: 己千 "Jiqian"
Leaf e	Inscription: 王己千 "Wang Jiqian"
Leaves b, c, d, e	Seal: 己千創稿 "Sketches created by Jiqian"

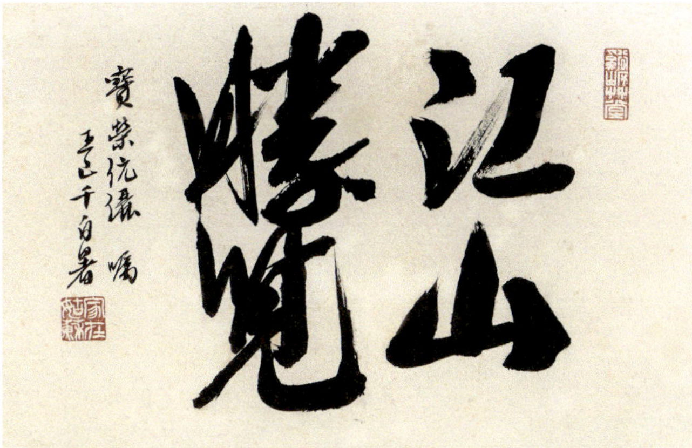

a

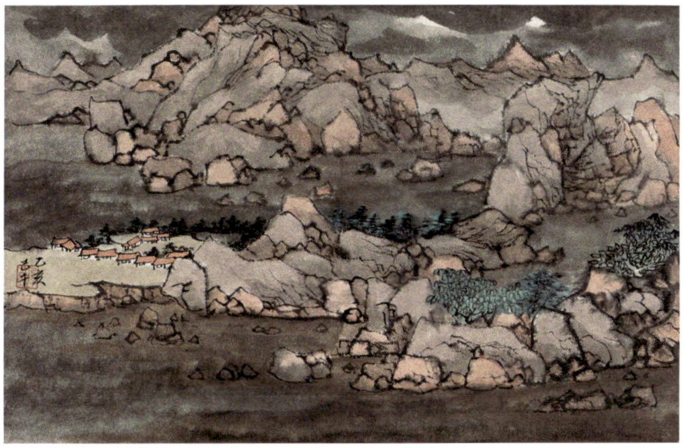

b

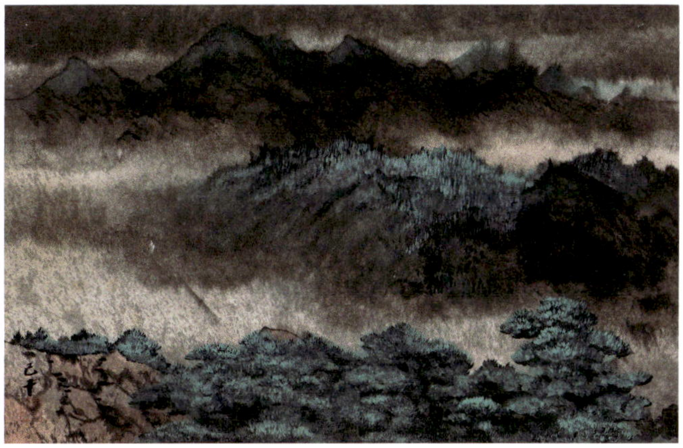

c

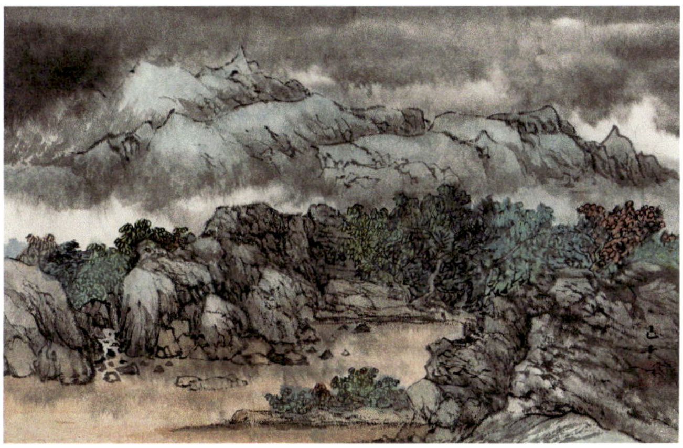

d

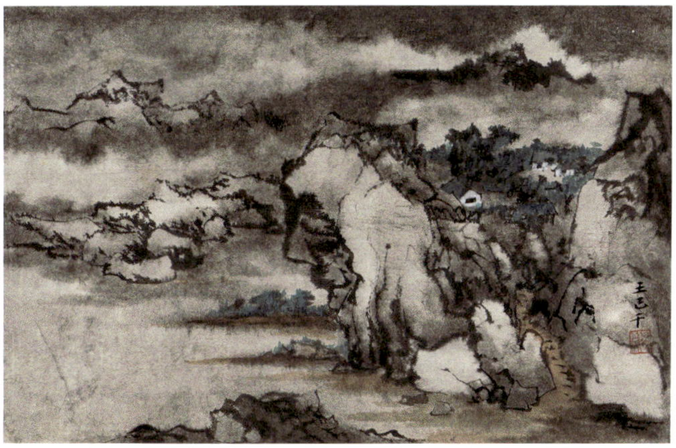

e

PLATE 14

Splendid Views of Rivers and Mountains, 1995–2001
16 painted leaves and 3 colophons
Ink and color on paper
Approximately 12 × 18 ½ inches (30.5 × 47 cm) each
Collection of Pao Yung Chao

Leaves f, g, h, i, j	Inscription: 己千 "Jiqian"
	Seal: 己千創稿 "Sketches created by Jiqian"
Leaf k	Inscription: 己千 "Jiqian"
	Seal: 王己千鉥 "Seal of Wang Jiqian"

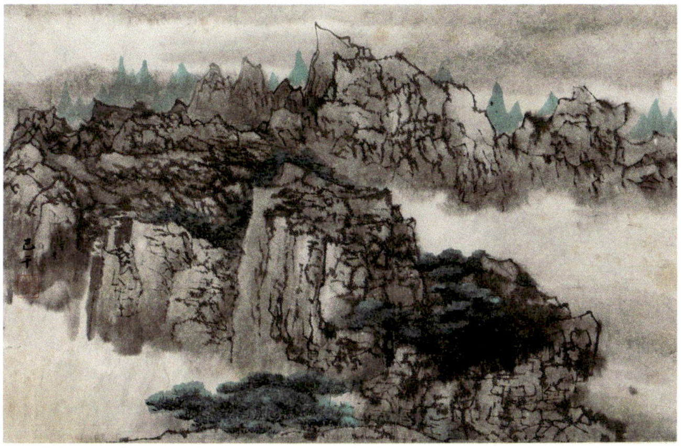

f

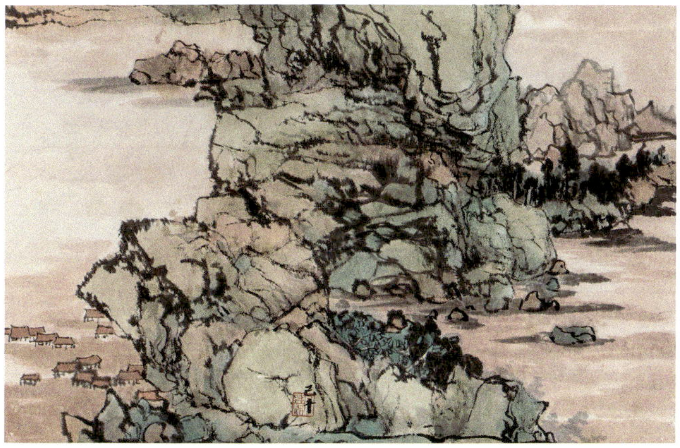

g

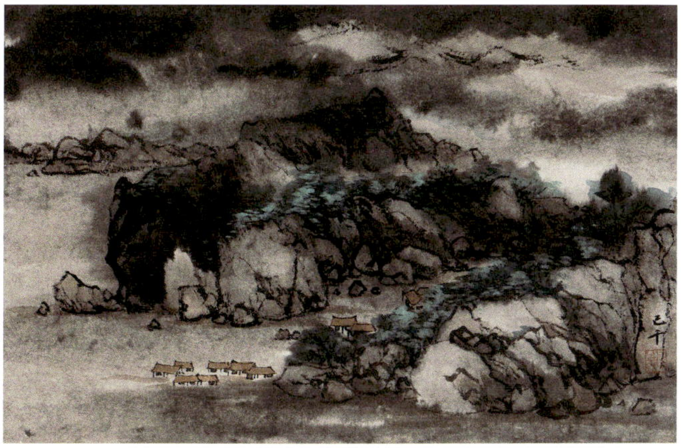

h

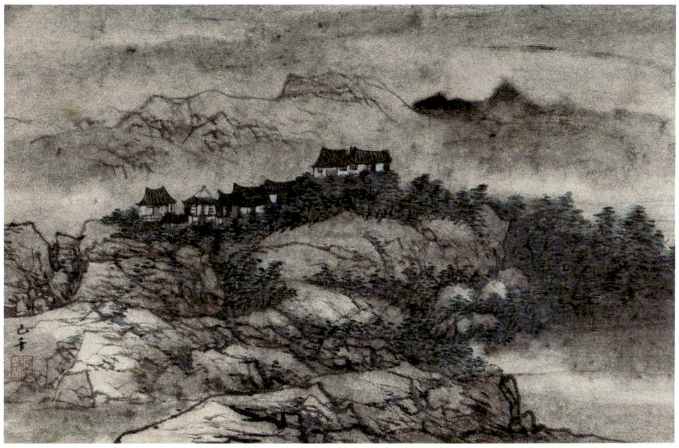

i

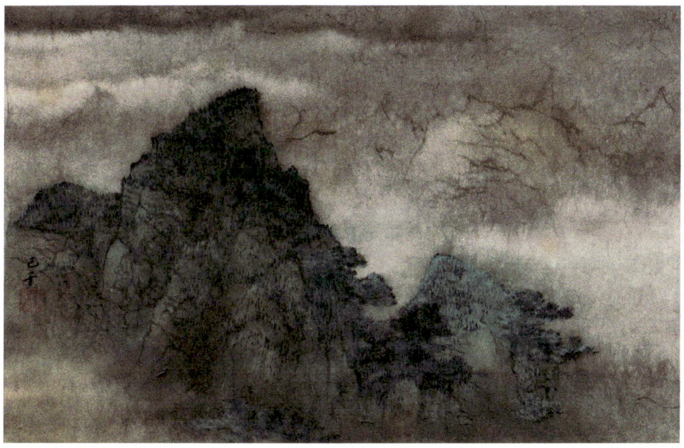

j

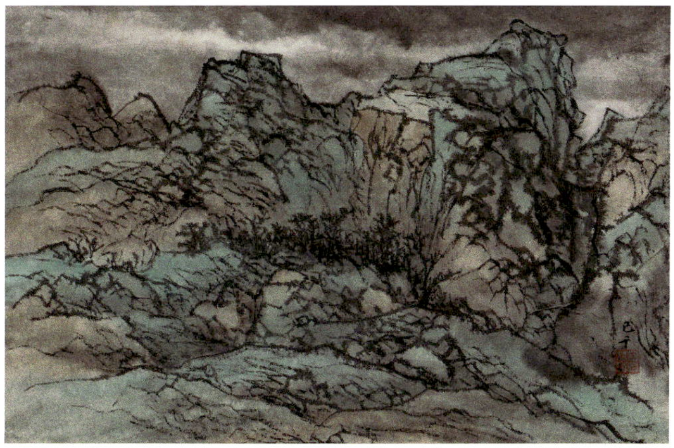

k

PLATE 14

Splendid Views of Rivers and Mountains, 1995–2001
16 painted leaves and 3 colophons
Ink and color on paper
Approximately 12 × 18 ½ inches (30.5 × 47 cm) each
Collection of Pao Yung Chao

Leaves l, m, o, p	Inscription: 己千 "Jiqian"
	Seal: 己千創稿 "Sketches created by Jiqian"
Leaf n	Inscription: 己千 "Jiqian"
	Seal: 王己千鉥 "Seal of Wang Jiqian"
Leaf q	Inscription: 辛巳正月,己千 "*Xinsi* [2001], January, Jiqian"
	Seal: 王己千鉥 "Seal of Wang Jiqian"

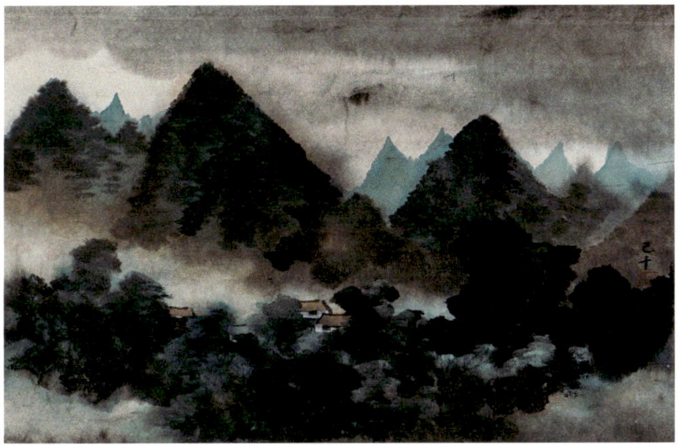

l

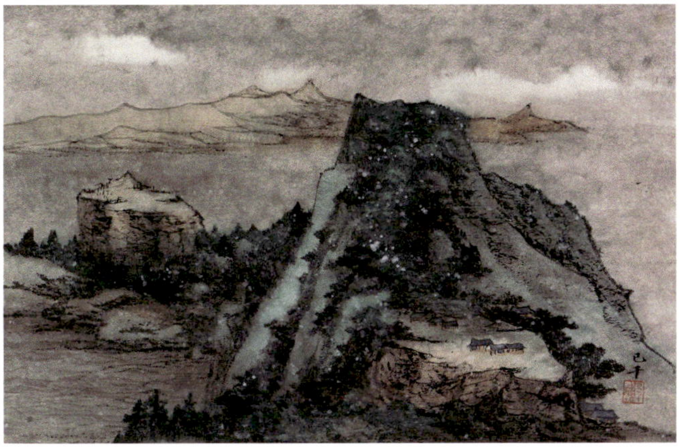

m

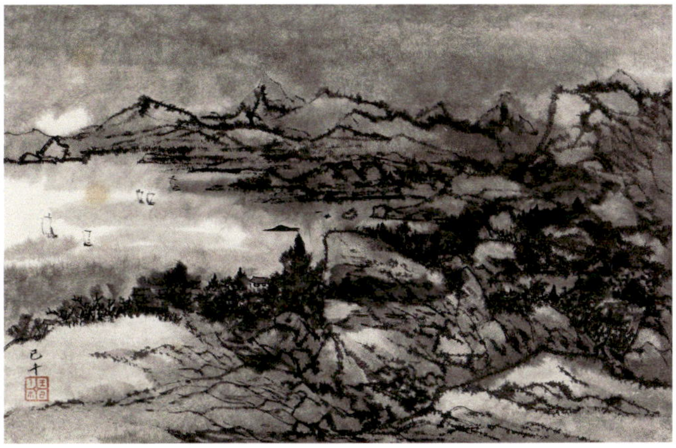

n

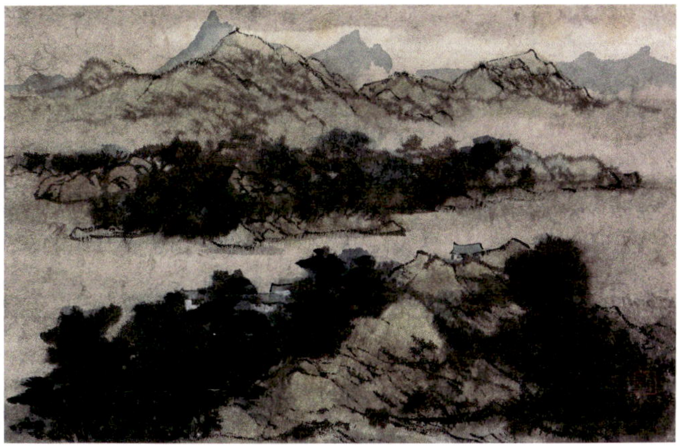

o

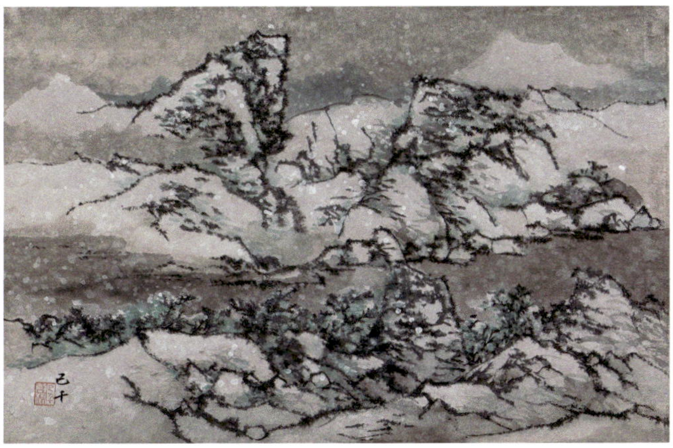

p

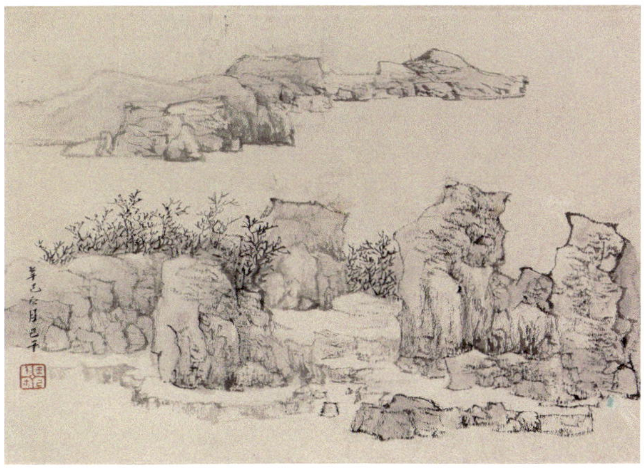

q

PLATE 14

Splendid Views of Rivers and Mountains, 1995–2001
16 painted leaves and 3 colophons
Ink and color on paper
Approximately 12 × 18 ½ inches (30.5 × 47 cm) each
Collection of Pao Yung Chao

First End Colophon r

Inscription:

寶榮趙兄為故友, 錢瘦鐵得意弟子, 好筆墨, 並工篆刻, 於余畫有嗜痂之癖, 屢囑寫畫冊以供清玩, 惟久違, 執筆應命. 乙亥初冬, 稍得餘閒, 漫筆此十頁, 即以奉踐宿諾, 並盼藝苑賢達有以教我也, 震澤王己千誌.

"My old friend Pao Yung Chao is one of Qian Shoutie's (1897–1967) beloved disciples. He enjoys painting and writing calligraphy and is adept at seal carving. Due to his fondness for my paintings, he urged me to paint him an album for his refined enjoyment. Having long neglected this duty, I took up my brush and responded to the request. In the early winter of the *yihai* year, I had some spare time to paint these ten leaves leisurely, which fulfilled my earlier promise. I sincerely appreciate comments from prominent and proficient members of the art community. Inscribed by Wang Jiqian from Zhenze."

Seal 1: 家在姑蘇 "Hometown in Suzhou"

Seal 2: 懷雲廔 "Hall where Ni Yunlin [Ni Zan] is treasured."

Second End Colophon s

Inscription:

己千翰墨兼神俊靈和之氣, 比諸前賢劇跡, 大都形異而神同, 不拘於虛, 無乖常理, 綱目存胸, 放膽佈局, 皴渲運筆, 著意經營, 是以日新又新, 變化無倪也.

己千一日舉所寶藏宋元卷冊, 謂余曰, 鑒之必精, 擬之貴似, 所以承先傳火也. 不蹈故轍, 日闢新疆, 所以立己啟後也. 今所努力, 敬業而已, 豈駭俗耶?

寶榮兄屬題己千大師畫冊, 因識所知, 十之張隆延.

"Jiqian's paintings and pieces of calligraphy are full of vigorous energy and enchanting harmony. Although his works look different from their ancient predecessors, they share the same spirit. His art is not groundless and conforms to the conventions. With both the general configuration and specific details in mind, he composes the painting in an audacious manner. By carefully planning his compositions, he manipulates his brush to create texture strokes and atmospheric washes. Due to this, his artwork continually develops inventiveness and embraces boundless change.

One day, Jiqian mentioned to me his collection of scrolls and albums from the Song and Yuan dynasties and said to me, 'In order to carry the torch of the forebears and pass it on, one needs to possess a strong understanding of connoisseurship as well as a strong sense of faithfulness when copying ancient masterpieces. But rather than traveling the beaten path, one should constantly open new borders in order to create distinctive artistic styles and inspire future generations. All of my hard work is merely dedication to my art. How is this extraordinary?'

My friend Pao Yung requested me to inscribe this album by master Jiqian. I therefore wrote what I knew about him. [By] Shizhi Zhang Longyan."

Seal 1: 隆延 "Longyan"

Seal 2: 法學博士 "Doctor of Law"

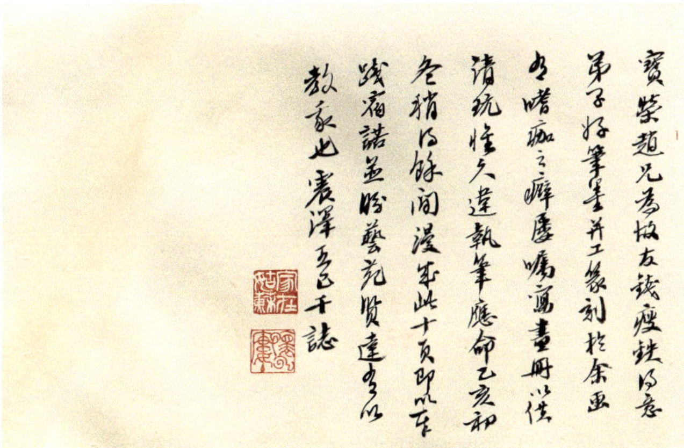

r

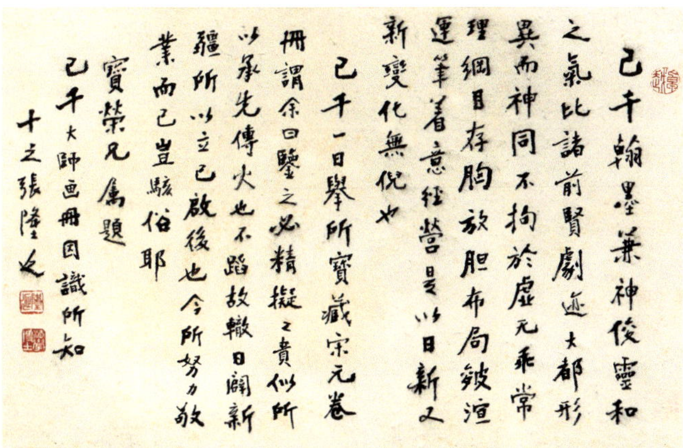

s

PLATE 15

no title (Abstract Work with Red), undated (ca. 1990s)
Ink and color on paper
22 ⅝ × 14 ¾ inches (57.5 × 37.5 cm)
Collection of Pao Yung Chao

Inscription: 己千為寶榮兄寫 "Jiqian painted for my friend Pao Yung"

Seal: 王己千鉥 "Seal of Wang Jiqian"

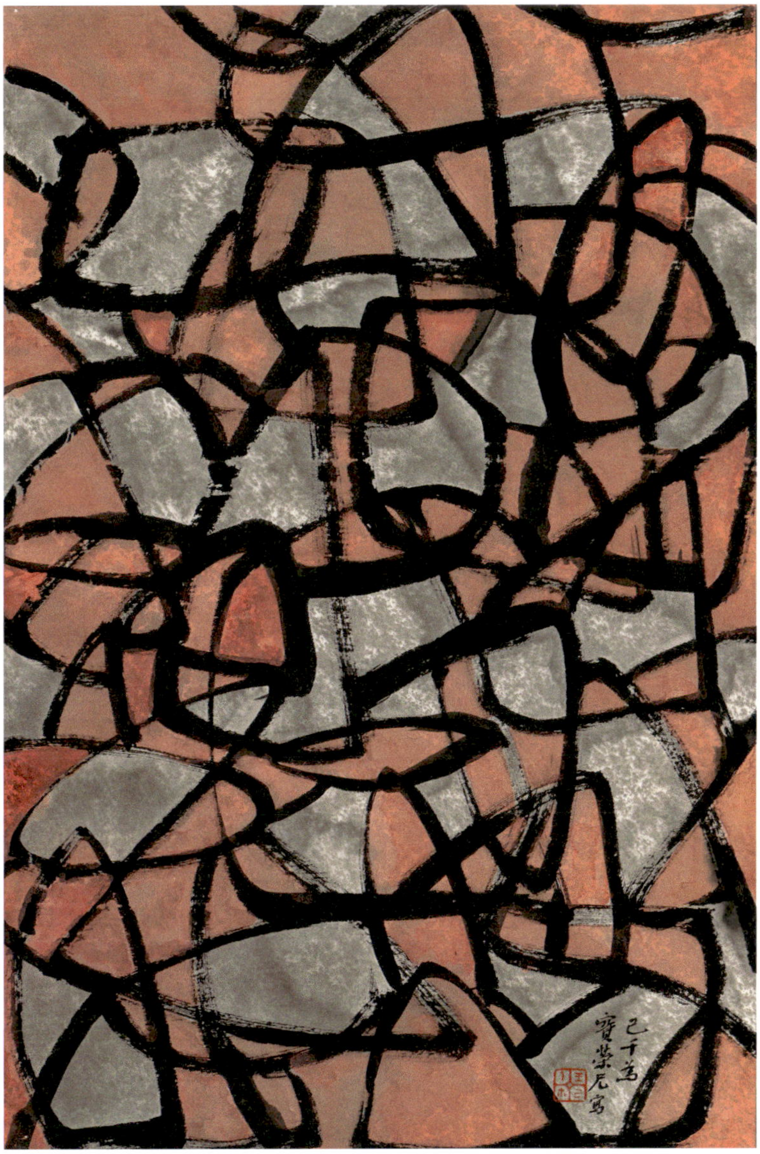

In the mid-1990s, Wang started to experiment with abstraction that integrated lines and brushwork drawn from both painting and calligraphy. This work was built upon a field of inky, light gray wash. Atop these mottled forms, the artist used a varied, quick-moving calligraphic line to execute repetitive mountain-like forms. In some areas, these shapes resonate against the variegated monochrome background to give a fleeting impression of depth and three-dimensionality, while other passages feature strong calligraphic lines in deep black or dull gray that interrupt the landscape contours and negate any illusion of depth. In some places, these overlying lines resemble Chinese characters, although they are ultimately illegible. Wang's abstract experiment thus hints at the ways that line can be used to construct deep orders of representational or textual meaning, but denies access to these traditional modes of understanding. Nevertheless, the power and beauty of the brushwork, necessarily connected to traditional forms of expression, is freed through abstraction to become something new.

PLATE 16

no title (Abstract Work with Blue and Green), 1998
Ink and color on paper
33 ¾ × 15 ⅝ inches (85.7 × 39.7 cm)
Collection of Pao Yung Chao

Inscription: 王己千, 戊寅十二月 "Wang Jiqian, *wuyin* [1998], December"

Seal: 己千創稿 "Sketches created by Jiqian"

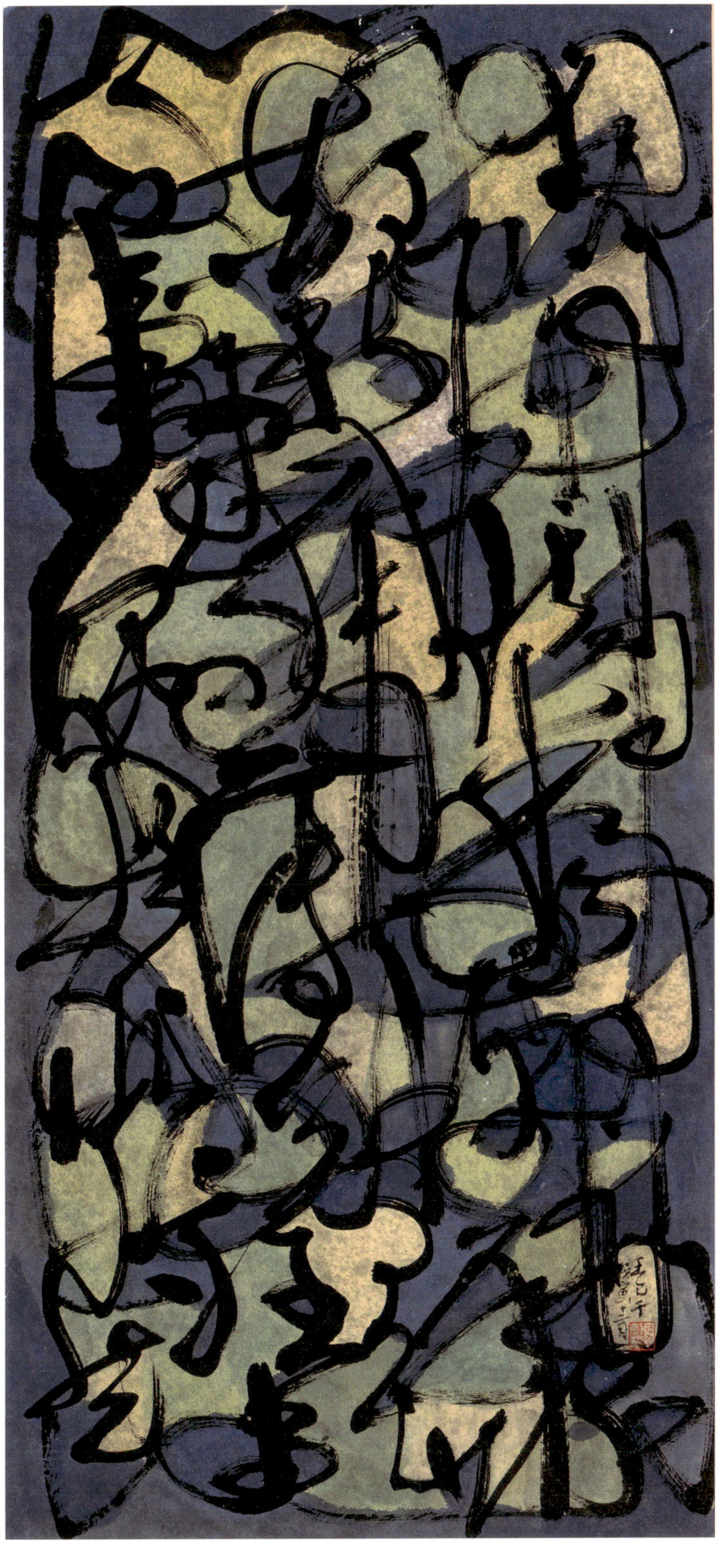

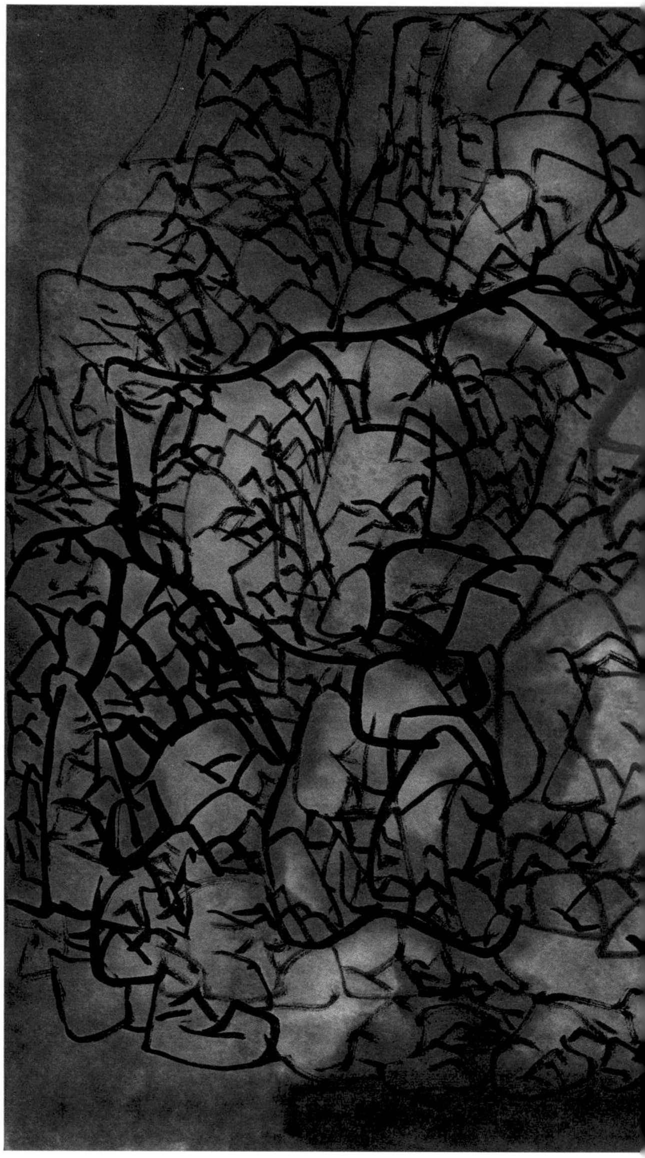

PLATE 17

no title (Abstract Work in Monochrome), 1998
Ink on paper
17 ¾ × 30 ¾ inches (45.1 × 78.1 cm)
Collection of Pao Yung Chao

Inscription: 己千, 戊寅 "Jiqian, *wuyin* [1998]"

Seal: 己千創稿 "Sketches created by Jiqian"

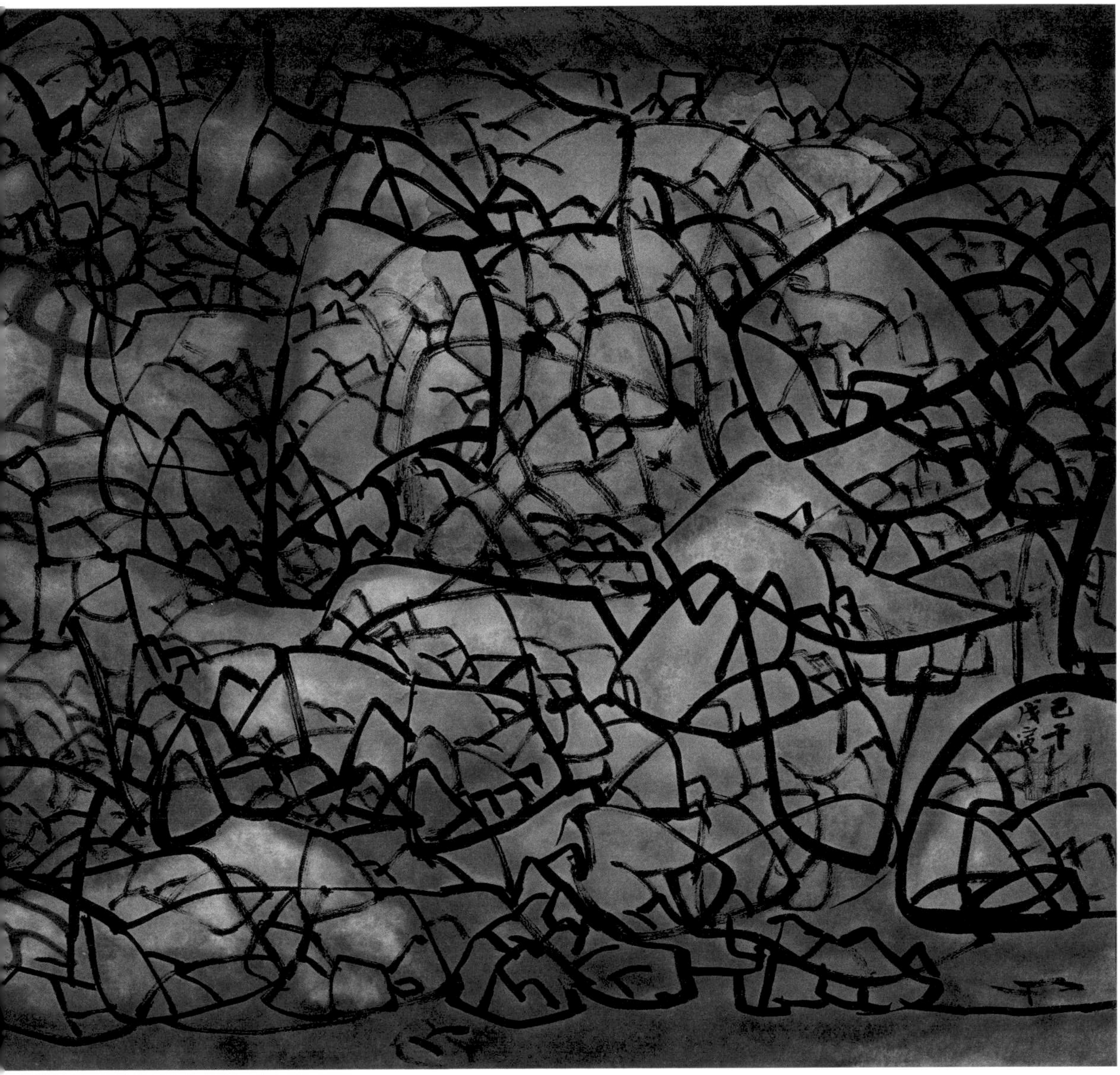

In the 1990s, Wang began a daily calligraphy practice on pages of outdated New York telephone books. The calligraphy includes familiar quotations from poetry, prose poems, and aphorisms that he would have memorized from his classical training, but over time some of his marks evolved from Chinese cursive script to illegible compositions. Through unconventional arrangements of lines that nonetheless retain the lyrical and fluid form of calligraphy, Wang's work emphasizes the inherent abstraction of the calligraphic form. The densely printed pages of the phone book, replete with reminders of the time and place in which Wang worked, capture the artist's playful discovery of calligraphic abstraction, a process that became the basis for his stand-alone abstract works (pls. 15, 16).

PLATE 18

no title (Phone Book with Artist's Calligraphy Practice), 1998
Ink on telephone book
10 ¾ × 19 ½ × 2 inches (27.3 × 49.5 × 5.1 cm)
Courtesy Private Collection

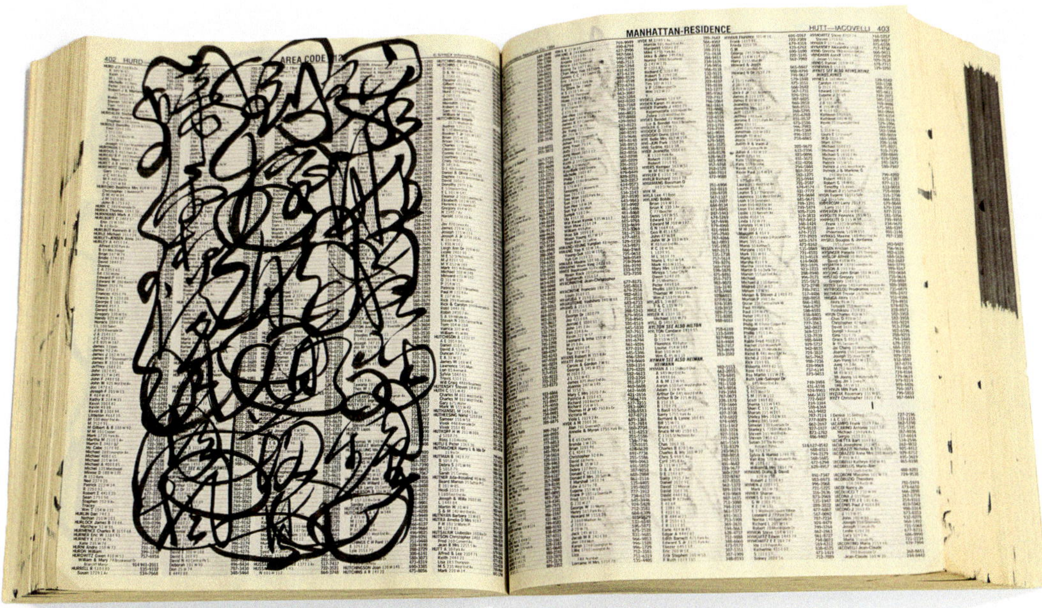
402 HURD
AREA CODE 212
MANHATTAN-RESIDENCE
HUTT—IACOVELLI 403

This abstract work explores the power and potential of Chinese calligraphic line. Brushwork in traditional Chinese calligraphy was always tied to a work's literary content or to historical writing styles. In *Abstract Calligraphy*, Wang used both artistic process and represented form to distance his art from these conventions so that the power of his calligraphic brushwork could be appreciated on its own. Using a flat-tipped Western-style brush, he created characters that seem to effloresce from seal-script calligraphy, producing a powerful but unorthodox effect. Hovering between legibility and nonsense, Wang's forms read as calligraphic even though they do not grant the viewer the ability to understand them based on their poetic content or specific stylistic model. The resulting abstraction is an exploration of line and forms that builds upon tradition even as it breaks from it, creating a work both familiar and surprising.

PLATE 19

no title (Abstract Calligraphy), 1998
Hanging scroll, ink on paper
Image: 53 ¼ × 26 ½ inches (135.3 × 67.3 cm)
Overall with mounting: 85 × 32 ⅜ inches (215.9 × 82.2 cm)
Courtesy Private Collection, New York
Reference no. 981200A

Inscription: 己千 "Jiqian"

Seal: 王己千鉥 "Seal of Wang Jiqian"

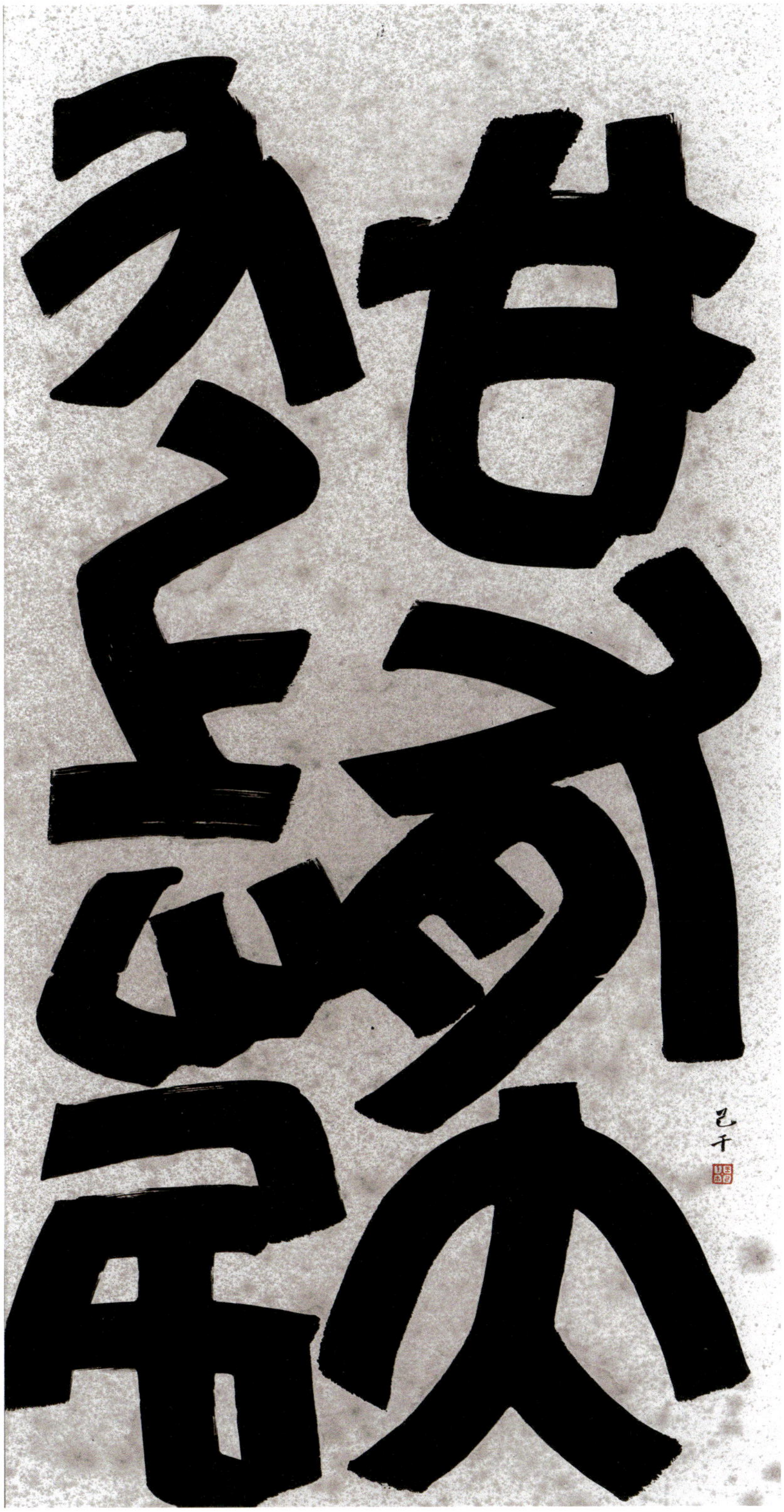

PLATE 20

no title (Abstract Calligraphy), 2000
Hanging scroll, ink on paper
Image: 41 ⅝ × 21 ½ inches (105.7 × 54.6 cm)
Overall with mounting: 74 ¾ × 26 inches (189.9 × 66 cm)
Courtesy Private Collection, New York
Reference no. 200403

Inscription: 庚午四月三日, 己千 "*Gengwu [sic]*, April 3, Jiqian"

Seal: 王己千鉢 "Seal of Wang Jiqian"

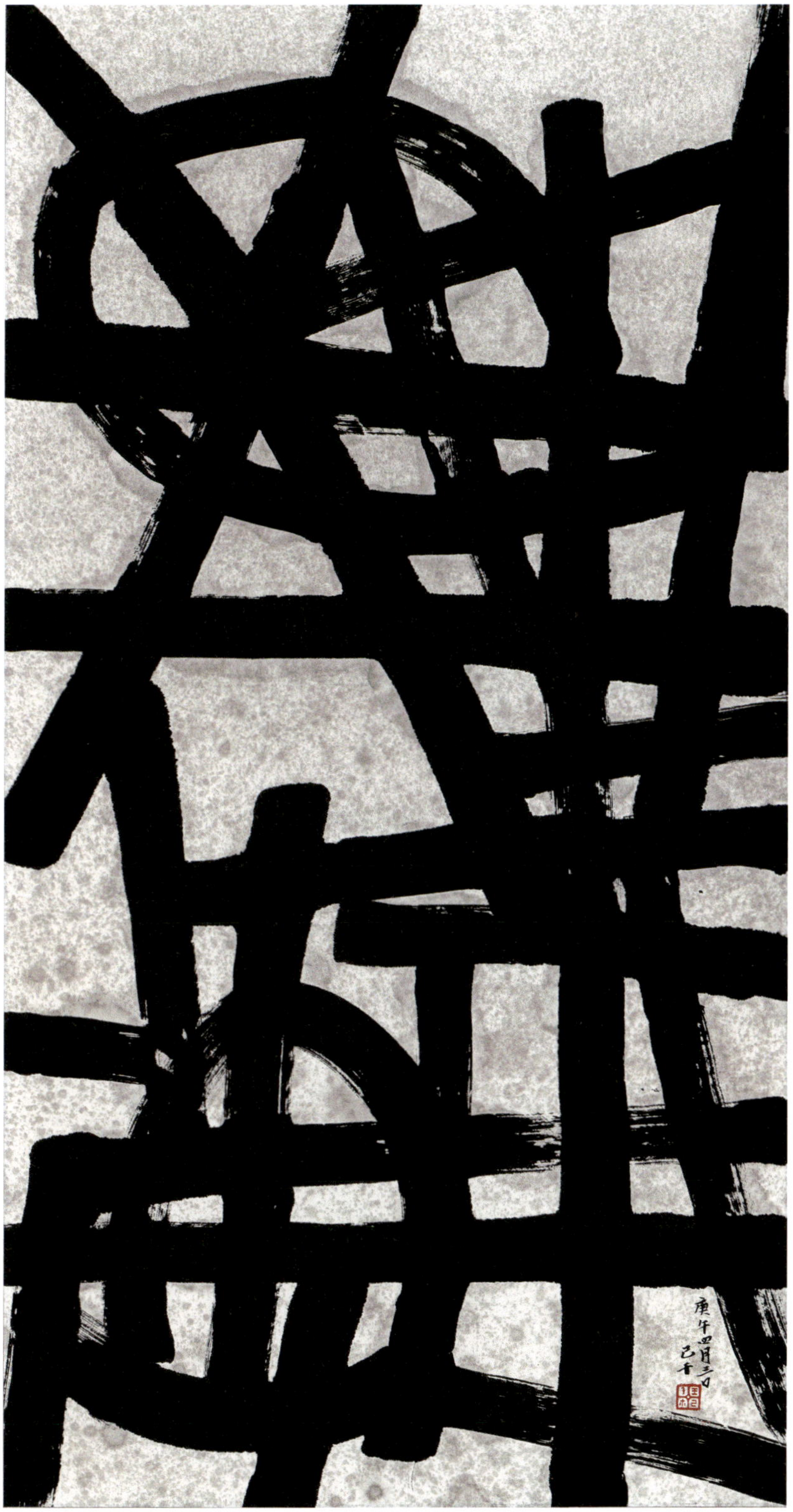
庚午四月三日
己千

Literati brushwork was the foundation of Wang's artistic and teaching practice. Created for his student Kathleen Yang, this album showcases a range of styles and techniques used to render rocks, trees, and other elements of traditional painting. Each leaf demonstrates a single idea: formal elements such as "withered trees and pines," technical skills such as "dry brush held upright," and stylistic models such as "Ni Zan's rocks" or "lofty mountains of Dong Yuan and Juran." Compositionally, each leaf pairs its central idea with a brief written description; the surrounding area is left deliberately unfinished. More than just a teaching tool, this album is a concrete representation of Wang's deep knowledge of classical painting as well as his practical mastery of these historical styles.

PLATE 21

Selection of leaves from:
C. C. Wang's Instructional Manual of Brushwork, undated, 2000–2002
Album of 17 painted leaves
Ink on paper
Courtesy Private Collection

Leaf a	9 ¾ × 13 ⅞ inches (24.8 × 35.2 cm) Inscription: 一般樹法用乾筆 "The conventional dry brushwork used to [depict] trees"
Leaf b	10 × 13 ⅞ inches (25.4 × 35.2 cm) Inscription: 董巨皴法 "Texture strokes in the style of Dong (Dong Yuan, 934–962) and Ju (Juran, fl. 10th century)"
Leaf c	9 ¾ × 14 inches (24.8 × 35.6 cm) Inscription: 倪雲林皴法 "Texture strokes in the style of Ni Yunlin (Ni Zan, 1301–1374)"
Leaf d	9 ⅜ × 14 ½ inches (23.8 × 36.8 cm) Inscription: 王蒙筆法 "Brushwork in the style of Wang Meng (1308–1385)"
Leaves a, b, c, d	Seal: 己千創稿 "Sketches created by Jiqian"

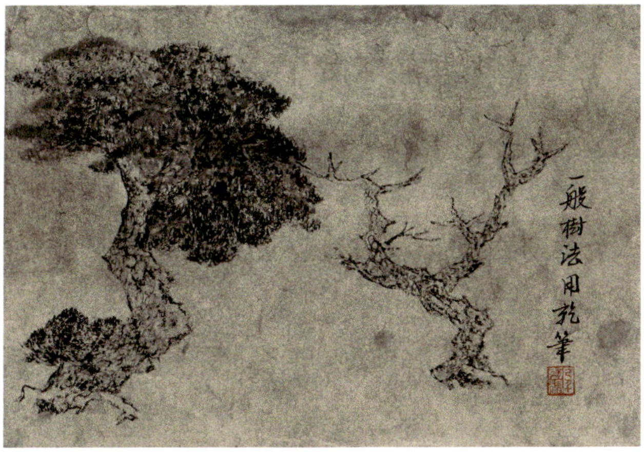

a

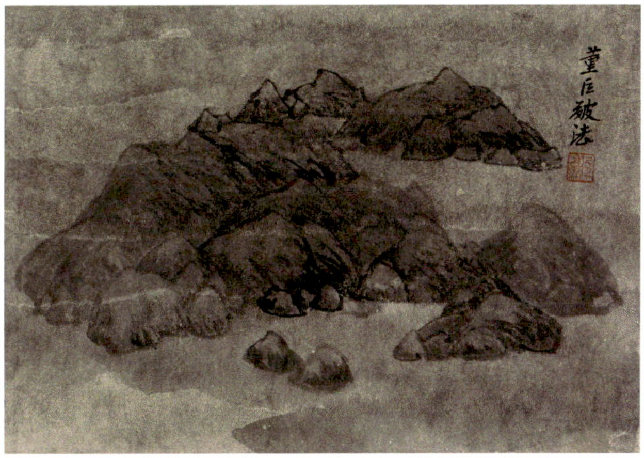

b

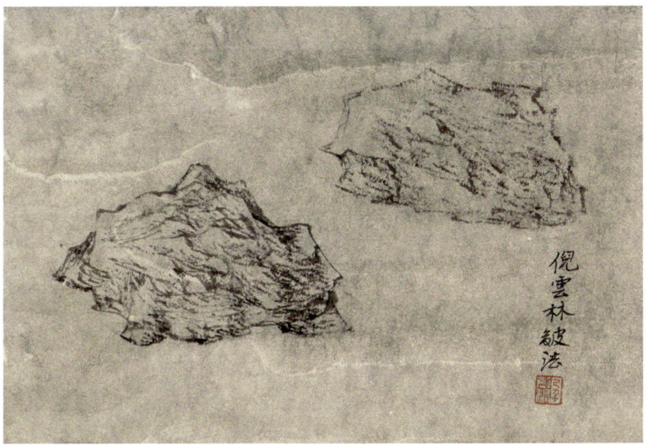

c

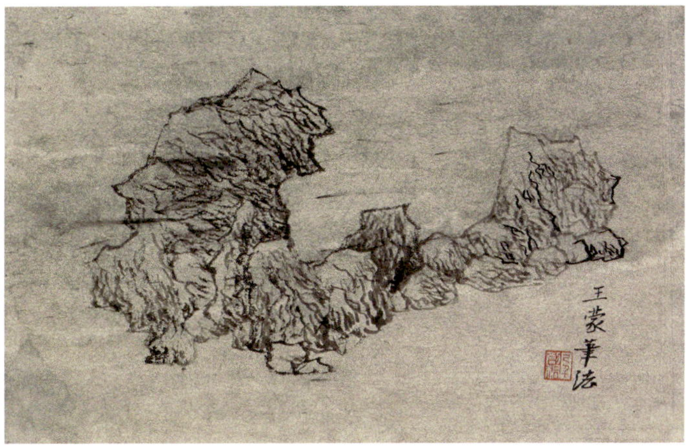

d

At the end of Wang's career, he painted this work in the style of Ni Zan. Wang admired Ni Zan because he made deeply self-expressive art through an artistic practice that revolved around restraint. Formally speaking, Ni Zan's works were characterized by sparse compositions, a limited vocabulary of representational forms, and strong brushwork.

All of these elements are visible here: Wang utilized simple, pared-down brushwork to create banks of rocks in the foreground. A copse of trees, with leaves executed in a variety of carefully controlled brushstrokes, stretches toward the middle ground. Wang, like Ni Zan, left a wide expanse of blank paper between this foreground mass and a softly rising mountain form in the background. Emulating the earlier artist's brush method, layers of dry brushstrokes provide subtle texture and the illusion of three-dimensionality in the distant rocks.

Even as he followed Ni Zan's artistic model, Wang also demonstrated his own mastery of the literati tradition. Wang's composition of landscape forms is not a copy of any specific painting, and his vocabulary of brushstrokes includes artistic phrases that are distinct from the Yuan master. This is especially evident in his use of a delicate ink wash in the far distance, a technique that is largely absent from Ni Zan's works. For Wang, the project of emulation was more than a reproduction of historical brush forms—it was a way to mirror Ni Zan's process of creation to express his own inner world.

PLATE 22

no title (Landscape in the Style of Ni Zan), 2001
Hanging scroll, ink on paper
Image: 29 × 18 ½ inches (73.7 × 47 cm)
Overall with mounting: 73 ⅛ × 23 ½ inches (185.7 × 59.7 cm)
Collection of Mr. and Mrs. Arnold Chang

Inscription: 辛巳冬己千 "*Xinsi* [2001], winter, Jiqian"

Seal: 己千創稿 "Sketches created by Jiqian"

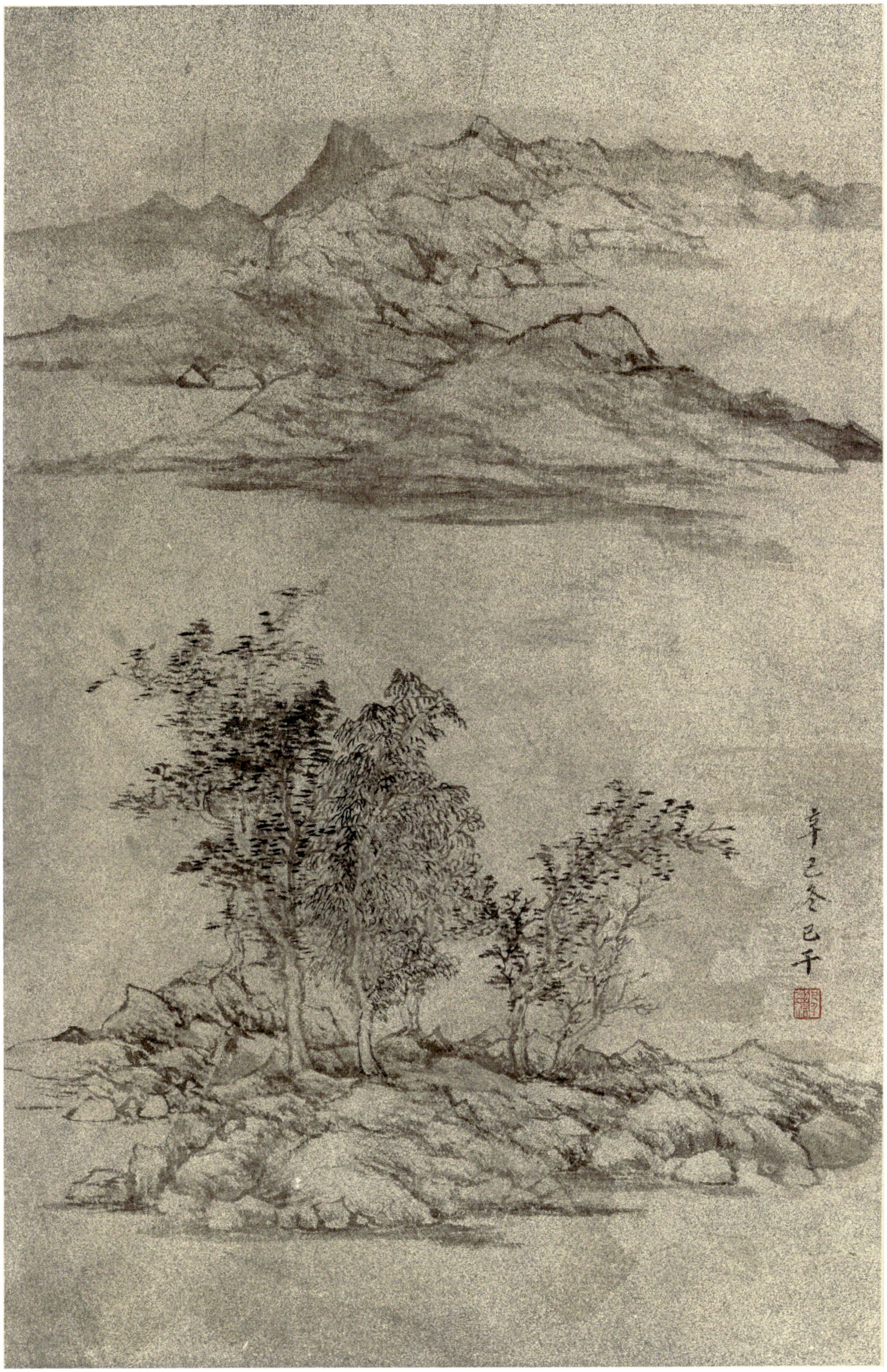
辛巳冬己千

PLATE 23

no title (Scholar's Rock), dated to the artist's 95th year, 2001
Hanging scroll, ink on paper
Image: 54 ¾ × 28 ½ inches (139.1 × 73. 2 cm)
Overall with mounting: 85 × 35 inches (215.9 × 88.9 cm)
Courtesy Private Collection, New York
Reference no. 210400

Inscription: 己千時年九十五 "Jiqian in [his] 95th year"

Seal: 己千創稿 "Sketches created by Jiqian"

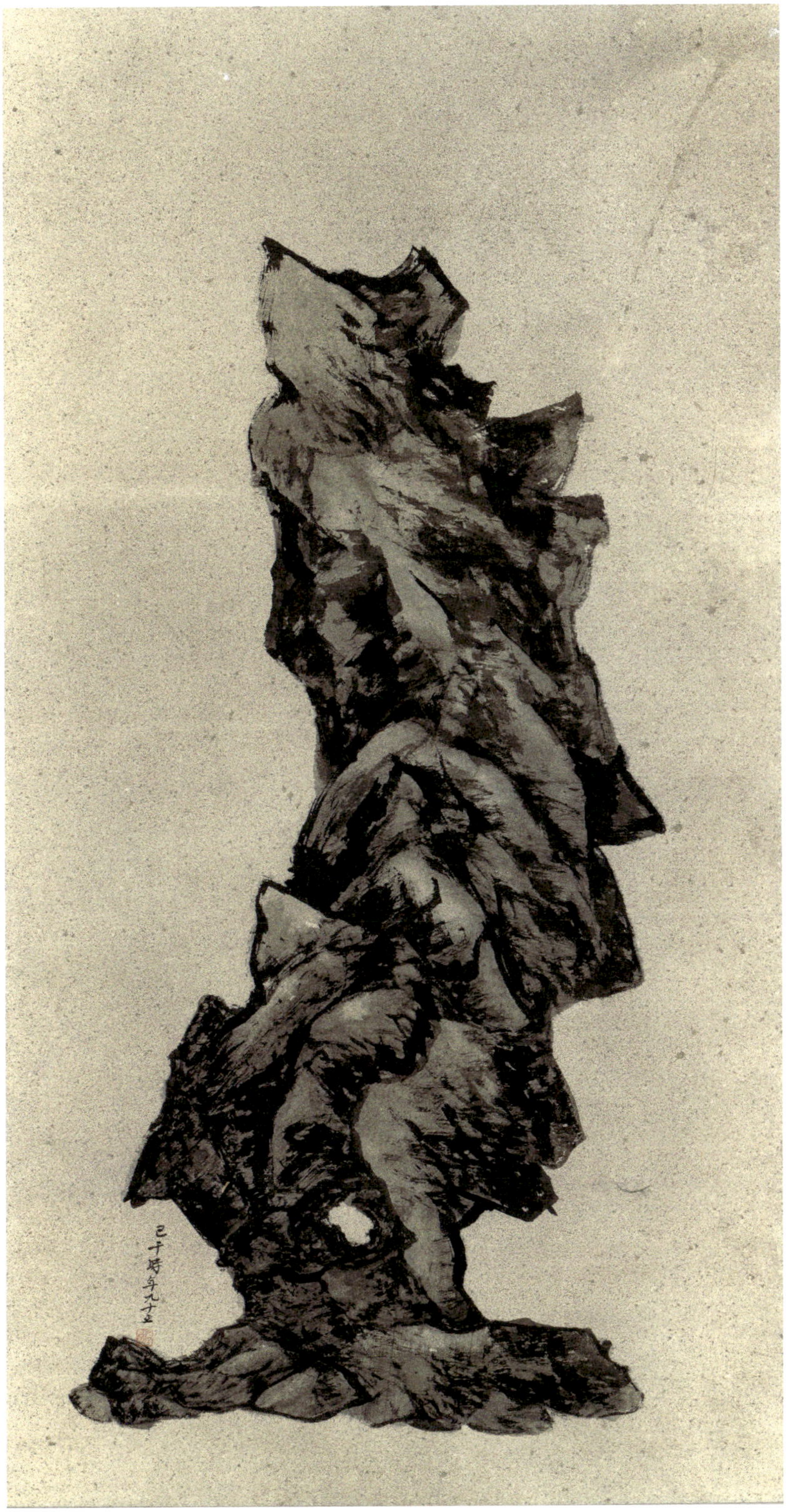

An Old Diehard? C. C. Wang's Deconstruction of Literati Line

DANIEL M. GREENBERG

> "I place great emphasis on the importance of brushwork in Chinese painting, and some may think I am just an old diehard. Doesn't putting so much importance on this traditional element inhibit the free development of Chinese painting?"—C. C. Wang[1]

C. C. Wang was a classically trained literati artist whose work deconstructed the concept of line in Chinese landscape painting and calligraphy. His art examined how line worked as a formal element, a system of meaning, and a marker of social class. In this essay, I will conduct a close visual analysis of Wang's early work in the literati tradition and early experimentation with mechanical processes to consider how he leveraged his mastery of traditional literati practice to question basic assumptions about line and its significance. Turning next to Wang's later works of painting and calligraphy, I will show how he created art that extends from the literati tradition even as it challenges it, creating new visual modes and refining traditional ones.

> "The quality of one's brushwork depends on one's innate talent as well as training. My experience tells me that an artist's brushwork can be cultivated and improved by studying and practicing."[2]

A single horizontal "hemp-rope" brushstroke, taken from a distant bank in an untitled 1934 painting by C. C. Wang (*Collected Landscapes after the Old Masters*), is emblematic of the artist's early line work in the literati tradition (fig. 1; pl. 1c). Appreciating this stroke requires a close look at the artist's brush mechanics, the artistic context of his composition, and the social context of Wang's copy. In fact, this line demonstrates Wang's connection to classical models, attests to the artist's training and social class, and forcefully argues for the continued relevance and lasting power of traditional landscape painting in twentieth-century China—all in the space of one square inch.

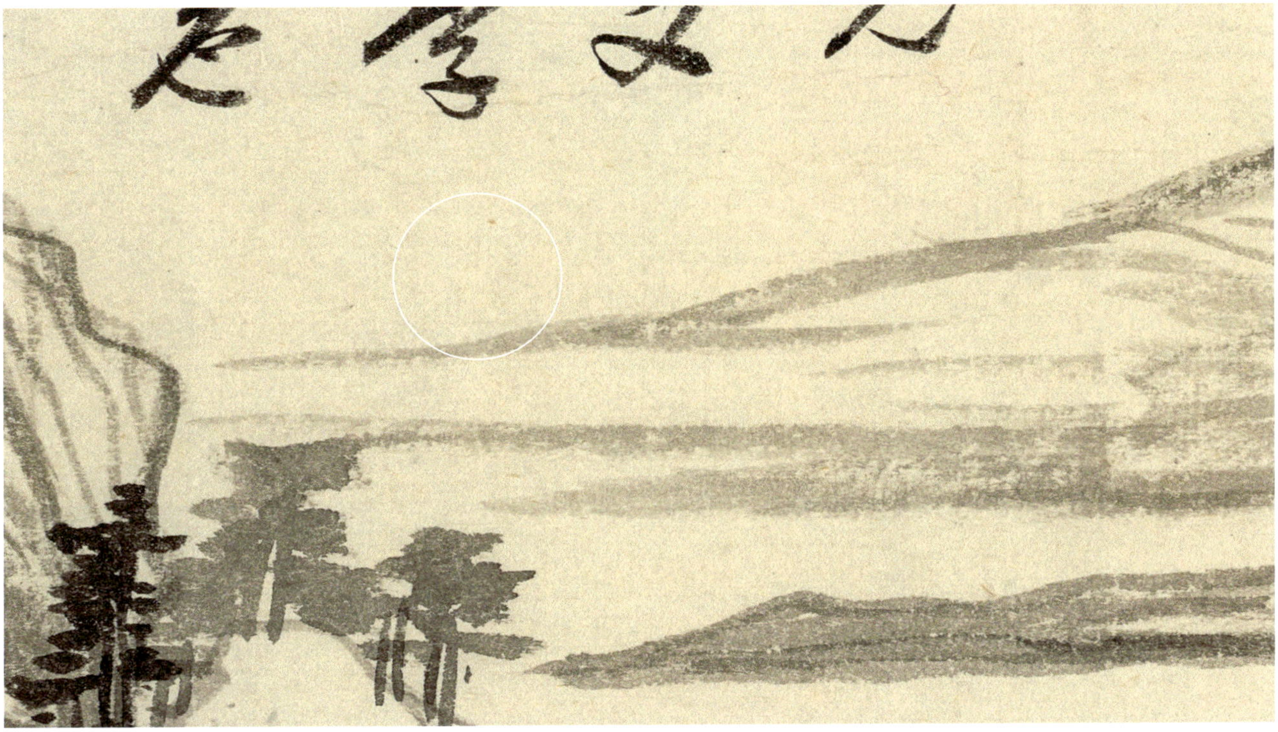

Fig. 1. Detail from no title (Collected Landscapes after the Old Masters), 1934–37. From the third painting (After Dong Qichang), 1934, pl. 1c.

The first path to understanding this line is to follow its creation. The artist's brush travels from left to right; we see a rounded *luobi* 落筆 where the brush first touches the paper, a softly undulating line that swells and recedes as our eye follows its extension, and a final rounded *tibi* 提筆 where the brush leaves the paper. This single stroke bears scrutiny on multiple levels. The ink tonality changes subtly between the dry, ethereal quality of its left side and its wetter, more saturated right side. The shape of the line is also elegant, as its top and bottom are soft and round, indicating a "centered" application of the brush point. And the shape of the line curves slightly in space, swelling and receding like a twisting wire.[3] Finally, the right side of this stroke is seamlessly connected to the next one, drawing a viewer's eye upward into the shape of a distant, rising mountain.

The form of this line and the artistic process used to create it were drawn from the literati tradition as transmitted to Wang through his study with Wu Hufan. Wang held his brush at a forty-five-degree angle above the paper, with his hand relaxed and thumb facing the ceiling, so that his brush tip was naturally oriented to work horizontally from left to right, and used gentle pressure to subtly vary the thickness of each centered line. The major painted features of *Collected Landscapes* are built from these characteristic lines, including the outlines and textured interiors of mountains, the trunks of trees, and the marshy banks of streams.

If we look beyond this single stroke to the painting as a whole, we see that Wang uses a diverse range of brush methods, each taken from the literati tradition. Tree leaves and branches are rendered with the tip of an upright brush held perpendicular to the paper, allowing for fine control in all four directions but creating sharp points and blunt ends where the brush touches the paper first and last. An upright brush is also used in both calligraphic inscriptions, where Wang writes that this work is a close copy that was created while examining an original work by the Ming-dynasty artist and founder of the Orthodox tradition, Dong Qichang, in the studio of his teacher, Wu Hufan.[4] Beside this inscription is Wang's copy of Dong Qichang's original inscription, rendered in a convincing replica of the earlier artist's distinctively fluid cursive script.

Wang's close copy of Dong's painting and calligraphic style demonstrate his claim to mastery of the technical and social skills at the core of literati tradition. Broadly speaking, literati art in dynastic China was tied to the elite class of educated officials that formed the core of China's state bureaucracy. From an early age, these men studied classical texts, calligraphy, and essay writing in hopes of passing the state-administered imperial examinations and attaining governmental office. The same practical skills and aesthetic standards at the heart of Chinese calligraphy—a required component of the exams—were used to create and judge the brushstrokes that comprised literati painting. Literati art rose with the examination system and emergence of this social class during the Northern Song dynasty and remained a feature of Chinese society until the collapse of the Qing dynasty in the twentieth century.

Wang's decision to copy a painting by Dong Qichang was a deliberate and conscious act of artistic self-definition in 1930s China. Before the fall of the Qing dynasty in 1912, making close copies of classical landscape masterworks was a necessary part of a literati artist's training. Not only did the successful completion of a side-by-side copy showcase technical mastery; it demonstrated good taste and social status.[5] Before photographic copies of classical masterworks became available in the twentieth century, only aspiring artists from elite backgrounds were granted access to view works in private collections, where their teacher or patron would help them to choose authentic paintings in an appropriate style.

But unlike artists working just fifty years before, Wang's copy represents a chosen allegiance rather than an inevitable rite of artistic passage. In 1930s

Shanghai, traditional landscape painting in the Orthodox tradition was just one of many competing artistic styles circulating in a rapidly developing and increasingly international entrepôt city. Aligning his artistic practice to Dong Qichang and the Orthodox School was no longer a straightforward declaration of social class and artistic ability—literati landscape was already considered somewhat retardataire, its future uncertain. How could an artistic practice so deeply grounded in centuries-old models of painting practice serve a modern artist in a new, post-dynastic China? Could literati ink landscapes still work as vehicles of personal expression? What could they communicate to audiences in China and abroad about the nature of Chinese art?

> "As an analogy, we can compare the painter's brushwork in Chinese painting to an opera singer's voice. . . . If we want to understand the true meaning of his art and to discover his inner world, we must learn to appreciate and penetrate deep into his brushwork, which is his primary means of expression."[6]

Questions of identity, process, and artistic meaning were at the heart of C. C. Wang's practice after he moved to the United States and are present in a first category of deconstruction: an attempt to challenge the specific artistic practices used to create literati line. Wang describes the literati tradition as an expression of two factors: breadth and depth. Breadth comprises "subject matter, compositional variety, etc.," while depth "refers to the inner spirit of the work, the personality of the artist as revealed in the brushwork, etc."[7] Wang's experiments in the early 1970s engaged with deconstructing "depth," exploring whether painting could still function to represent the inner spirit of the work and personality of the artist even when that artist surrenders some control to tools and processes outside the literati tradition.

One such experiment is clearly visible in a detail from another untitled painting (*Landscape after Fan Kuan*), from 1985 (fig. 2; pl. 7). Training our eyes on the shape of this fine, rounded line, we are primed to trace it from left to right like a single brushstroke in a traditional landscape painting. The beginning and end of this line are soft and rounded, with subtle changes in the wetness and thickness of ink across its length.

But while this is a beautiful line that fits squarely within the literati tradition, it was not created by a brush. Looking above it, a near-identical line can be seen—each has a similar distinctive peak at its middle. In fact, a similar shape

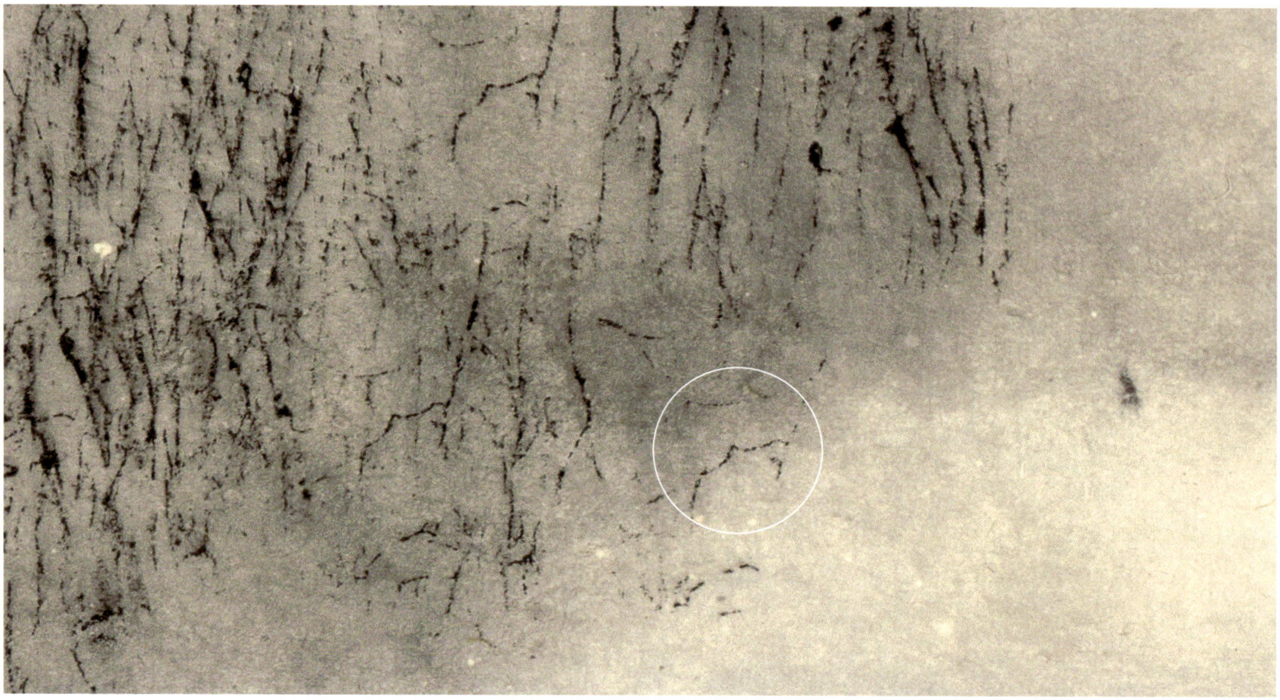

Fig. 2. Detail from no title (Landscape after Fan Kuan), 1985, pl. 7.

can be seen to the left and, indeed, repeating over the surface of this cliffside. These marks were created by inked paper wrapped around a roller, not a brush.

Looking more carefully at these marks in context, we can see that Wang has worked to integrate this mechanical mode of production into a traditional painting practice. Rolled lines were applied to the paper first, creating a web of repetitive strokes. Wang strategically created lines atop these strokes, complementing and extending some lines while working to obfuscate the unchanging repetition of these patterns as he built a larger landscape. The result is seamless and visually distinctive, a roiling network of mechanically produced randomness and tightly controlled, elegant brushwork.

Although Wang's process for creating this painting diverged from traditional methods, his goal was to interrogate the literati tradition rather than wholly break from it. *Landscape after Fan Kuan*, like *Collected Landscapes*, is a copy of a famous painting: *Travelers among Mountains and Streams* by the tenth-century master Fan Kuan. Wang's overall composition and his use of dense, inky brushwork to simulate patches of brush that cling to the ridges of the distant mountains mirror the spirit of this early model. Only close examination of the distinct visual components used to build this landscape reveals that a different process is being used.

Wang's *Landscape after Fan Kuan* is thus part of his larger exploration of the nature and significance of line at the heart of literati painting. By using rollers, daubing inked and crumpled paper stamps, and painting on folded paper, Wang explored how nontraditional methods could be integrated into an otherwise orthodox process of landscape painting. Moving away from the precision of a brush's direct intervention, these brushless lines cede part of the artistic process to chance. While other twentieth-century Chinese artists experimented with similar ideas, Wang was unique in his fixed efforts to create random *lines*, rather than washes or splashed ink.[8]

These changes to Wang's artistic process represent a theoretical as well as procedural deconstruction of literati art. Scholars have noted that the introduction of mechanical processes aligns the artist's work with the principles of pop art circulating in New York during the early 1970s, deconstructing the elevated notion of "fine art" by picking apart the direct connection between an artist and the production of art.[9] Importantly, Wang's work demonstrates that art in the Chinese tradition can be seen as part of the intellectual project of the New York School. For Wang, however, the target of inquiry was not just abstract expressionism or the Western canon—it was also Chinese literati landscape. If an artist creates both literati line and composition without a brush, does the resulting landscape painting still represent them in the same way? Is the "voice" of the artist still expressed in this work? If so, what does the artist actually contribute to the production of a painting?

> "In Chinese painting [brushwork] can sometimes be divorced from pictorial images and stand on its own, allowing an educated viewer to appreciate painting in a way that is analogous to the way we view calligraphy. We can ignore the pictures or the meaning of the characters, and simply enjoy the abstract beauty of the brushwork itself."[10]

Wang's interest in line, self-expression, and the literati tradition is further explored in a second deconstruction, which interrogates the connection between literati line and form. Building atop his previous experiments with randomized line, Wang pushed even further—creating work that stretched the

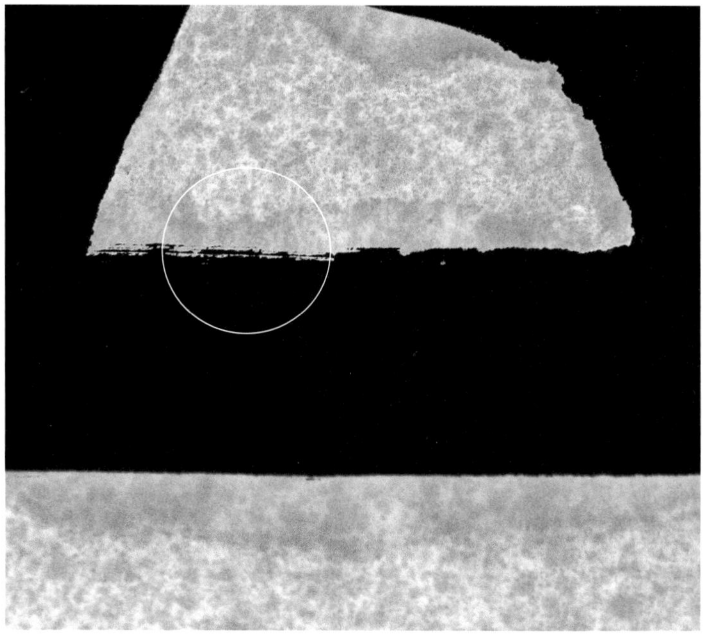

Fig. 3 (above). Detail of no title (Abstract Calligraphy), 2000, pl. 20.

Fig. 4 (right). C. C. Wang working in his studio, ca. 1990s.

boundaries of literati painting and calligraphy. This tension is seen in a detail from a third untitled work (*Abstract Calligraphy*), made around the year 2000, described by Wang as a piece of painted or manufactured calligraphy (fig. 3; pl. 20).

Looking carefully at a horizontal stretch of line, we can see how the visual qualities of Wang's art have changed since *Collected Landscapes* and *Landscape after Fan Kuan*. Unlike the rounded, undulating lines that characterize literati line in those works, the edges of this line are sharp, straight, and square. The upper border has an uneven, jagged quality where the dried edges of the brush dragged unevenly across the paper. Looking closely at this border, we can see that there is a complementary line of light gray, which bleeds into a dotted wash across the entire surface of the paper.

Wang's artistic process was completed in stages. First, he painted intersecting dark lines using a flat, Western-style sponge brush (fig. 4.) Only such a tool would allow him to create the sharp edges of his lines, including the square edge where his brush first meets the paper. The structure of a flat brush also explains the frequent areas of dryness, as this shape, unlike a Chinese brush, does not have a hollow core that holds a reserve of ink. Working from this skeleton of lines, Wang applied wet splotches of ink across the surface, perhaps by flicking a wet brush held a few inches above the paper's surface. Some areas of the paper absorbed this scattered ink, and the wet ink from his first layer interacted with this wash in unexpected ways that were beyond the artist's direct control. This application of randomized ink to the paper's surface echoes Wang's experiments with rollers and crumpled paper discussed above.

Wang's process raises deeper questions about the nature and function of this work of art. It is framed as a hanging scroll, inviting a viewer to consider it through the lens of Chinese calligraphy or painting. But what remains from the literati tradition? Wang has used randomness to sever the direct connection of artist, brush, and line. And he has substituted a Western painter's brush for that of a Chinese scholar. Using this distinctive, non-traditional brush, he has created powerful but un-orthodox lines that lack the soft, rounded qualities of literati line. Finally, he has removed all traces of three-dimensional and textual representation—this is neither a landscape nor a work of calligraphy.

Distanced from tradition but still in dialogue with it, Wang builds upon his previous experiments to play with a fundamental idea about line and its power: can a work of art created with randomness and un-orthodox line still be seen through the lens of literati art? Stacks of powerful but ragged lines, placed atop a ground of complementary wash and line, create a powerful composition, balanced in its abstraction. A viewer with a classically trained eye can still use Wang's criteria to find lines that invite closer looking even as they withhold a conventional beauty. There is still "depth" here, but it has evolved and changed to become something new and distinctly modern.

Wang's late abstract works are in dialogue with other contemporary Chinese artists who were working to explore the relationship between tradition and abstraction. His abstraction beyond character forms is in a loose theoretical dialogue with contemporary experiments by Gu Wenda and Xu Bing, even though Wang's experiments in this vein were never exhibited alongside work by these artists.[11] And his interest in painting with literati line without literati content presages the abstracted calligraphy painting of Wang Dongling. However, C. C. Wang was unique among his peers in that he continued to produce works of calligraphy and painting in a recognizably literati style at the same

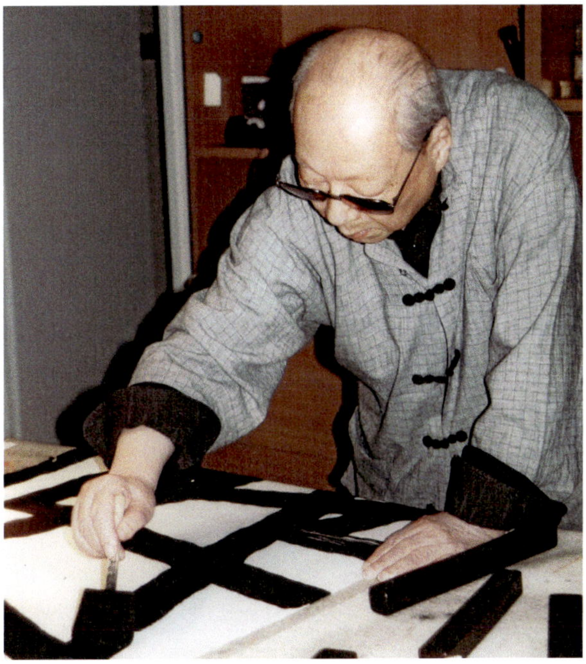

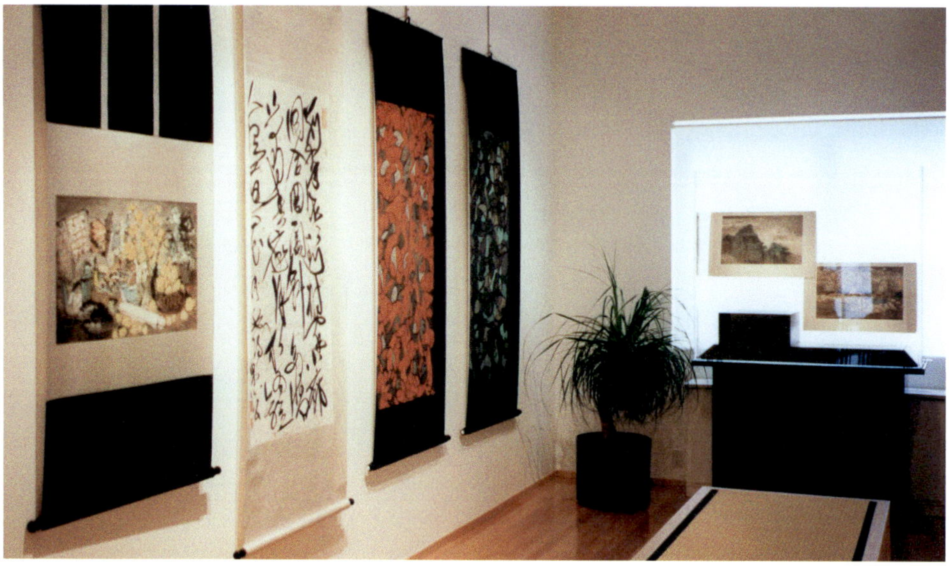

time as he was creating abstract works. A 1997 photograph of a gallery exhibition of Wang's painting shows two works of abstraction next to a work of traditional calligraphy, with two traditional landscapes on an adjacent wall (fig. 5).

Even as Wang experimented with randomness and unconventional tools to push the bounds of abstraction, he was using some of these same ideas to refine and reshape traditional landscape painting. In an untitled work from 2001 (*Landscape in the Style of Ni Zan*), we turn again to a detail of a single line drawn from a distant bank (fig. 6; pl. 22). The line itself is legible in the same way as that in *Collected Landscapes*: a round, delicately twisting line that extends from left to right following the path of the artist's hand. The dry, restrained quality of this brushwork consciously recalls the characteristically sparse line work of the fourteenth-century artist Ni Zan. But here our appreciation of Wang's line is complicated by a pattern of inky "noise" that extends across the entire surface of the paper. Like the background in the untitled work of 1990, Wang seems to have applied fine splashes of ink to the paper, creating a uniform matrix of dots and banks of solid gray. Although the pattern of the background in *Landscape in the Style of Ni Zan* is more regular than in *Abstract Calligraphy*, it seems to be a refined version of the same process. And like *Abstract Calligraphy*, Wang has built upon these patterns to subtly enhance the power of his brushwork. The extension of this distant ridge line is partly obfuscated by the pattern of background ink, giving it the quality of something perceived from afar. Behind this line, a solid patch of light gray is just visible enough to suggest a distant bank of clouds.

This tension between abstraction and representation represents a new stage in Wang's exploration of line and its limits. For while the play between the artist's brush and randomness is similar to the dynamic between roller and applied line in *Landscape after Fan Kuan*, treating the entire paper surface with fine slashes of ink moves beyond his previous experiments with mechanical processes and yields more of the painting's final visual program to chance. The result is a landscape that wrestles with a self-imposed matrix of obfuscation, its peaks and valleys emerging from a sea of inky noise that changes and tempers them as they rise upward like a sword from a smith's quenching pool.

Seen through the larger context of Wang's fully abstract works from this same period, the play between background and foreground becomes emblematic of the artist's larger interrogation of literati art. The inky matrix upon which the landscape is built is both deliberate and indexical, an integral part of the

Fig. 5 (left). Installation shot, *C. C. Wang at Ninety—A Kaikodo Celebration*, exhibition at Kaikodo Gallery, New York, spring 1997.

Fig. 6 (below). Detail from no title (Landscape in the Style of Ni Zan), 2001, pl. 22.

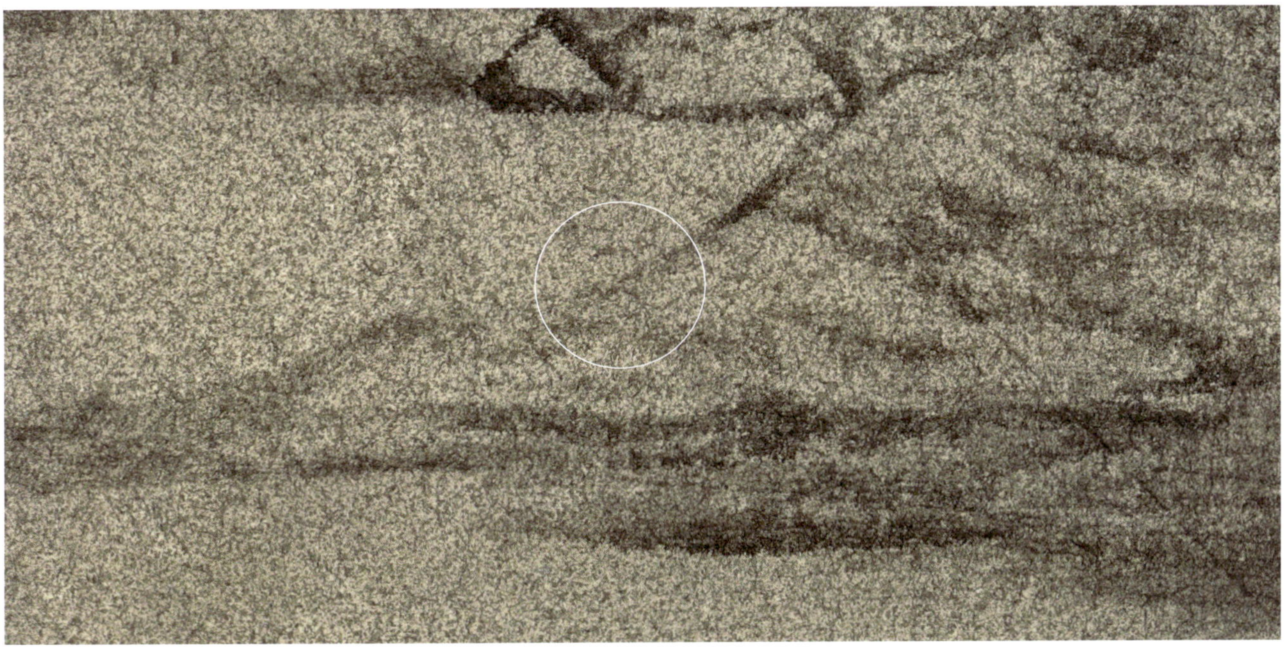

artist's process and his vision for the painting's function. Wang's field of ink and line works in tandem with his representational brushwork, each complementing the other. Just as the matrix of ink dots changes how we perceive Wang's painted landscape, perhaps the painted landscape can reframe our understanding of this abstracted ink field. We have seen that the artist explored how randomness could be integrated into indexical brushwork to present himself in a representational landscape. Perhaps the reverse is also true: Wang explored how brushwork could be integrated into indexical randomness to present himself in abstracted ink play.

Contrary to Wang's own loaded question, his single-minded focus on line and its limits did not make him an "old diehard." Rather, it became the core theoretical and practical method for a personal artistic practice in pursuit of the "free development of Chinese painting." Examining the nature of line and its limits allowed Wang to inhabit the boundaries of literati practice, using creative new artistic processes to express himself and his evolving vision of art. More than just the sum of his brushstrokes, C. C. Wang is present on every level of his late works—across randomness and representation, background and foreground, in calligraphy and painting alike.

NOTES

1. C. C. Wang, "The Importance of Brushwork in Chinese Painting," *Kaikodo Journal* 21 (Autumn 2001): 27.

2. Ibid., 30.

3. This metaphor is sometimes used to describe the quality of line in the calligraphy of Wang Xizhi 王羲之 (303–361). See Robert E. Harrist Jr., *The Embodied Image: Chinese Calligraphy from the John B. Elliott Collection* (Princeton, NJ: Art Museum, Princeton University; New York: Harry N. Abrams, 1999), 92.

4. Dong Qichang's inscription, in turn, states that his work emulates the style of Zhao Gan and Li Tang.

5. See Ming Hua, "Bridging the Tradition to the Modern, the East to the West: C. C. Wang and His Life in Art" (PhD diss., Arizona State University, 2014), 34.

6. Wang, "Importance of Brushwork," 27.

7. Ibid., 30.

8. Consider, for example, the use of splashed ink in the work of Chang Dai-chien 張大千 (Zhang Daqian) from the 1970s, as reproduced in Fu Shen and Jan Stuart, *Challenging the Past: The Paintings of Chang Dai-chien* (Washington, DC: Arthur M. Sackler Gallery, Smithsonian Institution; Seattle: University of Washington Press, 1991); or the use of wash in the painting of Fu Baoshi 傅抱石, illustrated in Anita Chung, *Chinese Art in an Age of Revolution: Fu Baoshi (1904–1965)* (Cleveland: Cleveland Museum of Art; New Haven, CT: Yale University Press, 2012).

9. See Mei Lan Yeung, "A New Traditionalist: C. C. Wang the Artist" (master's thesis, Ohio State University, 2006), 77–88.

10. Wang, "Importance of Brushwork," 27.

11. See Jerome Silbergeld, quoted in in Hua, "Bridging the Tradition," 280.

Transforming Tradition: C. C. Wang's First Two Decades in the United States

MARGARET LIU CLINTON

Mea culpa. In spite of ongoing attempts to override tendencies that prioritize Euro-American regimes of seeing, I admit a certain failure in my first encounter with the later work of C. C. Wang. Instinctively, I interpreted works akin to an untitled painting of 1998 (*Abstract Work with Blue and Green*) (pl. 16) through the formal frameworks of Western modernism. Like many unaccustomed audiences, I initially associated his continuous lines and small pools of color with—for example—Brice Marden's vermicular circuits or Lee Krasner's rounded forms and could not understand why Wang's work from the 1990s belatedly incorporated abstract expressionist strategies from the 1950s. Looking more deeply, however, I began to see that his practice in fact challenges my narrow notions of originality and aesthetic progress and introduces an entirely new set of stakes based on a highly sophisticated command of brush and ink.[1]

A brief foray into the cultural significance of the Chinese art of writing helps contextualize Wang's brushwork in *Abstract Work with Blue and Green* and reveals traces of cursive script, signaling a calligraphic genealogy that spans dynasties.[2] Wang's continuous line, painted on paper in one extended movement, required decades of training. Instead of reductively ascribing his lines to the influence of abstract expressionist painters—who often focused on the heft of materials—I now align Wang's lithe brush with a dancer's fluidity, a muscle memory developed over a lifetime of making strokes with the brush. In *Abstract Work with Blue and Green*, he forfeited legibility while balancing rupture and reference.[3] By boldly melding a calligraphic paroxysm, landscape palette, and swooning composition, Wang deftly combined his artistic training in Shanghai and New York. This raises the question, how did the twain meet?[4] Born in Suzhou in 1907, C. C. Wang lived and worked primarily in New York City from 1949 until his passing in 2003. While much has been written about his early training in China, this essay delves into the art historical climate of the 1950s in the United States to underscore a Western failure to recognize the traditional elements of Wang's practice that prompted his breakthrough transformations in the 1960s and ultimately led Wang to invigorate literati and abstract traditions throughout the rest of his career.[5]

Wang's art in the 1950s has been characterized by Jerome Silbergeld as a study or "digestion" of Western painting styles and described by the ink artist Arnold Chang, a devoted pupil of Wang, as a vague period of creative gestation alongside his ongoing collecting.[6] Both authors note visible "results" of experimentation in the 1960s. Looking closely at Wang's experience in the 1950s, it becomes clear that the constraints of his circumstances significantly contributed to his later experiments. Wang began his formal study of Western painting at the Art Students League in 1949. The following year he held his first US solo exhibition of Chinese literati paintings at the Warren E. Cox Gallery in New York. In contrast to galleries exhibiting contemporary artwork, Cox's focus on what were once called Oriental antiquities earned him a reputation as a tastemaker in the spheres of ceramics, lighting, and interiors, which often included chinoiserie. Meanwhile, an international conversation set against antiquity and tradition was forming in prominent New York galleries and museums. Avant-gardist modernisms that were irreconcilable with premodern traditions were prioritized—an unfavorable condition for many Chinese diasporic artists whose work required active dialogue with the past. These constraints later generated a series of adaptations in Wang's work.

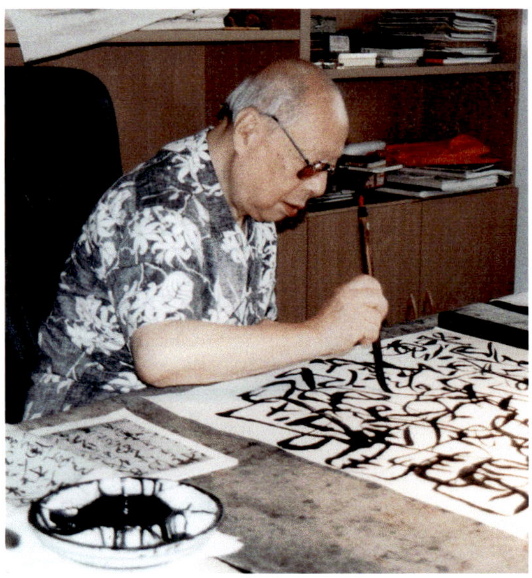

In a gallery announcement introducing Wang's 1959 solo exhibition at Mi Chou Gallery—the first US gallery to exhibit contemporary Chinese art exclusively—James Cahill noted: "I am afraid that the subtle stylistic allusions in his painting, and others of their most admirable qualities, may escape some casual Occidental viewers. Much of the finest Chinese painting of any period, alas, is likely to suffer the same handicap."[7] Mi Chou Gallery's founder, Frank Fulai Cho, recounted a visit between C. C. Wang and the Chinese artist Chang

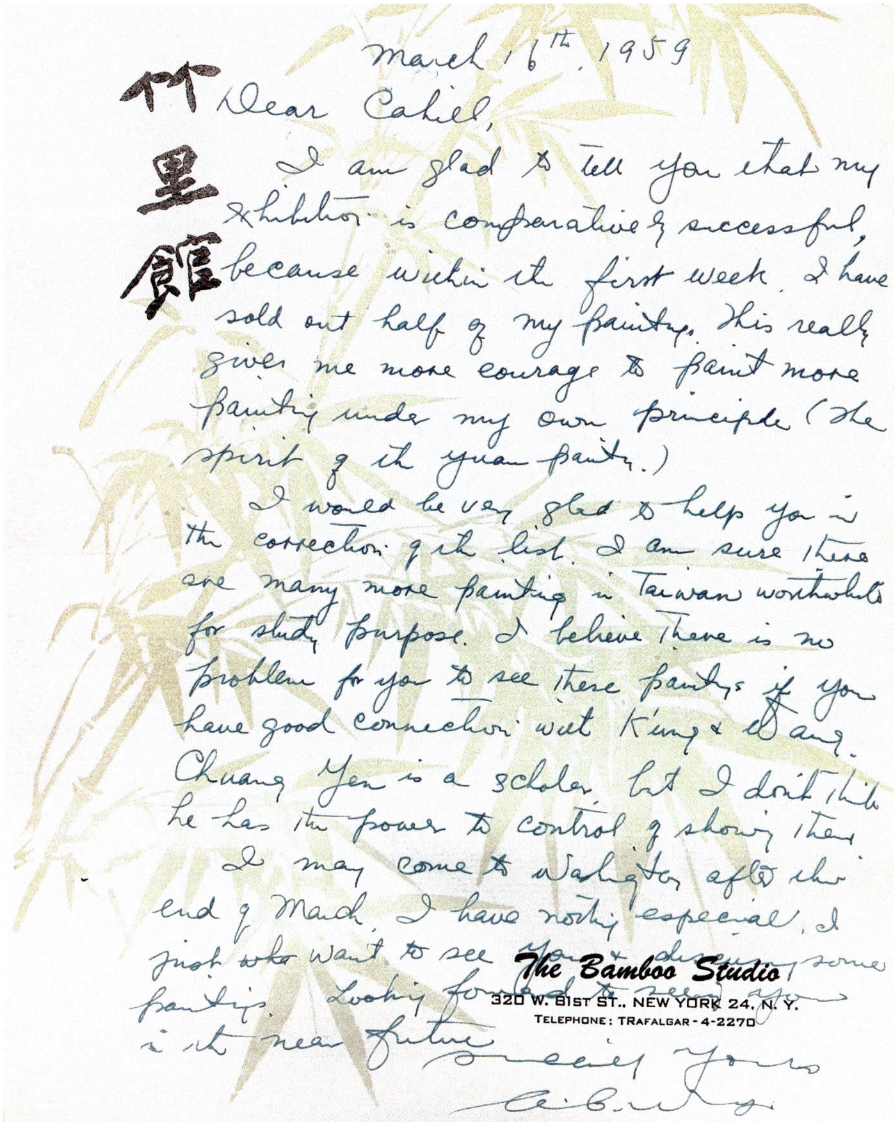
竹
墨
館

March 16th. 1959

Dear Cahill,

I am glad to tell you that my exhibition is comparatively successful, because within the first week, I have sold out half of my paintings. This really gives me more courage to paint more painting under my own principle (the spirit of the yuan painting.)

I would be very glad to help you in the correction of the list. I am sure there are many more painting in Taiwan worthwhile for study purpose. I believe there is no problem for you to see these paintings if you have good connection with King & Wang. Chuang Yen is a scholar but I don't think he has the power to control of showing them.

I may come to Washington after the end of March. I have nothing especial, I just want to see you & discuss some paintings. Looking forward to seeing you in the near future.

Sincerely Yours

C. C. Wang

The Bamboo Studio
320 W. 81st St., New York 24, N. Y.
Telephone: TRafalgar-4-2270

Fig. 1 (left). Photograph of C. C. Wang working in his studio, ca. 1990s.

Fig. 2 (above). A letter from C. C. Wang to James Cahill dated March 16, 1959. James Cahill papers, Freer Gallery of Art and the Arthur M. Sackler Gallery Archives. Gift of James Cahill, 2001, FSA. A2001.11.

Dai-chien 張大千 (Zhang Daqian). In response to Wang's frustrations regarding "the difficulty of explaining Chinese painting to Western audiences," Chang Dai-chien responded, "It is of course an insurmountable handicap for those who have never touched a brush" (fig. 1).[8] Again, the word *handicap* appears, this time referring to the viewer, not the painter.

One wonders how Wang might have felt about these conditions. In a letter to Cahill dated March 16, 1959, Wang wrote: "Dear Cahill, I am glad to tell you that my exhibition is comparatively successful, because within its first week, I have sold out half of my paintings . . . this really gives me more courage to paint in the spirit of the Yuan painters" (fig. 2). However, the art historian Ming Hua's research states otherwise. Hua notes Wang's disappointment with the Western reception of his exhibitions at Warren E. Cox Gallery in 1950 as well as Mi Chou Gallery in 1959 and explains that these failures "prompted Wang to reconsider his art in the Western context. In the city, the Western audiences' eyes were accustomed to watercolors and oil paintings. Traditional Chinese landscape painting, with its ink on paper, looked unfamiliar."[9]

Silbergeld also details certain challenges that New York presented during Wang's earliest years in the city. Noting the popularity of decorative "flower-and-bird paintings," Wang painted wallpaper and lampshades to make ends meet.[10] The financial pressures facing Mi Chou Gallery and its artists are evidenced by certain stylistic adaptations that Wang made in his own work.[11] While his 1959 exhibition included traditional landscape paintings, the works that sold were "decorative" still life paintings executed in the style of the painter Qi Baishi.[12] Without any deep understanding of brushwork, Western audiences could easily discern the materiality of the ink in "strong brush gestures" that at the time would have been emblematic of abstract expressionist painters such as Franz Kline, Mark Tobey, or Robert Motherwell.[13]

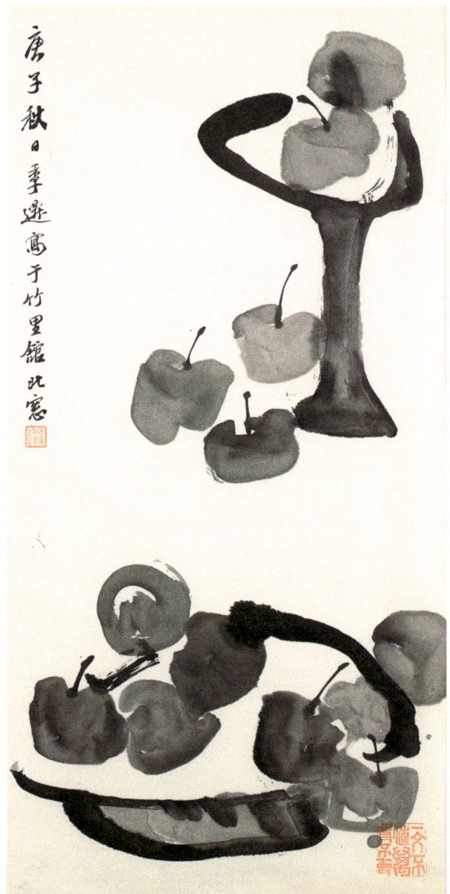

While nothing in the composition of his still life works suggests that Wang begrudged the need to pare down his wide skill set to one style, his choice of seals hints at internal strife. In his 1960 painting *Apples*, the seal states: "Even if not worth a penny, I would not sell it for ten thousand strings of cash"—a proud disclaimer that denies the true reason for painting in this style (fig. 3). Another still life portrays a tantalizing array of brushes, awaiting deployment. Wang's seal plaintively asks: "How can I work completely according to other people's conceptions?"[14] We can interpret this as a lament about the narrow scope of style and limited legibility.

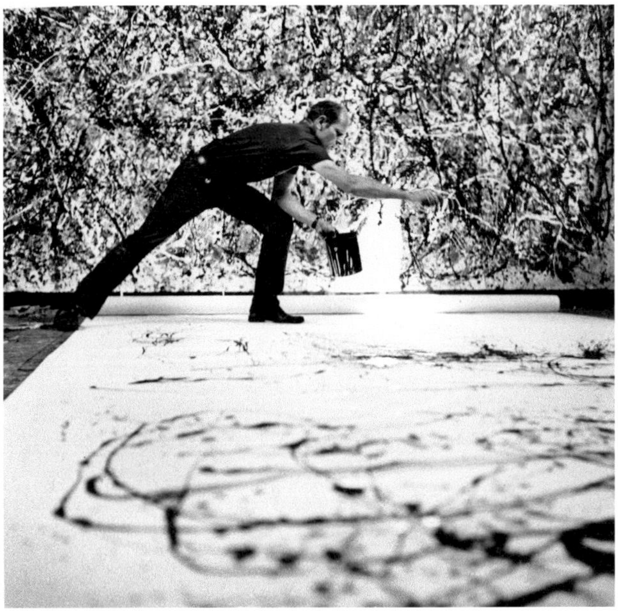

Alongside geopolitical priorities, a critical context was coalescing in the United States. Abstract expressionism became widely recognized in the years between 1947 and 1958, a period that approximates C. C. Wang's first two solo exhibitions in New York. To understand the reigning visual sensibility of this New York-centric movement, we must recall that while Howard Rosenberg would write about Action Painters in 1952, an emphasis on materiality had already been established by Clement Greenberg's essay "Towards a Newer Laocoön," published in 1940, which argued against the "linguistic" or "poetic" references that might shape interpretation. Relying instead upon the inherent truth of a medium's materials in their "purest" form, Greenberg asserted: "Purity in art consists in the acceptance, willing acceptance, of the limitations of the medium of the specific art. To prove that their concept of purity is something more than a bias in taste, painters point to Oriental, primitive and children's art as instances of the universality and naturalness and objectivity of their ideal of purity. . . . Painting abandons chiaroscuro and shaded modelling. Brush strokes are often defined for their own sake."[15]

What Greenberg meant was that the stroke recuses itself from any duty to representational or narrative content. For Greenberg the material was the content, an ethos embodied by abstract expressionism's most recognized poster boy, Jackson Pollock. Featured in the August 8, 1949, issue of *Life* magazine, Pollock became a household name when the feature's tagline asked, in a roundabout proclamation, "Is he the greatest living painter in the United States?" Pollock's ruggedly individual and unapologetically non-representational painting symbolized a defiant rejoinder to the social realist styles of the United States' Cold War counterparts.[16] In a 1950 interview Pollock considered paint's materiality to be so deeply essential that he retracted his brush and circumvented the mark of his own hand to showcase the medium's tendencies (fig. 4): "Most of the paint I use is a liquid, flowing kind of paint. The brushes I use are used more as sticks than brushes—the brush doesn't touch the surface of the canvas, it's just above."[17]

Fig 3 (left). C. C. Wang. *Apples*, autumn 1960. Hanging scroll; ink on paper, 36 ⅞ × 17 ⅞ inches (96.2 × 45.3 cm). Ching Yüan Chai Collection, on extended loan to the University Art Museum, University of California, Berkeley. Inscription: 庚子秋日季遷寫於竹里館北窗 "1960, Autumn Day. Inscribed by Jiqian at the north window of the Bamboo Studio." Seals: (left) 季遷旅美之作 "Done by Jiqian in America"; (lower right) 一文不值, 萬貫不賣 "Even if not worth a penny, I would not sell it for ten thousand strings of cash."

Fig. 4 (above). Photograph by Hans Namuth. *Jackson Pollock*, 1950.

Pollock's physical removal of the brush could not be more distinct from Wang's physical connection to it. In this context, how can we reconcile the first encounters by a US audience with a cross-generational tradition of Chinese "brushwork" or "brushstroke?" Wang himself stated: "The first two important things that I learned about Western painting are that it is meant to be seen from a distance, so composition is crucial, and that the 'touch' of an oil painter is similar to our brushwork, but not exactly the same because of the nature of the materials, and brushwork is the one aspect that Chinese painters have explored in much greater depth."[18] Wang's attention to disparities between viewing distances is telling. Viewing, in the premodern Chinese context in which Wang was trained, meant private viewing (fig. 5). The *bimo* (brush and ink skills) that Wang mentions are studied within the scope of inches—not at the span of feet. Within the landscape tradition, a dramatic play of geological scale unfolds in key details. Any serious scholar or practitioner of *bimo* inspects every inch to uncover the skills embedded in the construction of image and script alike. As is the case with artwork titles in Western traditions, the literati's inscription and choice of seal inflect tone and guide interpretation. We can infer that these three registers—the mark of an experienced hand, a stylized inscription, and equally sophisticated seals—would have been virtually imperceptible to a Western audience accustomed to large-scale compositions.[19]

In the early 1950s, Wang also studied the work of leading abstract expressionist painters, including Mark Tobey, who took extended interest in various Asian painting traditions. Tobey acknowledged that his early calligraphic studies with Chinese diasporic artist Teng Gui in the 1920s, as well as his continued studies of Japanese calligraphy in the 1930s, impacted his practice. In his writing about Tobey's *Universal Field* (fig. 6), former

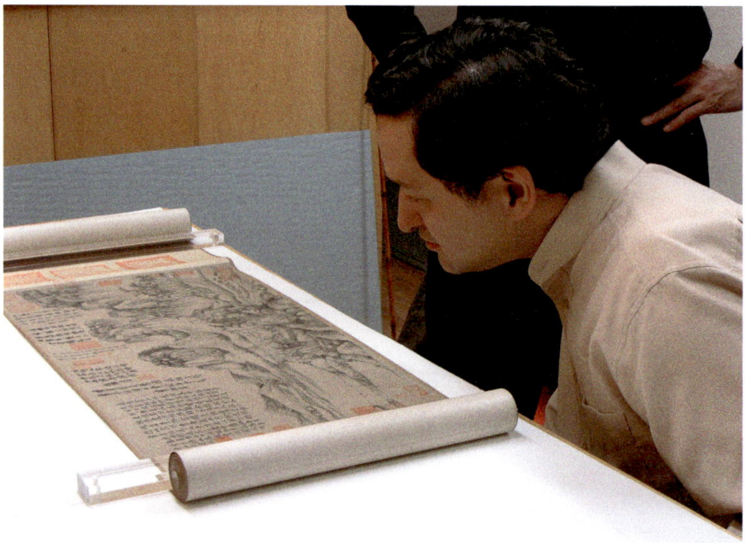

Museum of Modern Art curator William C. Seitz noted: "The image of Tobey's religious views on his work is evident in his fusion of calligraphic brush strokes against a background built of numerous washes of paint, as in *Universal Field*, which he may have been referring to when he spoke about 'Oriental fragments—characters which twist and turn drifting into western zones forever speaking of unity of man's spirit.'"[20] Tobey's reference to the inherently spiritual qualities of "Oriental fragments" echoes Greenberg's orientalism. Meanwhile, Wang did not reciprocate Tobey's enthusiasm and felt that the abstract expressionists were overrated when compared to predecessors whom he considered far more groundbreaking, such as the impressionists.[21]

Wang was not merely rejecting the unfamiliar. Reflecting on his earliest viewings of abstract expressionist painting, he stated (with his characteristically upper-class politesse): "I knew of Pollock, Kline, Motherwell, and Tobey. I saw what they were doing, but I didn't really understand it at the time."[22] On the contrary, Wang did understand and he detailed disparate methodologies with alacrity: "In Western art, the brush is a tool, which is used to illustrate the object's volume, texture, structure, light and darkness, and shadows. The Chinese brush, on the other hand, has a unique tip that can produce pointy, round, flat and bold strokes, and it is developed to suit the different needs for both calligraphy and painting . . . thus as the artist searches for formal aesthetics, he must also pay serious attention to the ink work and brush work."[23]

Fig. 5 (left). Arnold Chang inspecting a handscroll at the Museum of Fine Arts, Boston, 2006.

Fig. 6 (above). Mark Tobey. *Universal Field*, 1949. Tempera, opaque watercolor, and fiber-tipped pen on cardboard, 27 ⅞ × 44 ⅝ inches (70.8 × 113.3 cm). Whitney Museum of American Art, New York. Purchase, 50.24.

For Wang, and his literati contemporaries, the flinging, dripping, or dragging of paint across a surface simply for the sake of breaking with the past must have felt confusing, if not to say unconsidered. Wang's statement also underscores certain nuances of the literati tradition. Scholar-artists are trained to assess all components of a work—symbolic references, the choice of paper, colophon, seals, the wetness or dryness of the ink (pl. 21, leaf a), and most especially the method by which lines have been "drawn" (linear strokes), "cut" (texture strokes), or dotted in (accents).[24] Emulation of the brushwork, thematics, poetics, or compositional references of past masters is purposely deferential and conveys the depth and breadth of an artist's visual lexicon (pl. 21, leaf d).[25]

In his discussion of this challenging decade, Silbergeld also noted that while Wang did not feel masterful in Western styles, the artist later credited his Western education with the development of his compositional skills. It was Wang's forays into new techniques, not new subjects, that loosened his approach to the landscape tradition. Evidence of his experimentation surfaces in works from the early 1960s as Wang turned his attention to the paper itself (fig. 7):

> I did some sketches on watercolor paper, a very rough paper which gives a natural feeling. Why is it rough? Because that makes it natural. If it was smooth, then the lines wouldn't be natural, there wouldn't be anything natural in it. I discovered that Western artists also want this natural roughness. Then I began to use this roughness. Accidental effects, which give this natural feeling, depend partly on the paper. This gave me the idea that if I could get some of that natural feeling by using wrinkled paper, I might come up with the same result.

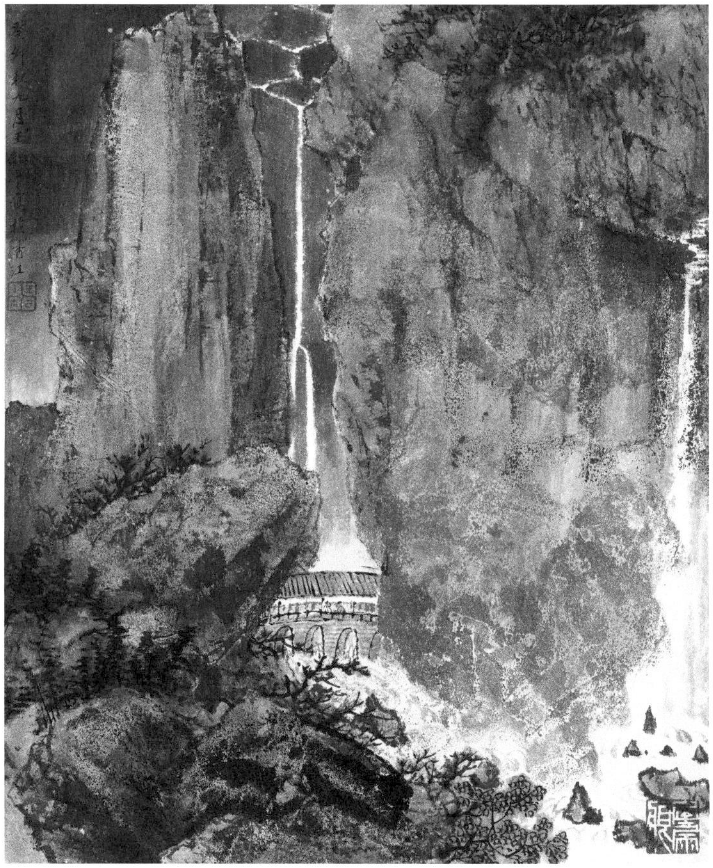

Fig. 7. C. C. Wang. *Landscape with Pavilion at the Foot of a Waterfall*, 1963. Hanging scroll; ink and colors on paper, 19 5⁄16 × 15 ¾ inches (49 × 40 cm). Berkeley Art Museum and Pacific Film Archive, University of California; on extended loan from the Ching Yuan Chai Collection. Inscription: 癸卯秋九月王紀千寫於香江 "1963, Autumn, 9th month. Inscribed by Wang Jiqian in Hong Kong." Seals: (left) 王己千鉥 "Seal of Wang Jiqian"; (lower right) 屋漏痕 "Stains from a leaky roof."

Wang's choice to start wrinkling paper forced a temporary surrender to chance that opened up new potentials. He would go on to blot the "ground" of his landscape compositions with foundational ink marks and then deploy his brushes to compose a landscape around the underlying texture (pl. 6). A "call and response" dialogue ensued. In this interplay between chance and control, one appreciates Wang's many references to jazz improvisation, a tradition that is often misinterpreted as completely spontaneous or free form.[26] In jazz ensembles, a song often passes from one band member to the next, as each musician launches into an interpretive solo before they rejoin the harmonic fold of the original composition. Inventiveness within the given framework—not a complete break from it—demonstrates mastery.

By virtue of his world-class art collection, Wang was perceived first and foremost as a connoisseur rather than as an artist. Yet he and his peers not only introduced literati art and history to the United States—they were also building the conceptual scaffolding through which their own artistic practices could be understood.[27] Until recently, narrow readings and false attributions have dogged the reception of numerous twentieth-century artistic practices that evolved on the margins of prevailing US and European centers. In terms of cultural heritage, Wang's fidelity to his literati training should be commended as a dual act of preservation and expansion. C. C. Wang's work is a credit to American art history, in spite of itself.

NOTES

1. In the first half of the twentieth century, the predominant Western model of artistic progress was associated with the historical avant-garde. The logic of this vanguard was premised on notions of teleological advancement in which a new garde (or front line) superseded an old garde—with the implicit understanding that the old garde was outmoded. This diachronic model, which requires new advances, is insufficient for interpreting a cross-generational dialogue between Chinese literati artists whose practice actively engaged precedents that spanned dynasties. Wang wrote, "Within my abstract works, which merged calligraphy and painting, I search for new interactions where the hand and mind can unite in *harmony*. It is not my intention to start something new in order to be different. Instead, without abandoning the basic elements of Chinese art, all I want to express through my brushwork are what my heart desires and the content of my thoughts." C. C. Wang, "Notes on Calligraphy and Painting," August 1999, accessed November 16, 2022, http://www.echinaart.com/Advisor/adv_ccwang_landscape.htm.

2. See Richard Barnhart, "Chinese Calligraphy: The Inner World of the Brush," *Metropolitan Museum of Art Bulletin* 30, no. 5 (April–May 1972): 230–41.

3. "Functionally, the essential principle underlying the cursive script is to write each character as quickly and simply as possible while still conveying the essence of its form; in other words, to reduce a standard form to an abstraction that can be imparted in continuously flowing movement." Ibid., 235.

4. "Oh, East is East, and West is West, and never the twain shall meet, / Till Earth and Sky stand presently at God's great Judgment Seat; / But there is neither East nor West, Border, nor Breed, nor Birth, / When two strong men stand face to face, though they come from the ends of the earth." Rudyard Kipling, "The

Ballad of East and West" (1889), https://www.kipling-society.co.uk/poem/poems_eastwest.htm.

5. The catalogue for the exhibition *Mountains of the Mind: The Landscapes of C. C. Wang* (Washington, DC: A. M. Sackler Foundation, 1977) offers first-person accounts of Wang's upbringing and early life in Suzhou; but for a detailed view of his connoisseurship, see the copious notes Wang kept about paintings that he studied throughout his life: Kathleen Yang, ed., *Through a Chinese Connoisseur's Eye: Private Notes of C. C. Wang* (Beijing: Zhonghua shuju, 2010).

6. See Jerome Silbergeld, *Mind Landscapes: The Paintings of C. C. Wang* (Seattle: Henry Art Gallery and University of Washington Press, 1987), 26–27. Chang's statement that "the decade of the 1950s was very fruitful for C. C. Wang the collector" stands in high contrast to his declaration that "the 1960s was a period of tremendous creativity for Wang." Arnold Chang, "C. C. Wang at Ninety: A Kaikodo Celebration," *Kaikodo Journal* 3 (Spring 1997): 12.

7. Quoted in Frank Fulai Cho, "Reminiscences of Mi Chou: The First Chinese Gallery in America," *Chinese American Forum* 1, no. 3 (May 1985): 7.

8. Frank Fulai Cho, "The Question of Brushwork (Bi-Mo) in Chinese Painting," *Chinese American Forum* 12, no. 2 (October 1996): 3–10.

9. Ming Hua, "Bridging the Tradition to the Modern, the East to the West: C. C. Wang and His Life in Art" (PhD diss., Arizona State University, 2014), 50. Silbergeld (*Mind Landscapes*, 69) notes that the 1959 exhibition of his paintings at Mi Chou Gallery, "including flowers, genre paintings, and traditional landscapes scrolls . . . was by his own admission unsuccessful, even depressing."

10. Silbergeld, *Mind Landscapes*, 23.

11. Ibid., 67.

12. For a well-trained literati painter, this genre would have been considered less skilled or less "serious" than landscape painting. Wang was encouraged to work in this style by his friend the gallerist Alice Boney, who believed it would appeal to Western audiences. Ibid., 66.

13. Ibid., 27.

14. Ibid., 27, illus. 7.

15. Clement Greenberg, "Towards a Newer Laocoön," *Partisan Review* 7, no. 4 (July–August 1940): 305.

16. "And in the institutional world of both museum and government cultural policy, Pollock and the other abstract expressionists began to be seen as important emissaries of the American experience: wildness was now starting to be recoded as freedom—a liberated sensibility increasingly deemed as setting a good example for the cause of democracy in Cold War-torn Europe." Hal Foster et al., *Art Since 1900: Modernism, Antimodernism, Postmodernism*, (New York: Thames & Hudson, 2016), 350.

17. Jackson Pollock, interview by William Wright, in *Abstract Expressionism*, ed. Katy Siegel (London: Phaidon, 2011), 239.

18. Quoted in Chang, "C. C. Wang at Ninety," 11.

19. For further analysis of Chinese literati painting, see Jerome Silbergeld's *Chinese Painting Style: Media, Methods, and Principles of Form* (Seattle: University of Washington Press, 1982).

20. William C. Seitz, *Abstract Expressionist Painting in America* (Cambridge, MA: Harvard University Press, 1983), quoted in Siegel, *Abstract Expressionism*, 107.

21. Quoted in Silbergeld, *Mind Landscapes*, 29.

22. Quoted in Chang, "C. C. Wang at Ninety," 12.

23. Wang, "Notes on Calligraphy and Painting."

24. For technical illustrations of brushstrokes, see Molly Schardt, "Brushstrokes: Styles and Techniques of Chinese Painting," ed. Richard Mellott and So Kam Ng, November 1995, https://education.asianart.org/wp-content/uploads/sites/6/2019/09/Brushstrokes.pdf, 40–45.

25. See the discussion of Fan Kuan's *Travelers among Mountains and Streams* in Wen-shing Chou's essay in this volume, 22.

26. For a discussion of Wang's embrace of chance in an untitled work from 2001 (*Landscape in the Style of Ni Zan*), see Daniel M. Greenberg's essay in this volume, 96–97.

27. Kathleen Yang (*Through a Chinese Connoisseur's Eye*, 2) outlines a significant learning curve: "Before the 1950s, the problem with Western appreciation of Chinese paintings was lack of access. The situation changed when C. C. Wang opened the door to his collection and willingly shared his connoisseurship. From 1950 to 1970, one could visit him in New York City and see Song, Yuan, Ming, and Qing masterpieces. The purchase in 1973 of twenty-four Song and Yuan paintings from his collection by the Metropolitan Museum was a monumental event. Accessibility had passed from the largesse of a private collector to the responsibility of a public museum."

Writing the Unfamiliar Landscape: Analyzing the Calligraphy of C. C. Wang and Its Connections to New York City Graffiti

JORDAN HOMSTAD

"The fundamental inspiration of calligraphy," stated the poet and calligrapher Chiang Yee, "as of all arts in China, is nature . . . . Every stroke, every dot suggests the form of a natural object."[1] Some of the earliest forms of Chinese characters were actually pictograms, clear and graphic representations of the objects they stood for; over time the characters were abstracted and standardized but never lost their ties to the natural world.[2] How, then, did the calligraphy of collector and scholar-artist C. C. Wang change when he immigrated to the urban landscape of New York City in 1949?[3] To many, New York City is fundamentally separated from the natural world, and in the latter half of the twentieth century it was the quintessential concrete jungle. Nevertheless, the city is its own form of landscape. *Hills and Ravines in Running Script* (fig. 1) shows how Wang's calligraphy may have responded to the urban environment; rather than the flowing strokes normally associated with ink-brush calligraphy, the characters are blocky and sharp, sardined together on the paper as if they are passengers on an overcrowded subway. This cramped feeling is only exacerbated by the wide brush that Wang used, which creates angular, condensed characters that pile together like New York City buildings, merging into one amorphous mass that is more texture than text.

In the 1960s, following Wang's arrival in New York City, a trend began to emerge that would forever change the urban landscape: "tagging," or the act of writing one's alias on public property, began to take off.[4] By the 1980s, graffiti was a near-ubiquitous part of the city, as much a part of the landscape as concrete paving stones or rusty fire escapes. Tags covered subway cars both inside and out, and this stylized form of writing took on an omnipresence akin to that of calligraphy in China, where it filled shops, homes, temples, and palaces (figs. 2, 3).

The artist, curator, and art historian Arnold Chang, Wang's disciple, recalls showing his master *Subway Art*, a book by Martha Cooper and Henry Chalfant about graffiti first published in the 1980s: "[He] was fascinated by these images, many of which took the form of stylized lettering written with spray paint—a type of urban calligraphy using the written word as the basis for personalized graphic designs. . . . Though thankfully Wang avoided vandalizing public property, the quick pace and frenetic energy of New York and its inhabitants are similarly reflected in the meandering lines and agitated rhythms of his late calligraphic works."[5] Graffiti images were illicit and sometimes insular, often incorporating writing styles and motifs that held meaning only within the street-art community, while calligraphy was a historic, integral, and almost universal part of Chinese culture. However, both were wholly inescapable within their respective urban landscapes. Taking inspiration from the street art that was so

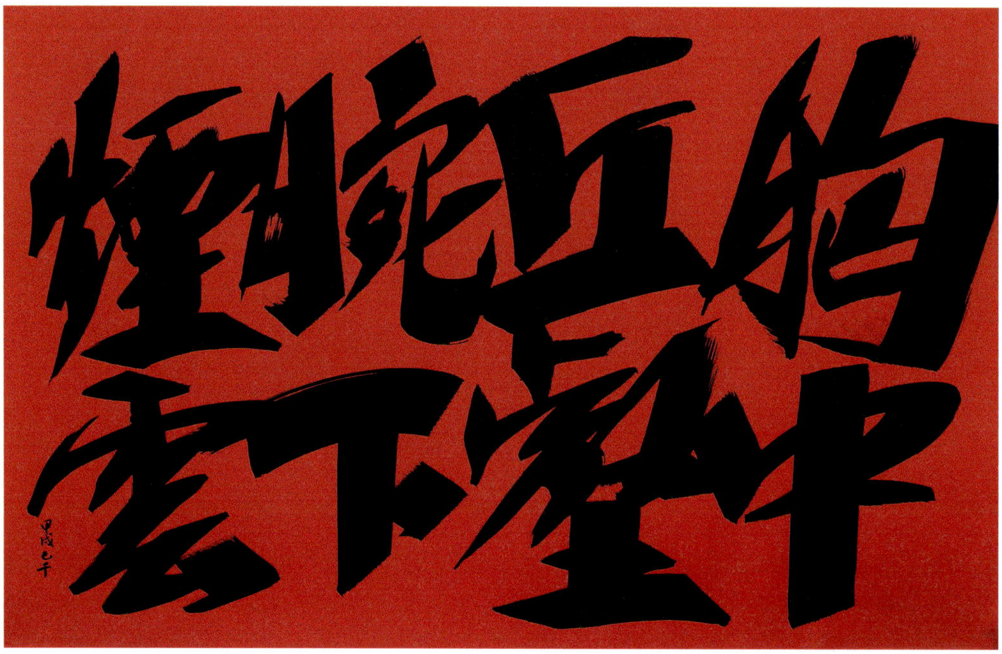

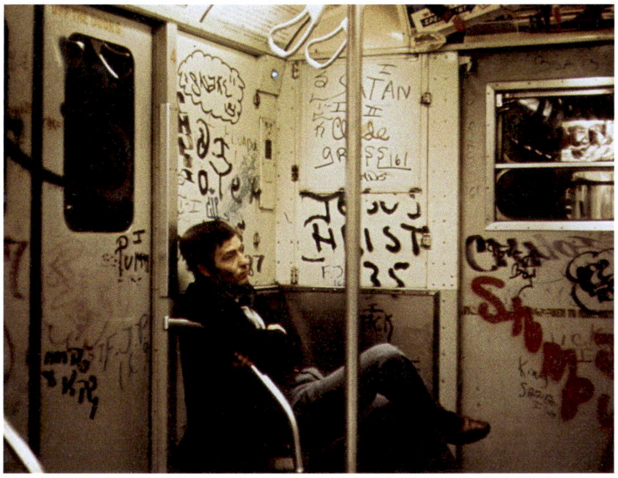

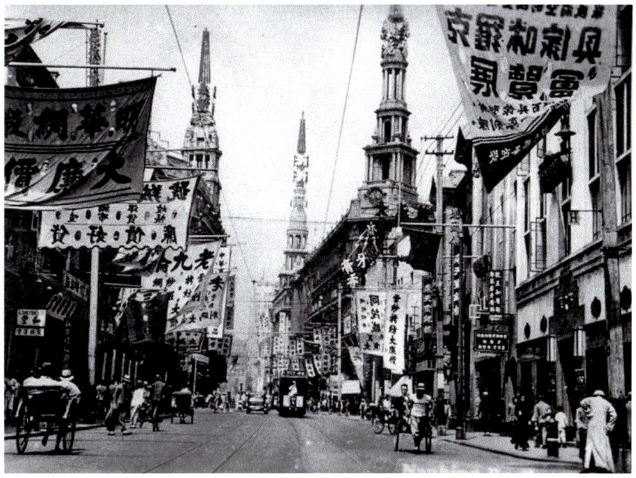

Fig. 1 (left). C. C. Wang. *Hills and Ravines in Running Script*, 1994. Chiseled sponge brush with black ink on red construction paper, 40 × 26 inches (101.6 × 66 cm). Private Collection and Fu Qiumeng Fine Art, New York. Script reads: 胸中丘壑, 腕下煙雲 "Hills and Ravines of the Mind, Clouds and Mist beneath the Wrist." Inscription: 甲戌己千 "*Jiaxu* [1994], Jiqian.

Fig. 2 (above left). Erik Calonius. *Subway Car*, May 1973. Collection of the National Archives and Records Administration.

Fig. 3 (above right). Shanghai's Nanjing Road in the 1930s.

fundamental to the landscape of the latter half of his life, Wang merged graffiti techniques with the decades of study and literati scholarship that informed his perspective to create a truly international reinterpretation of Chinese calligraphy.

According to Chang, Wang turned to practicing calligraphy in New York telephone books so as not to waste paper (pl. 18). Within these pages Wang practiced calligraphy on a daily basis, reinvigorating a habit first established when he was a young child learning characters. With each turned page, a new style of calligraphy emerges: on one, bold running-script blazes across listings of businesses starting with the letter *A*; on another, confident cursive script is overlaid on a map depicting the city's regional calling area. Yet another page shows evidence of Wang's experiments with abstraction, where cursive script knots into lines and flourishes that are nearly impossible to untangle. Wang learned calligraphy through copying, much as he did painting; as Chang states, "he practiced for an hour or two every day, gradually memorizing the content of the texts he was copying and simultaneously internalizing the brush movements required to duplicate the forms of the original models." Nevertheless, Wang always considered himself a painter, rather than a calligrapher, and was therefore much less beholden to traditions of calligraphy than to the immense history of Chinese landscape painting.

Wang's experiments within the pages of this phone book were just that: experiments. He thought little of the book as a piece of art, and instead considered it an easy way to continue the calligraphic practice that had been part of his life since childhood. However, Chang notes that the book was received positively by others, despite Wang's own belief in its experimental nature: "I'm sure that [Wang] was genuinely surprised when he learned that students and friends found [the phone book experiments] to be charming and engaging works of contemporary art." This daily practice of experimentation extended beyond the binding of the phone book, impacting Wang's formal works of calligraphy as well.

In one such formal, untitled work of calligraphy in running script, (*Chanting of Dragon and Roaring of Tiger*) (fig. 4), the characters are a mixture of standard and cursive scripts not uncommon in Chinese calligraphy,[6] but the splattered-ink background separates the characters from the paper itself. Because of the ink's texture, the paper takes on an entirely new character that feels both modern and urban; the splatters recall those from a can of spray paint, nearly empty following a long night spent painting subway cars, or the pocked and gritty pavement of a metropolis. One could easily imagine strolling down a sidewalk and looking down, only to be surprised by 龍吟乕嘯 scrawled brashly across the pavement underfoot. The characters would not seem out of place, considering how much of the city at that time was covered in street art, tags, and even classic graffiti such as lovers' initials and ". . . was here." Through this work Wang performs a sort of cultural exchange, using a splattering technique like that employed by some abstract expressionists and by artists working with spray paint, to recontextualize characters that are integral to Chinese history within a uniquely New York environment, resulting in the dissolution of preestablished artistic hierarchies and disciplines. Wang considered himself a landscape painter, the genre held in the highest regard in traditional literati painting. At the same time, his experiments with calligraphy combined one of the most storied Chinese art forms with street graffiti, a form of expression largely practiced by working-class communities of color—and by artists who embraced abstract expressionism—a celebrated movement of painting that prevailed from about 1947–58 and was visibly dominated by white men.

An explicit subset of Wang's graffiti-inspired calligraphy includes his works with felt-tipped marker, bristle brush, and sponge painting brushes. To many practitioners of traditional Chinese calligraphy, the use of anything but an animal-hair ink brush would be tantamount to sacrilege. Chiang Yee—who, like Wang, spent many years abroad—claimed that a good calligraphic stroke could not be made with an ink pen or a pencil: "The brush alone—the same brush as the painter uses—can effectively reproduce the movements of clouds and trees."[7] The materials of brush and ink are often considered the most fundamental elements of Chinese art, but not using those materials exclusively does not mean he did not make "Chinese calligraphy." In fact, he broadened the scope of what can

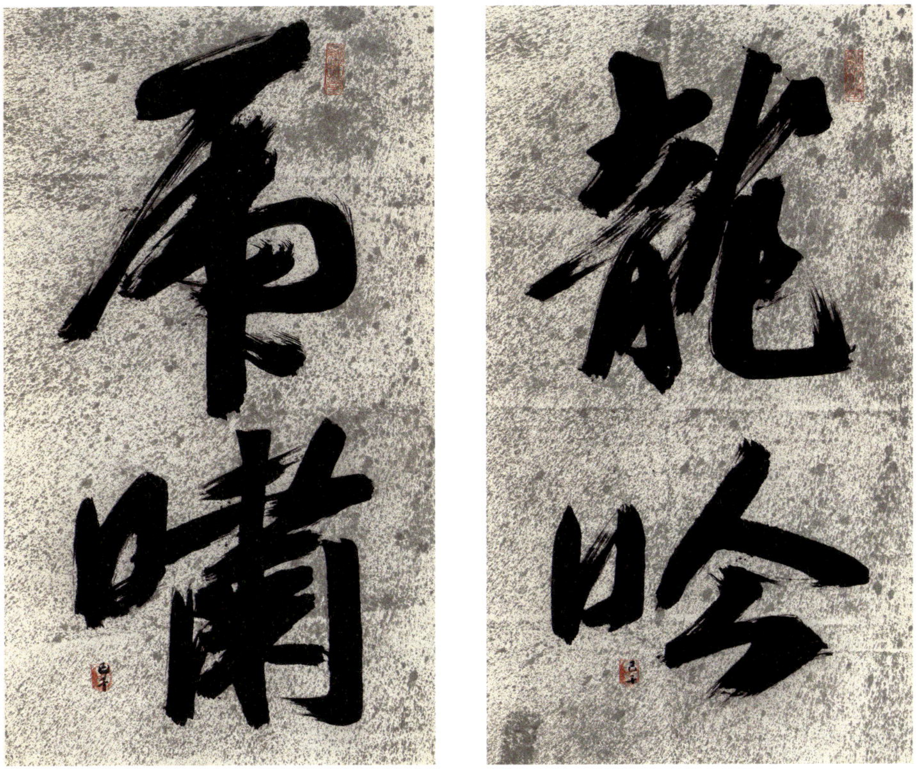

Fig. 4. C. C. Wang. no title (Chanting of Dragon and Roaring of Tiger), undated. Pair of hanging scrolls; ink on paper, left: 47 ½ × 27 ¼ inches (120.7 × 69.2 cm); right: 47 ⅝ × 27 ¼ inches (121 × 69.2 cm). Courtesy Private Collection. Script (left): 龍吟 "Chanting of Dragon"; Script (right): 乕嘯 "Roaring of Tiger." Inscription (both scrolls): 己千 "Jiqian." Seals (both scrolls, upper right): 谿岍草堂 "Thatched Cottage by Riverside"; (both scrolls, lower left): self-portrait of the artist.

be considered Chinese calligraphy, incorporating markers and paint-splattered gestures that recall urban graffiti.

Wang's calligraphic work in *Chanting of Dragon and Roaring of Tiger* is less sharp than in *Hills and Ravines in Running Script*. In both examples, the unusual background does most of the work in recontextualizing Wang's calligraphy beyond its lineage in Chinese literati culture. *Chanting of Dragon and Roaring of Tiger* was written with a relatively dry brush—the ink shows large amounts of variation and texture, from the darkest of blacks to a patchy stroke that is more background than ink, skipping over the page as a brush might skip over rough pavement. Wang's use of wetter, darker ink in *Hills and Ravines* lends it a more graphic quality. Wang refilled his brush frequently during the writing process, making it difficult to see much variation in texture. The characters are powerful, imposing, and very flat. Although upon close inspection slight traces of bristle marks can be seen, at first glance the characters look as if they were scrawled with a chisel-tipped permanent marker. The angularity of the running script recalls the complex forms of "wildstyle" graffiti tags, a comparison heightened by the vibrant background.[8] The combination of the deep-red construction paper—unusual for Chinese calligraphy in both its material and brilliant color—and the

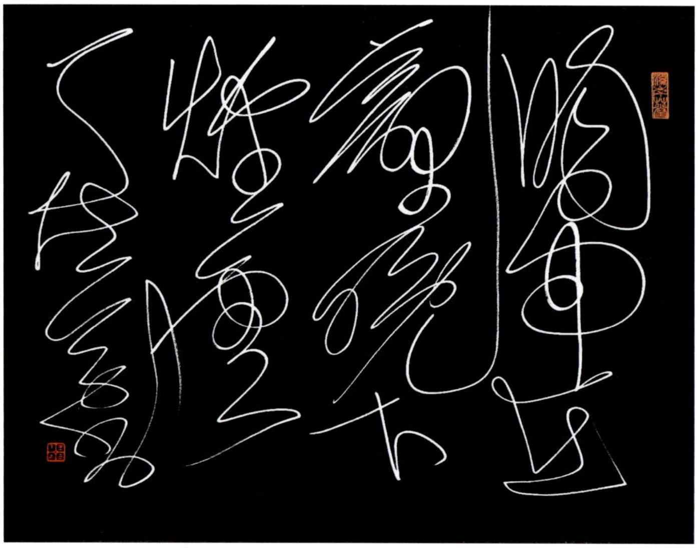

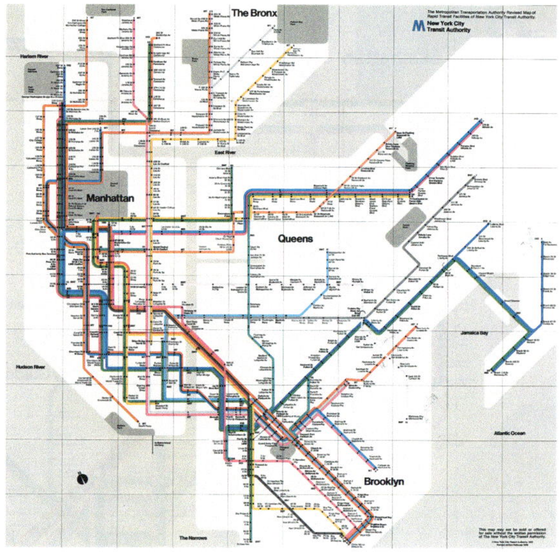

graphic characters bridges the gap between the seemingly disparate crafts of ink-brush calligraphy and street graffiti.

While calligraphy is often used to convey meaning, Wang's late calligraphic works often teetered on the edge of, if not totally embraced, complete abstraction. *Fragrant Foliage in Cursive Script* (fig. 5), written on black construction paper with a silver felt-tipped marker, is one example; the cursive script conveys a definite meaning, but it is so loosely and fluidly drawn that it is nearly illegible, even to audiences familiar with Chinese characters. While such loopy cursive script has precedents in earlier works by masters such as Wang Duo (王鐸, 1592–1652),[9] the knotted, fevered lines of C. C. Wang's characters recall the tangle of subway lines that cut through New York City (fig. 6). Wang's completely abstract works, such as *Ink and Gold Abstract Calligraphy* (fig. 7), display a similar level of intricacy, although they focus less on the lines of the brush and more on the spaces between; if *Fragrant Foliage in Cursive Script* suggests a simplified graphic of subway lines, *Ink and Gold* suggests a complete map, showing the arbitrary divisions within neighborhoods separated by those lines.

Wang's experiments with abstraction were often done in spite of, rather than because of, the actual meanings of the characters. Chang notes that "the literary content of these images was secondary, even irrelevant, to their visual impact. . . . C. C. Wang took the poetic rhymes of his youth, added a touch of

Fig. 5 (above left). C. C. Wang. *Fragrant Foliage in Cursive Script*, undated. Double-sided work; silver and gold metallic ink on black construction paper, 19 ¾ × 25 ½ inches (50.2 × 64.8 cm). Private Collection and Fu Qiumeng Fine Art, New York. Seals: (upper right) 溪岸草堂 "Thatched Hut by the Riverbank" (lower left) 王己千鉥 "Seal of Wang Jiqian."

Fig. 6 (above right). Massimo Vignelli, Michael Hertz Associates, New York City Transit Authority, Joan Charysyn, and Bob Noorda. *New York Subway Guide*, 1978. Foldout map, 22 × 18 inches (55.9 × 45.7 cm).

Hip Hop, and reconfigured them to match the dynamic rhythms of his late years."[10] Wang's disregard for legibility shares some elements of 1980s graffiti culture, although they have different motivations. Kase2, one of the leading pioneers of wildstyle graffiti in the 1980s, declared, "I throw 'em off with the camouflage. That way they can't bite [steal] my style."[11] Tagging was a sort of turf war in the New York City graffiti scene, with participants plastering their aliases across subway cars at sizes and in colors as large and eye-catching as possible. The obscuring of meaning within the individual's tag was essentially a way to protect, or even trademark, their own identity on the streets; Wang's abstraction, on the other hand, was often applied to famous prose written by historical Chinese scholars. Also a manner of self-fashioning, this may have been Wang's way of laying claim to the texts he copied, emphasizing their relation to him and to literati culture; it could also have been his own method of studying the texts, making sense of the characters by letting them flow through his own hand. Whatever the motivation, Wang's forays into abstraction seem to interrogate the long-established meanings of Chinese characters, reflecting on the changing world in which historical texts exist. Furthermore, Wang's use of abstraction highlights the inherently powerful forms of Chinese characters, which from their earliest instances of usage were designed to mimic nature. While this abstraction renders the calligraphy less legible, the characters mirror their

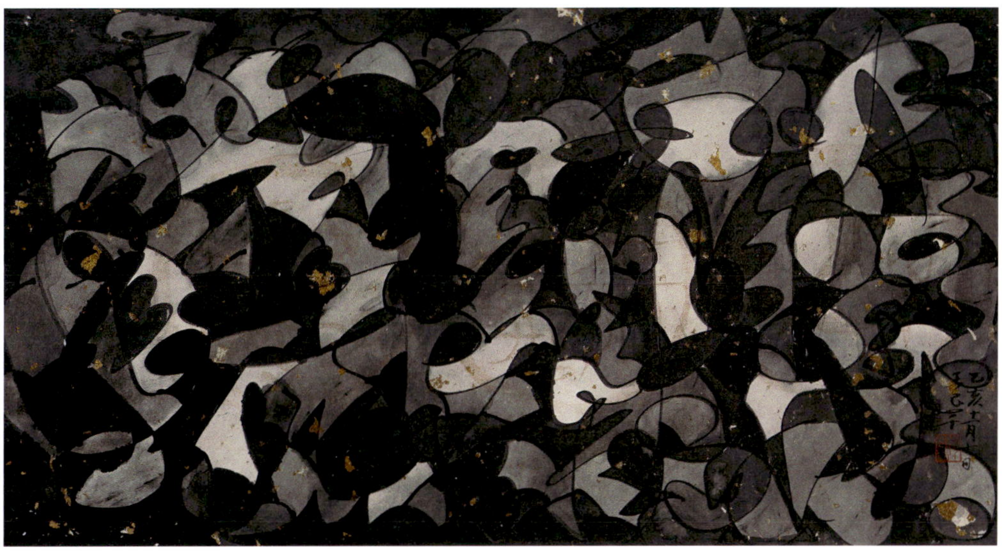

Fig. 7. C. C. Wang. *Ink and Gold Abstract Calligraphy*, 1995. Chinese brush with ink on gold flake rice paper, 12 × 23 inches (30.5 × 58.4 cm). Private Collection. Inscription: 已亥十一月十日王己千 "*Yihai* [1995], November 10, Wang Jiqian." Seal: 己千創稿 "Sketches created by Jiqian."

surroundings just as they have always done, reflecting tangled messes of subway lines, chaotic graffiti on the sides of train cars, and the rivers of people who stream in and out of New York streets. Thus, Wang's works continue to uphold the tradition of calligraphy, recontextualizing centuries of practice and scholarship within a new landscape.

It is impossible to say how much Wang was consciously influenced by New York City graffiti. He may have been on the lookout for eye-catching tags every time he took the subway, hoping to find calligraphic inspiration in the landscape of an urban metropolis; he could just as easily have seen the books on graffiti shown to him by Arnold Chang, flipped through them a few times, and then gone back to his painting feeling relatively unchanged. Whether consciously or not, C. C. Wang was influenced by the city's culture of graffiti tagging, and his work exists on a precipice between East and West, old and new, legible and abstract. Showing a willingness to experiment beyond the confines of his training as a scholar of Chinese arts, Wang combined thousands of years of history with an emerging form of American self-expression to create a new form of calligraphy that could only have been made by an artist whom many consider to be the last of the Chinese literati.

NOTES

1. Chiang Yee, *Chinese Calligraphy: An Introduction to Its Aesthetic and Technique* (Cambridge, MA: Harvard University Press, 1938), 111.

2. Ouyang Zhongshi, introduction to *Chinese Calligraphy*, ed. Wang Youfen (New Haven, CT: Yale University Press; Beijing: Foreign Languages Press, 2008), 33–46.

3. See *C. C. Wang: Recent Works* (New York: EastWest Studios, 1993), 35.

4. Martha Cooper and Henry Chalfant, *Subway Art* (New York: Owl Books, Henry Holt, 1984), 14.

5. Arnold Chang, "New York Rhythms, Suzhou Rhymes," Fu Qiumeng Fine Art, January 14, 2022, https://fuqiumeng.com/news/54-article-new-york-rhythms-suzhou-rhymes-author-arnold-chang/. The two subsequent quotations from Chang are also from this source.

6. Wang Shizheng, "The Evolution and Artistry of Chinese Characters," in *Chinese Calligraphy*, ed. Wang Youfen, 47–66.

7. Yee, *Chinese Calligraphy: An Introduction*, 112.

8. Cooper and Chalfant (*Subway Art*, 27) define *wildstyle* as "a complicated construction of interlocking letters."

9. See, for example, Wang Duo, *Free Copy of Xu Jiaozhi's calligraphy,* 1635, hanging scroll, ink on satin, 8 ft. 10 in. × 20 1/16 in. (269.2 × 51 cm), Guanyuan Shanzhuang Collection, on loan to the Metropolitan Museum of Art, New York.

10. Chang, "New York Rhythms, Suzhou Rhymes."

11. Quoted in Cooper and Chalfant, *Subway Art*, 71.

C. C. Wang and Chinese Painting Studies in the West

JOSEPH SCHEIER-DOLBERG

It is a striking fact: examine the key episodes in the formation of Chinese painting studies in the West—from the 1930s to the 1990s—and there you will find C. C. Wang. He is among the teams selecting objects for important exhibitions; with the scholars wrangling over authenticity and dating; on the long trek to the remote museum storeroom; at the symposium. His persistent presence throughout these decades is all the more striking for the fact that his own voice is so little preserved. Wang published sparingly, leaving those who would assess his influence to seek other metrics of evaluation. If one looks closely, though, the conclusion that his impact on the field was great—perhaps uniquely so—becomes inescapable. The C. C. Wang manner of understanding art is so densely woven into the way we look at and talk about Chinese paintings that it operates as a kind of ambience, imperceptible but ubiquitous. This essay is an examination of some key episodes that made it so.[1]

Long before he had the opportunity to travel outside China, Wang began to interact with the nascent field of Chinese painting studies abroad. The first milestone came thanks to his teacher Wu Hufan, with whom Wang studied painting and connoisseurship in Shanghai in the 1930s, when he was invited to participate in the selection committee for the *International Exhibition of Chinese Art* to be held at London's Royal Academy from 1935 to 1936. The *International Exhibition* was the Chinese government's first attempt to marshal its artistic patrimony for the purpose of cultural diplomacy, and the stakes were accordingly high.[2] Over the course of three months in 1935, along with Wu and other well-connected connoisseurs, the twenty-eight-year-old Wang gained the privilege of access to the collections of the Palace Museum—the erstwhile Qing imperial collections—for the purpose of selecting painting and calligraphy to be shown in London.[3] Noting the rarity of the occasion, the American scholar of

Chinese art history Jerome Silbergeld has remarked that "no private citizen of China had *ever* had this opportunity before."[4] Though he had by this point been exposed to many fine paintings in Shanghai's private collections, the volume and quality of the palace collections afforded the young Wang a major leap in connoisseurial exposure and experience.

This first episode in our story is ambiguous, as the paintings sent to London by the selection committee were recognized as disappointing even at the time.[5] Many have wondered why the committee sent such an underwhelming group of artworks, especially given the importance of the enterprise. Could such gifted connoisseurs truly have seen this as a worthy representation of Chinese painting history, or was a decision made—for whatever reason—to withhold the best pieces from travel abroad? James Cahill has argued that it was the latter, noting that a preview exhibition held in Shanghai included a rich selection of masterpieces that were not sent to London.[6] Whether this tactic was conceived by government officials overseeing the process or by the committee itself is not known, but this foray into institutional politics and intercultural communication must have provided an indelible learning experience—along multiple registers—for the young C. C. Wang. First and foremost, he gained the chance to study thousands of important paintings to which access had been tightly controlled for centuries. Second, he played a role in representing China—both government and culture—to the larger world, and he saw firsthand both the stakes and the difficulties of doing so. Finally, he had the chance to work in an intercultural environment, as one of his colleagues on the committee was the German scholar Victoria Contag, who became an important collaborator in years to come.[7]

In the course of debates among the committee members, both Wang and Contag were struck by the subjective nature of connoisseurship—how it relied upon a single viewer's interpretation of visual data and therefore was subject to near-constant disagreement. Both felt that objective standards could aid the field as it sought to coalesce around a canon, and they settled on the photographic reproduction of authenticated seals and signatures as a worthy contribution. The two young scholars embarked on a project to collate and publish such a resource. After processing the photographs of the Palace Museum collection they had made for the Royal Academy survey, in 1937 Wang and Contag began to traverse wartime China in search of other important collections to supplement their book. For seals and signatures to have value in the process of authentication, they must themselves come from accepted works, so Wang's and Contag's connoisseurial training was critical to the success of their enterprise.[8] The project had the added benefit of gaining them entrée into China's most important collections. The resulting book, published in a German-Chinese edition in 1940 and later in an expanded, English-Chinese edition in 1966, became an indispensable tool for the collector and student of Chinese painting and calligraphy.[9] A well-thumbed copy can be found on the shelf of nearly every professional in the field, and it remains in regular use today.

In 1947, C. C. Wang made his first trip abroad, traveling first to Japan and then to the United States. In New York, he found work at the Metropolitan Museum of Art (the Met), where curator Alan Priest employed him to authenticate paintings in the collection, particularly the recently acquired A. W. Bahr collection.[10] For Priest, the viewing sessions must have provided an eye-opening window into a manner of connoisseurship practiced by few if any at that time in the United States. As Arnold Chang has reflected elsewhere in this volume, when C. C. Wang instructed students in how to look at Chinese paintings, he nearly always focused on details of brushwork rather than composition—so much so that, according to Chang, his slides never even featured overall images of the paintings in question. For Wang, working in the tradition of Wu Hufan and generations before him, the heart of a painting lay in the interplay of brush, ink, and paper—the *bimo* 筆墨—and this had to be examined at close range to be understood. Priest, unschooled in this manner of analysis and following credulously the attributions of and signatures on the paintings themselves, had rated the collection worthy of purchase for a significant sum. Wang's evaluation was, on the contrary, severe—he deemed fewer than 10 percent of the artworks authentic—but his judgment has been borne out by subsequent generations of study. Thus began his career as a leading connoisseurial adviser to American collections, public and private, a capacity that allowed him to refine the canon of paintings suitable for study in the United States.

Wang returned to China in 1948, but it quickly became clear that the future there would be painful for someone who so revered the past. Leaving his homeland, Wang settled in New York City, where he attempted to establish a new life. One of his first influential ventures was to support the founding of Mi Chou Gallery, the first art gallery in the United States devoted to works by Chinese artists. Established by his student Frank Fulai Cho, the gallery was initially located on the ground floor of Wang's townhouse on the Upper West Side, where it served as a rallying point for the elite, culturally minded Chinese immigrant community in New York City. Notably, Mi Chou was not a venue (only) for nostalgic, conservative art—its exhibition program included cutting-edge architecture and design, photography, and printmaking, along with stars of ink painting such as Qi Baishi and Chang Dai-chien.[11] Thanks to C. C. Wang, it also presented at least one important exhibition of premodern Chinese painting at a time when such shows were exceedingly rare—a 1959 exhibition of paintings by the Four Monks of the early Qing dynasty (Bada Shanren 八大山人[ca. 1626–1705], Shitao 石濤 [1642–1707], Hongren 弘仁 [1610–1663], and Kuncan 髡殘 [1612–after 1674]), drawn entirely from Wang's own collection.[12] It would be many years before other galleries took up the mantle of this pioneering enterprise.

From 1949 to 1956, Wang remained in the United States awaiting conferral of citizenship. He continued to build relationships with people who were interested in Chinese painting, most consequentially James Cahill, whom Wang met when Cahill was a curator at the Freer Gallery of Art in Washington, DC. At the time, Cahill was a young, enterprising graduate student at the University of Michigan, but he would go on to be one of the defining figures of Chinese art history in the twentieth century—a curator, collector, and longtime professor at the University of California, Berkeley. Cahill reflected often in print and in lectures how profoundly C. C. Wang impacted his intellectual development. Their friendship began during this period in New York, when Cahill was on a fellowship at the Met, from 1953 to 1954. Describing these early encounters, Cahill wrote that they provided him with his "first glimmerings of understanding of the Chinese tradition of connoisseurship, through weekly sessions with C. C. Wang."[13]

Once able to move freely in the late 1950s, Wang resumed travel to Europe and Asia, often in search of paintings to supplement his growing collection. In 1959 he participated in an important trip that enabled him to affect the direction of the field in subtle but important ways: a visit to Taiwan with Cahill, where Wang advised the American scholar in the selection of works for his general history, *Chinese Painting* (1960), written for Skira's *Treasures of Asia* series.[14] Over the course of a month, Cahill and Wang, accompanied by members of the National Palace Museum staff, combed through paintings in the bunker-like temporary storerooms created to house the collection in Taichung 台中, near the village of Pei-kou 北溝 (fig. 1). In his reminiscences of this time, Cahill recalls Wang's constant companionship, noting that National Palace Museum scholar Li Lin-ts'an 李霖燦 referred to the trio as the "Three Painting Worms" for their relentlessness during viewings.[15] The length of the trip and the tenacity of the visitors won them the opportunity to look beyond the well-studied

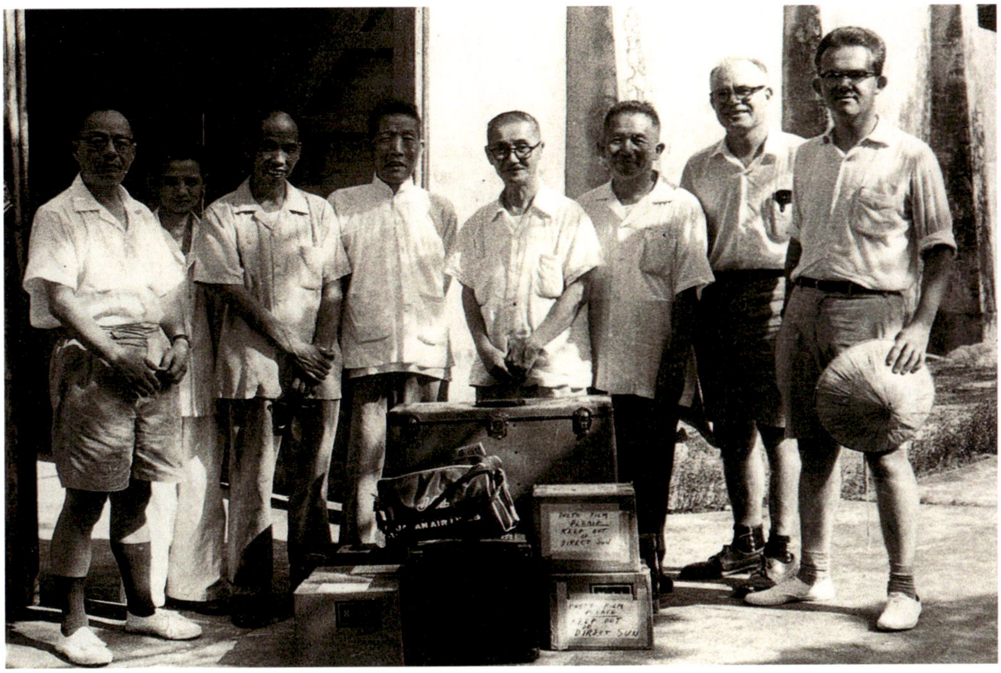

Fig. 1. Survey and photography team for James Cahill's 1959 survey of the National Palace Museum collection for his book *Chinese Painting.* From left to right: C. C. Wang, Zhang Deheng, Li Lin-ts'an, Liang Tingwei, Chuang Yen, Tan Danjiong, Henry Beville, and James Cahill. Pei-kou, Taiwan, 1959.

areas of the collection into lesser-known crates, where they discovered important works that had never been published; Wang's knowledge of the collection, gained during the 1935 survey, was no doubt helpful in brokering these viewings and elucidating what emerged. The work done during this trip was instrumental in defining the canon of paintings available for study in reproduction, as *Chinese Painting* became one of the most widely available introductory resources on the topic, and one of the few to reproduce works in color.

Wang and Cahill's 1959 visit to the National Palace Museum in Taiwan would have further reverberations. By the time of their journey to Pei-kou, planning was already underway for a major exhibition of artworks to travel from the National Palace Museum to the United States—a momentous act of cultural diplomacy intended to solidify the Republic of China's position as the steward of Chinese culture in international eyes.[16] The idea would come to fruition with the five-city extravaganza *Chinese Art Treasures* in 1961–62, for which Cahill played a key role in both object selection and catalogue writing.[17] For the scholarly community, the exhibition was epochal. The opportunity to study so many important, early paintings—in particular a group of monumental landscapes of the Northern Song dynasty—altered the careers of a number of scholars and enticed some not yet in the field to pursue careers in Chinese art history.[18] The selection also helped to delineate the canon of important early works from the palace collections that students in the States would study intensively.[19]

Though C. C. Wang has never been formally acknowledged as a contributor to this exhibition, it is worth considering how the discussions of 1959 affected Cahill's thinking and even that of colleagues from the National Palace Museum as they considered how to shape *Chinese Art Treasures*. Not only was Wang already established as one of the world's preeminent connoisseurs—and perhaps the only person to have seen the important collections in Asia, Europe, and the United States—but he was also the only member of the 1935 Burlington House exhibition selection committee to whom Cahill could turn for counsel. Whether Wang's experience translated into explicit advice or worked its way more subtly into the final object selection, Cahill's writings make clear that the elder scholar had a significant impact on his thinking, and therefore Wang's voice must be considered as an important contribution to the *Chinese Art Treasures* story.

Back in New York in the 1960s and into the early '70s, C. C. Wang's own collection of paintings became an important resource for the burgeoning field of Chinese painting studies in the United States. In the words of Silbergeld, "Wang's apartment provided an open, modern environment in which Wen Fong and his students, as well as many other American scholars, were treated to long, invaluable study sessions."[20] Wang was not the only New Yorker to make his collection so available—John Crawford, John Elliott, Earl Morse, Wang Fang-yu, and Wan-go Weng provided similar access to students—but his collection had unusual scope, ranging from the tenth century through the eighteenth. For a field still defining its canon, especially the corpus of locally available masterworks, Wang's collection was essential, and for many young scholars it provided formative encounters with Qing-dynasty artists such as Ni Zan, Wang Meng, and Wang Yuanqi. These encounters had reverberations beyond the environment of the academic seminar, as both professors and students began to use paintings from C. C. Wang's collection in seminal exhibitions, catalogues, and books that defined the young field's concerns.[21] The important early statement on the Orthodox School of the Qing dynasty—Wen Fong and Roderick Whitfield's 1969 exhibition and catalogue *In Pursuit of Antiquity*—was deeply influenced by C. C. Wang, from whose collection many of the key works in the exhibition were borrowed.[22]

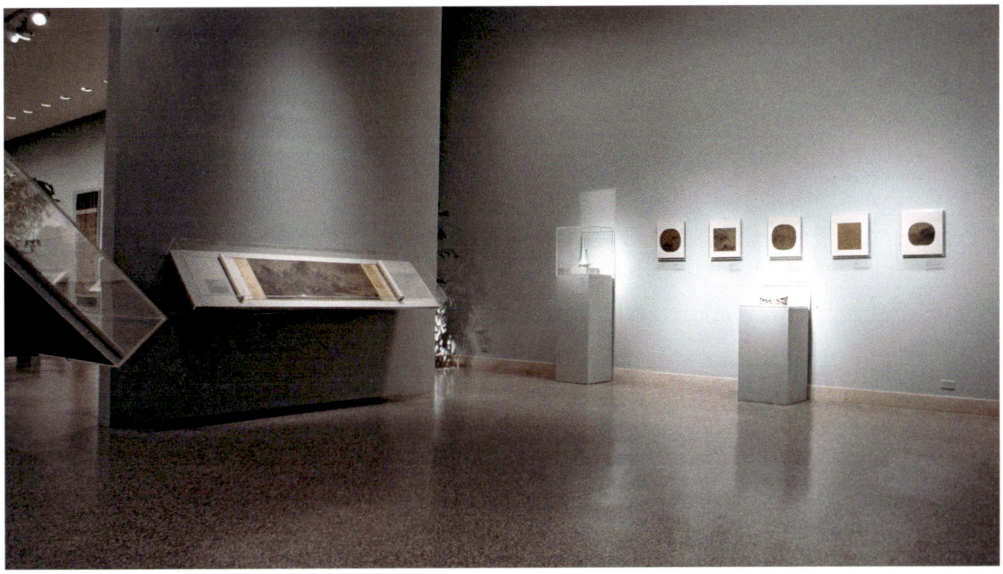

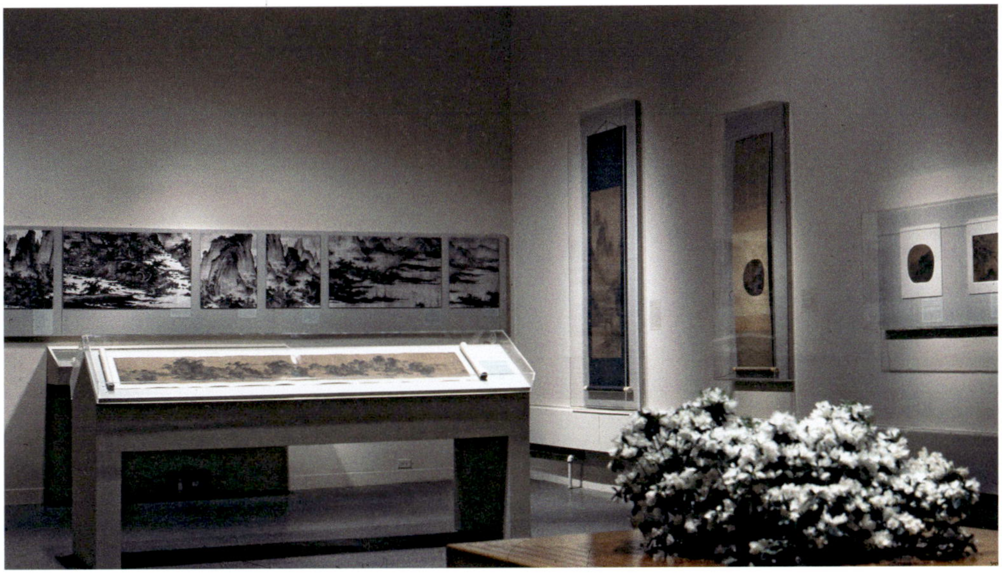

Fig. 2 (above). Installation shot, *Sung and Yüan Paintings: Exhibition of Newly-Acquired Chinese Paintings*, The Metropolitan Museum of Art, New York, 1973–74.

Fig. 3 (right). Installation shot, *Summer Mountains: The Timeless Landscape*, The Metropolitan Museum of Art, New York, 1976.

In 1973, Wang entered wider public consciousness with Wen Fong's acquisition of twenty-five important artworks from his collection for the Met. The acquisition was considered controversial at the time—the museum was still reeling from the disappointment of the Bahr Collection, which Wang had helped to discredit—and it was loath to make another, even higher-profile mistake. With this in mind, the museum took the extraordinary step of having the collection publicly vetted by independent experts: Richard Barnhart (Yale

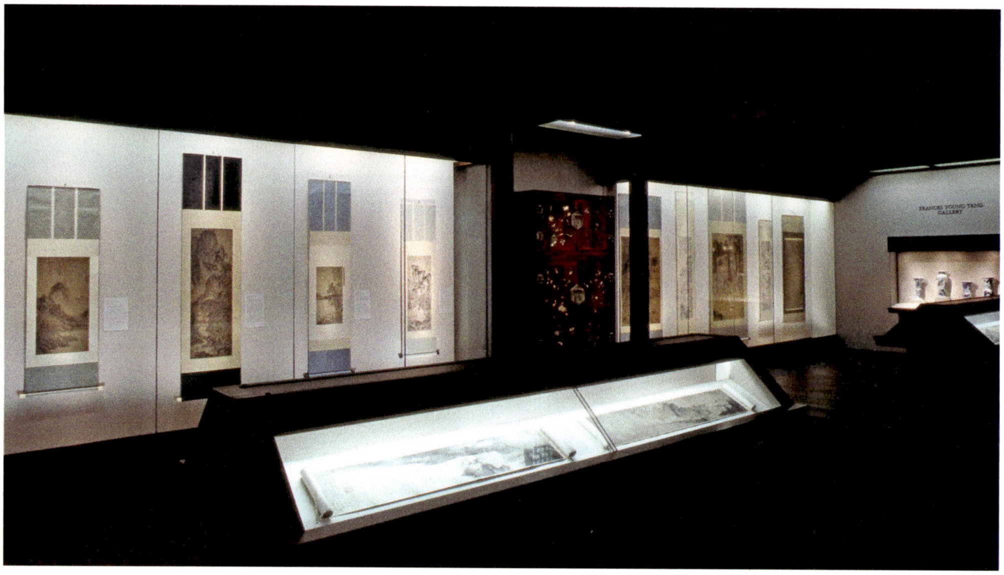

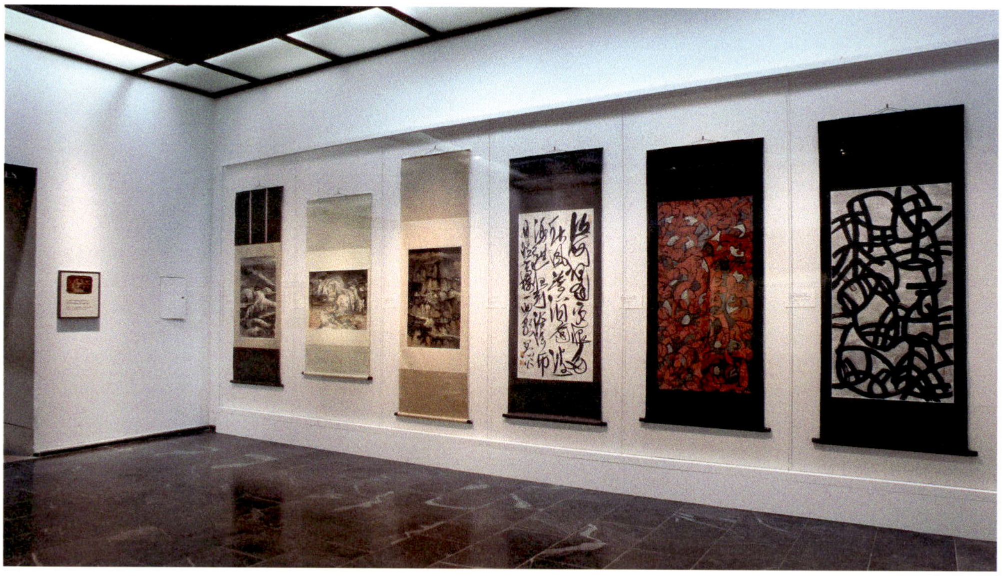

Fig. 4 (top). Installation shot, *The Artist as Collector: Masterpieces of Chinese Painting from the C. C. Wang Family Collection*, The Metropolitan Museum of Art, New York, 1999–2000.

Fig. 5 (above). Installation shot of C. C. Wang's own paintings shown in *The Artist as Collector*.

University), Sherman Lee (Cleveland Museum of Art), and Laurence Sickman (Nelson Gallery, Kansas City). Barnhart's evaluation that, for the Met, "the transition from non-entity to major collection would be sudden and dramatic with this acquisition" captured the generally positive tenor of the reports, which convinced museum trustees to invest major funds in this area despite a lack of expertise within the board itself.[23]

For the museum to acquire the group en bloc amounted to a remarkable ratification of Wang's personal taste. Where the other major public collections of Chinese painting in the United States had been built over time from multiple sources, the Met's core group of early paintings now reflected the vision of a single private collector.[24] Naturally, not everyone in the field agreed with all of Wang's attributions, nor with changes to these attributions made by Fong after they were acquired, but the paintings quickly became central to the field's discussions; even those who disputed attributions devoted significant time to the collection.[25] Wang's sensibility was further canonized in formative exhibitions, catalogues, and books: *Sung and Yüan Paintings* (1973–74; fig. 2); *Summer Mountains: The Timeless Landscape* (1976; fig. 3); *Along the Border of Heaven* (1983); Fong's magnum opus *Beyond Representation* (1991); and *The Artist as Collector* (1999–2000; figs. 4, 5), and its catalogue, *Along the Riverbank* (1999).[26] The symposium that accompanied this final exhibition, held on December 11, 1999, hinged on debates over the authenticity of *Riverbank*, the early landscape masterpiece that was among the final group of paintings purchased from Wang's collection for the Met by museum trustee Oscar Tang. This event and its proceedings, *Issues of Authenticity in Chinese Painting*, produced original research by major scholars that remains essential reading for students of Chinese painting, weaving the C. C. Wang collection and sensibility even more densely into the fabric of the field.[27]

Wang's impact on Chinese painting studies came also through the market, an arena of particular importance to a young discipline still adding works to its canon. He advised dealers, including C. T. Loo (1880–1957) and his successor Frank Caro, who had extensive experience with antiquities but less with paintings. Wang helped to establish New York as a key site for auctions of Chinese painting through his work as a consultant with Sotheby Parke Bernet (later Sotheby's), where he collaborated for many years with Arnold Chang. Though he was still building his own collection at the time, Wang was generous with advice to other collectors, a number of whom named him as a key influence in their own collecting journey. Earl Morse, whose collection formed the basis of

In Pursuit of Antiquity, noted C. C. Wang's "counsel, helpfulness, and friendship," and recalled being advised by Wang to purchase an important Wang Hui 王翬 (1632–1717) painting "found in a dark corner of the saleroom at an auction."[28] R. W. Finlayson, who collected seventeenth- and eighteenth-century painting, cited Wang's guidance in the building of his own collection, which was exhibited at the Royal Ontario Museum in 1963.[29] If you were collecting Chinese paintings in New York during this period, it was nearly impossible to escape Wang's influence. Many of the works that are today essential to the field were brought to market or placed in homes thanks to his expertise.

How does one assess the impact of a person on a field of study? The terms are amorphous, the metrics imprecise. C. C. Wang's achievements as a collector are widely celebrated. Increasingly, his accomplishments as a painter are being recognized. His impact on Chinese painting studies as an academic discipline remains underappreciated, but the episodes explored here suggest that his contribution was great. What is clear is that Wang touched many, in ways both overt and subtle, with his understanding of Chinese painting. His influence was felt in exhibitions large and small, in catalogues and books, and in the objects that are available today for study. According to Kathleen Yang, an independent scholar who studied with C. C. Wang, more than 150 paintings from Wang's collection currently reside in museums in the United States, Europe, and Australia, and many more have come to light thanks to his work as a consultant to dealers, auction houses, and collectors.[30] Fifty years on from the initial purchase of Song and Yuan paintings by the Met in 1973, works from the C. C. Wang collection are among the most requested by scholars for research viewings and for teaching, testimony to their ongoing position in the core curriculum for scholars in the United States and beyond. These are all important, tangible contributions. But perhaps the most enduring impact that C. C. Wang had on the field was also the most subtle, the hardest to quantify: generations of scholars and collectors talked with him, looked at paintings with him—some even learned to paint from him. They listened to him expound on his collection and the collections of others, and in the process they gained access to a tradition of connoisseurship—not just authentication, but appreciation—to which few could lay claim. At a time when mainland China was inaccessible to most, this gave Wang an outsize voice in the development of the field. If that voice is difficult to perceive today, it is perhaps because it is has become such an integral part of our practice as a field.

NOTES

1. I am indebted to scholars who have published on the life and career of C. C. Wang: Hsu Hsiao-hu (Joan Stanley-Baker), Ming Hua, Kathleen Yang, and especially Jerome Silbergeld. For more comprehensive biographical narratives, please consult their publications: Hsiao-hu Hsü, "Wang Chi-ch'ien: An Appreciation," in *Mountains of the Mind: The Landscape Painting of Wang Chi-ch'ien*, ed. Meredith Weatherby (New York: Weatherhill, 1970), 11–18; Ming Hua, "Bridging the Tradition to the Modern, the East to the West: C. C. Wang and His Life in Art" (PhD diss., Arizona State University, 2014); Kathleen Yang, ed., *Through A Chinese Connoisseur's Eye: Private Notes of C. C. Wang* (Beijing: Zhonghua shuju, 2010); and Jerome Silbergeld, *Mind Landscapes: The Paintings of C. C. Wang* (Seattle: Henry Art Gallery and University of Washington Press, 1987).

2. On the *International Exhibition of Chinese Art*, see Jason Steuber, "The Exhibition of Chinese Art at Burlington House, London, 1935–36," *Burlington Magazine* 148, no. 1241 (August 2006): 528–36. On the perspective of expatriate Chinese scholars regarding the exhibition in London, see Liya Fan, "The 1935 London International Exhibition of Chinese Art: The China Critic Reacts," *China Heritage Quarterly*, no. 30–31 (September 2012): 1–8.

3. On the composition of the selection committee, see Clarissa von Spee, *Wu Hufan: A Twentieth Century Art Connoisseur in Shanghai* (Berlin: Reimer, 2008), 48–51.

4. Silbergeld, *Mind Landscapes*, 17.

5. Unsatisfied with the overall quality and unconvinced by the attributions, the European curators of the exhibition provided their own dates for many paintings in the catalogue, setting off a contretemps between defenders of the selection committee and their critics. See Leigh Ashton, "Some Notes on the Chinese Exhibition," *Burlington Magazine for Connoisseurs* 68, no. 395 (1936): 86–91; and John C. Ferguson, "Reflections on the London Exhibition of Chinese Art," *T'ien-Hsia Monthly* 2, no. 5 (May 1936): 433–42.

6. Cahill speculated that the committee may have chosen minor works in order to shield important pieces from the unpredictable sea journey to London. Whether the selections were made in good faith or with a dose of cynicism about European audiences' discernment cannot be known from the record, but Cahill's skepticism that this group of connoisseurs would have considered the chosen group of paintings to be a worthy representation of the glories of Chinese art is well-founded. See James Cahill, "London 1935/36 Exhibition: 'Early' Paintings from China," accessed September 21, 2022, https://jamescahill.info/the-writings-of-james-cahill/london-193536-exhibition-early-paintings-from-china.

7. On Victoria Contag, see Clarissa von Spee, "Victoria Contag: Pioneer, Scholar and Collector of Chinese Paintings," in *Modern Chinese Painting and Europe: New Perceptions, Artists* [sic] *Encounters, and the Formation of Collections*, ed. Michaela Pejčochová and Clarissa von Spee (Berlin: Reimer, 2017), 61–80. See also Clarissa von Spee, "Wu Hufan, Victoria Contag, and C. C. Wang—A Passion for Paintings and a Lifelong Friendship," lecture recorded April 27, 2019, accessed February 10, 2022, https://www.youtube.com/watch?v=Dmc8z7nJ3y0.

8. This was also sensitive work, as Wang and Contag could not offend their hosts by explicitly dividing collections into authentic and inauthentic prior to photography and documentation. To navigate these difficulties, they developed secret hand signals that allowed them to communicate evaluations of authenticity discreetly and therefore include only those works they both deemed to be authentic. Silbergeld, *Mind Landscapes*, 21.

9. Wang Chi-ch'ien and Victoria Contag, *Ming-Qing huajia yinjian* 明清畫家印鑑 / *Maler-und sammler-stempel aus der Ming-und Ch'ing-zeit* (Shanghai: Shangwu, 1940); Chi-ch'ien Wang and Victoria Contag, *Seals of Chinese Painters and Collectors of the Ming and Qing Periods*, rev. ed. (Hong Kong: Hong Kong University Press, 1966). According to C. C. Wang's student and friend Kathleen Yang, Wang wished to expand the book further in his later years, and he worked with Yang and her husband Denis toward that end, but the project did not come to fruition. Yang, *Through A Chinese Connoisseur's Eye*, 2.

10. Silbergeld, *Mind Landscapes*, 22.

11. Wang himself had a show of his own paintings at Mi Chou in 1959, but according to him the work did not resonate with the audience. Frank Fulai Cho, "Reminiscences of Mi Chou: The First Chinese Gallery in America," *Chinese American Forum* 1, no. 3 (May 1985): 4–8.

12. Ibid., 8.

13. James Cahill, "2004 Brief Talk Given at New York Chinese Scholar's Garden Society," April 27, 2004, accessed August 14, 2022, https://jamescahill.info/the-writings-of-james-cahill/cahill-lectures-and-papers/61-clp-61-2004.

14. James Cahill, *Chinese Painting* (Geneva: Skira, 1960). See also James Cahill, "Albert Skira and Chinese Painting," accessed September 30, 2022, http://jamescahill.info/the-writings-of-james-cahill/responses-a-reminiscences/143-21albert-skira-and-chinese-painting.

15. James Cahill, "The Place of the National Palace Museum in My Scholarly Career," accessed February 21, 2022, https://jamescahill.info/the-writings-of-james-cahill/cahill-lectures-and-papers/81-clp-117-2005.

16. John Alexander Pope, Aschwin Lippe, and James Cahill, *Chinese Art Treasures*, exh. cat. (Geneva: Skira, 1961). On the story of *Chinese Art Treasures*, see Noelle Giuffrida, "The Right Stuff: Chinese Art Treasures' Landing in Early 1960s America," in *The Reception of Chinese Art across Cultures*, ed. Michelle Ying Ling Huang (Newcastle upon Tyne: Cambridge Scholars Publishing, 2014), 201–28. On the Cold War implications of the exhibition, see Jane Ju, "Chinese Art, the National Palace Museum, and Cold War Politics," in *Partisan Canons*, ed. Anna Brzyski (Durham, NC: Duke University Press, 2007), 115–34.

17. Giuffrida, "The Right Stuff," 206; Cahill, "The Place of the National Palace Museum."

18. Richard Barnhart, for instance, has written that his encounter with the paintings of Guo Xi and Fan Kuan at the *Chinese Art Treasures* exhibition so moved him that he decided to pursue a career in the field of Chinese art history. See Richard Barnhart, "The Song Experiment with Mimesis," in *Bridges to Heaven: Essays on East Asian Art in Honor of Professor Wen C. Fong*, ed. Jerome Silbergeld et al. (Princeton, NJ: P. Y. and Kinmay W. Tang Center for East Asian Art, Department of Art and Archaeology, Princeton University, 2011), 1:115.

19. Wang's notes from his 1959 visit and subsequent trip with Cahill in 1962 were collated and published by Kathleen Yang in *Through A Chinese Connoisseur's Eye*.

20. Silbergeld, *Mind Landscapes*, 32. Wen Fong was one of the leading figures of Chinese art history during the twentieth century. In addition to founding the earliest doctoral program in Chinese art in the United States at Princeton University (1959), Fong also built the collections of the Princeton University Art Museum and, beginning in 1971, the Met, where he served as leader of the Asian Art Department even as he taught at Princeton. Fong regularly brought his students to see artworks in the homes of private collectors.

21. Paintings from Wang's collection or recently acquired by others from Wang were included in a number of early exhibitions, including: Martie W. Young et. al., *The Eccentric Painters of China* (Ithaca, NY: Andrew Dickson White Museum of Art, Cornell University, 1965); Richard Edwards, *The Painting of Tao-Chi* (Ann Arbor: Museum of Art, University of Michigan, 1967); and Roderick Whitfield, *In Pursuit of Antiquity: Chinese Paintings of the Ming and Ch'ing Dynasties from the Collection of Mr. and Mrs. Earl Morse* (Princeton, NJ: Art Museum, Princeton University, 1969).

22. Roderick Whitfield was professor of Chinese and East Asian Art at the University of London, 1984–2002, and curator in the Department of Oriental Antiquities at the British Museum, 1968–84.

23. Metropolitan Museum of Art, "Metropolitan Museum Acquires Twenty-Five Important Chinese Paintings," press release, July 13, 1973, Museum Archives.

24. This situation would evolve in 1989 with the bequest of the collection of John M. Crawford Jr., but even with those significant additions, the early paintings from the C. C. Wang collection remain the core of the Met's holdings in this area.

25. In his 1987 book on C. C. Wang, Jerome Silbergeld documented well the debates that ensued over attributions in the wake of the collection's acquisition. Silbergeld, *Mind Landscapes*, 32–34.

26. Wen Fong and Marilyn Fu, *Sung and Yüan Paintings* (New York: Metropolitan Museum of Art, 1973); Wen Fong, *Summer Mountains: The Timeless Landscape* (New York: Metropolitan Museum of Art, 1975); Richard M. Barnhart, *Along the Border of Heaven: Sung and Yüan Paintings from the C. C. Wang Family Collection* (New York: Metropolitan Museum of Art, 1983); Wen Fong, *Beyond Representation: Chinese Painting and Calligraphy, 8th–14th Century* (New York: Metropolitan Museum of Art, 1992); Maxwell K. Hearn and Wen Fong, *Along the Riverbank Chinese: Paintings from the C. C. Wang Family Collection* (Metropolitan Museum of Art, 1999).

27. Judith G. Smith and Wen Fong, eds., *Issues of Authenticity in Chinese Painting* (New York: Department of Asian Art, Metropolitan Museum of Art, 1999).

28. Earl Morse, preface to Whitfield, *In Pursuit*, 14, 11.

29. Reginald William Finlayson, foreword to *Catalogue of the Exhibition of Individualists and Eccentrics: The Mr. and Mrs. R. W. Finlayson Collection of Chinese Paintings*, by Hsio-yen Shih, Reginald William Finlayson, and Henry Trubner (Toronto: University of Toronto Press, 1963), ii.

30. Yang, *Through a Chinese Connoisseur's Eye*, 299–301.

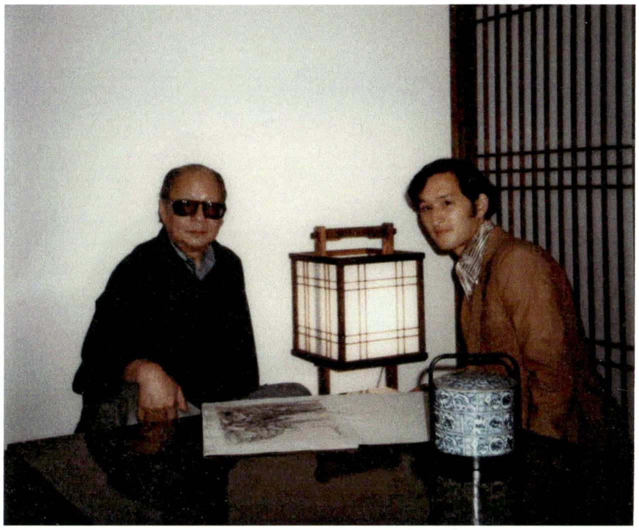

Remembering the Master

ARNOLD CHANG

I have a very vivid memory of the first time I met C. C. Wang, in the summer of 1977. I was a graduate student at the University of California, Berkeley, studying the history of Chinese painting with the eminent art historian James Cahill. One day, when I was doing research in the study room adjacent to Professor Cahill's office, he came into the room and introduced me to his old friend C. C. Wang—in English, everyone referred to him as C. C. (based on his given name as written in Wade-Giles, the standard romanization of the time, Chi-ch'ien 季遷,己千). I was quite familiar with his name because he was a famous collector who owned many of the paintings that were published in our textbooks. C. C. was visiting the Bay Area and had come to Berkeley to see Professor Cahill and to view a work painted by Wu Hufan that had just been donated to the Berkeley Art Museum (now the Berkeley Art Museum and Pacific Film Archive). Wu Hufan was one of the most highly regarded connoisseurs and collectors of the twentieth century, as well as a fine painter, and C. C. Wang was his first student. Although he had already studied painting with several masters before meeting Wu Hufan, it was under Wu's mentorship that C. C. had sharpened his eye and developed a taste

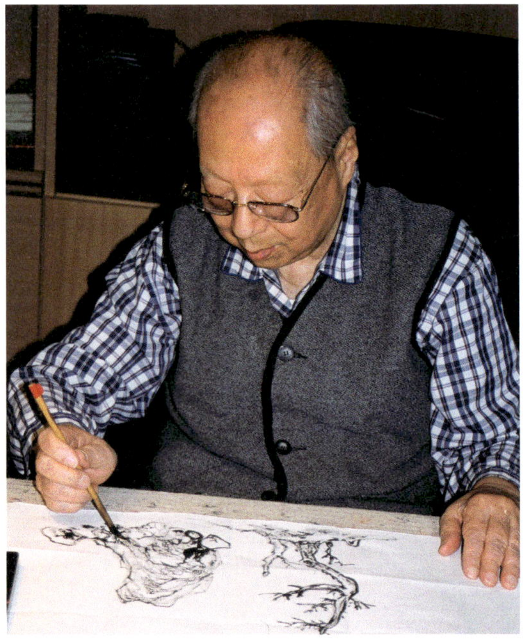

for the works of old masters that would ultimately form the basis of his own creative endeavors. I learned that C. C. was staying in San Francisco for a few weeks and was offering two classes at the Chinese Culture Center, located at the edge of Chinatown, one on "Techniques of Chinese Painting" and the other on "Appreciating Chinese Painting." I enthusiastically enrolled in both classes (fig. 1).

I had previously studied with two teachers of Chinese brushwork—while still in high school I learned Chinese calligraphy from Wang Jiyuan 王濟遠 (Wang Chi-yuan) in New York, and as a college student I took Chinese painting classes with Guo Yanqiao 郭燕嶠 (Kuo Yen-ch'iao) in Taipei, Taiwan. Typically, a beginning student learns by copying the works that their teacher has created as a model. In both calligraphy and painting, the student is meant to copy each model as closely as possible, stroke by stroke. This is the tried-and-true method of learning to use the brush correctly—a practice that forces the student to look closely at the model and train his hand to regulate the direction, angle, pace of movement, and amount of pressure applied to the brush, in order to control the flow of ink in a way that matches the original. The teacher demonstrates the proper way of holding the brush, and the student attempts to mimic his brush movements.

Fig. 1 (previous page). C. C. Wang and Arnold Chang, San Francisco, summer 1977.

Fig. 2 (above). C. C. Wang painting, New York, ca. 2000.

C. C. Wang employed the same basic approach. For his "Techniques" class of about ten pupils, he had prepared a variety of models to copy, using photocopies of his own landscape compositions. Like my previous teachers, he first demonstrated his technique for painting simple landscape elements, such as trees and rocks. I immediately noticed that the way he wielded his brush was fundamentally different from that of my other teachers. Rather than holding the brush upright, perpendicular to the surface of the paper—as I had been taught and as most painting manuals prescribe—most of the time his brush was held at an oblique angle to the paper (roughly thirty degrees) as he painted, with only the very tip of the brush touching the surface (fig. 2). The direction of the brush movements was generated by his shoulder, while his relaxed fingers and wrist controlled the pressure of the brush, and thus the flow of ink, through micro-movements. Watching him paint was like observing a master of *Taiji quan*

太極拳 (tai chi) practicing graceful gestures that conceal enormous inner power masquerading as slow-motion dance. By regulating the pressure of the brush tip, the artist retains the energy of the stroke centered within the line itself, just as the *qi* 氣 of the Taiji master circulates within the body rather than dissipating externally. C. C. began painting and all the students were mesmerized as mountains, valleys, and waterfalls magically materialized before our eyes!

As we attempted to copy the sample images, he would move from student to student, like a chess master playing ten simultaneous games, offering encouragement and making suggestions to each individual, often making corrections directly on a student's work or demonstrating a particular technique on a separate sheet of paper. I had more experience painting than most of the others, so when it was my turn, C. C. would generally take out a new sheet of paper and start painting. Somehow, whatever he demonstrated for me seemed to respond to a question I had in my mind about a particular technique or style but had not yet verbalized. I immediately sensed that, when it came to Chinese painting, we had an almost telepathic connection.

C. C. Wang's class on "Appreciating Chinese Painting" was unlike any class I have ever taken. He began by showing slides of paintings, as is typical in art history classes. Ordinarily a professor might begin with an overall image of the entire composition, discussing various aspects of the work and its place within the individual artist's oeuvre and within a broader art historical context. They might then show a series of details of individual sections of each work to demonstrate salient points concerning technique, composition, and other formal characteristics of the work. In C. C.'s class, however, it became clear after viewing a few slides that he showed *only* details of the paintings, never the overall composition! Also, the slides appeared in no particular order—not chronologically, not divided by school, dynasty, region, or even style.

He had an encyclopedic knowledge of the entire history of Chinese painting, from its earliest times to the present day, but he judged each work on its own merit, as a personal expression of the individual artist who created it. For C. C. Wang, looking closely at details revealed the artist's character, personality, and spirit. The medium of ink brushed on absorbent paper is extremely sensitive—the paper provides a continuous record of every mark made by the movement of the brush. Wet and dry, dark and light, thick and thin strokes are woven together by the artist into a tapestry of textures, through *bimo* 筆墨 (brush and ink), or "brushwork." Studying these lines and patterns up close is the most direct conduit to the artist's *xin* 心 (mind/heart).

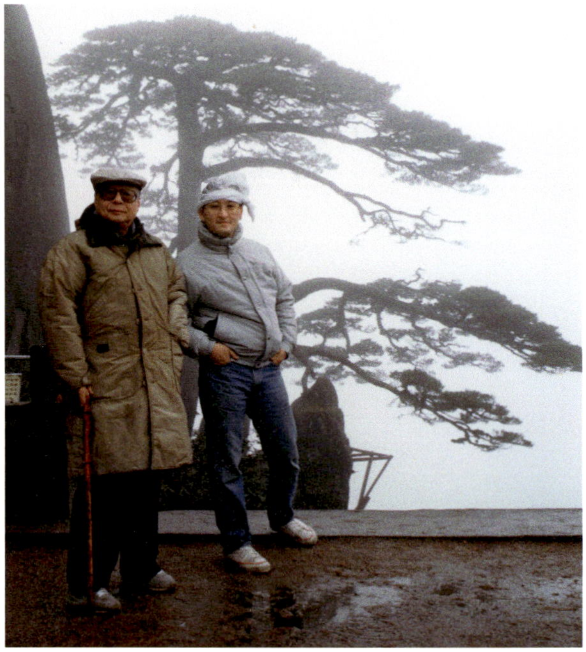

Fig. 3. C. C. Wang and Arnold Chang, Huangshan, Anhui, China, 1987.

The classes at the Chinese Culture Center were taught in English, but once C. C. discovered that I also could communicate in Mandarin, that became our default language, and from then on, I always addressed him as *Wang laoshi* 王老師 (Teacher Wang). I'm not sure if all the students benefited from these two classes as much as I did, but attending them changed the course of my life. I had just completed my master's degree in Asian studies at Berkeley and was preparing to enter the PhD program in art history to continue my education with James Cahill. The two classes at the Chinese Culture Center, however, made me realize that the study of the *history* of art did not satisfy my need to paint. I decided to postpone my entry into the doctoral program, travel back to my native New York City, and continue to learn painting technique and the "appreciation" of Chinese paintings from C. C. Wang. My plan was to study with him for a year or so and then reapply to Berkeley. Little did I know that I would remain C. C.'s student for the next twenty-five years, until his passing in 2003, and by that time Professor Cahill had already retired!

Meeting C. C. in San Francisco was the start of a decades-long conversation about Chinese painting and painters, and art in general, that extended to New York, Shanghai, Huangshan, Hong Kong, and beyond (fig. 3). Whenever we would meet up, whether we had seen each other the day before or hadn't seen each other for months, we would pick up our conversation from wherever we had left off.

For the first two or three years after moving back to New York in 1978, I spent at least two days a week at C. C.'s studio. In the morning I would arrive in his apartment building on 68th Street and Lexington Avenue—appropriately named Imperial House—wave to the doorman, traverse the gigantic lobby to the elevator, which was manned by a neatly attired attendant, and make my way up to the ninth floor. C. C., usually dressed in a casual indigo *yukata*, would greet me at the door, often holding a bunch of rolled-up scrolls under his arm. "Zhang Hong [my Chinese name], what would you like to paint today? (張洪你今天要畫什麼?)" I could not believe how fortunate I was!

I had anticipated that I would continue to learn painting techniques by copying C. C.'s own paintings, as I had in San Francisco, but when I arrived in New York he explained to me that to really learn to paint well I shouldn't just follow his style; rather, I should learn directly from the old masters by studying and copying their works. I should learn what makes them great and gradually develop my own style—find my own voice within the tradition. C. C.'s private collection of ancient Chinese paintings and calligraphy was world-renowned, and he possessed some of the greatest masterpieces by artists of the Song, Yuan, Ming, and Qing dynasties (dating from the eleventh to the nineteenth centuries). He invited me, on a weekly basis, to choose whatever original works I wanted to study and copy. It was like having an open invitation to an all-you-can-eat buffet at a five-star restaurant!

As a general rule, one day a week I chose to copy smaller works—album leaves or handscrolls—and the second day I would copy a larger hanging scroll. Although C. C. owned many fine Song-dynasty paintings, most of which were painted on silk, I was mostly drawn to works on paper derived from Yuan-dynasty styles. C. C. suggested that I initially concentrate on landscapes by the more conservative painters of the Qing-dynasty Orthodox School because their brushwork was extremely refined, but their compositions tended to be more orderly and easier to replicate. The ultimate goal of copying is not to make an exact facsimile of the original, but by retracing the original artist's methods you learn to internalize his creative process. Nevertheless, it is gratifying when you learn enough to capture the essential qualities of the original work.

Of all the copies that I made during those first few pivotal years of study with C. C. Wang, there is one that is particularly meaningful—a copy of an album of ten *Landscapes in the Manner of Old Masters* by the seventeenth-century painter Dong Qichang. This marvelous album is now in the collection of the Nelson-Atkins Museum of Art, but I was able to copy the original paintings when the album was still in C. C.'s collection. Over a period of several months, I made close freehand copies of each leaf. The most challenging leaf to copy was a landscape after the Yuan-dynasty master Wang Meng, particularly difficult because the composition is intricate and the unusual application of color adds an additional layer of complexity (figs. 4, 5).

I was pleased that I was able to produce a decent likeness of each of the original Dong Qichang album leaves, but more importantly, by copying them I was not only emulating Dong's own brushwork, I was also able to see the old masters through Dong's eyes. How did he internalize and transform the original

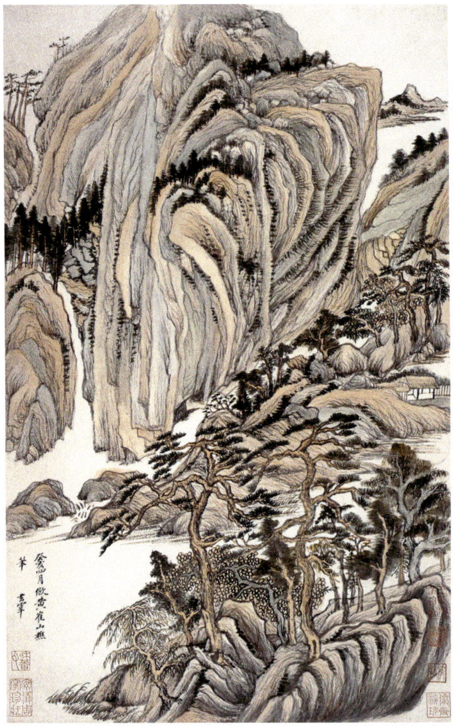

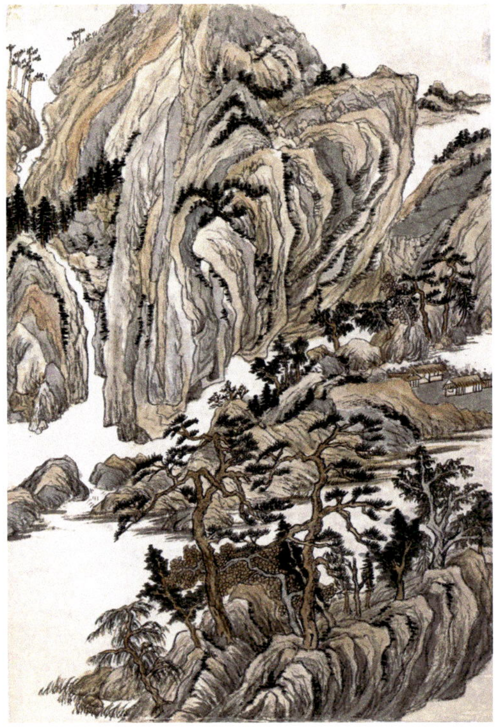

models into his own unique vision? How did he create an individual style that was personal but embodied the spirit of the old masters? I now had a deeper understanding of what I had previously known intellectually—to be a real artist I would have to be more than a copyist; I would need to transform my models and develop a personal style. Fortunately, I had C. C. as a guide.

During the decade of the 1980s, I was director of the Chinese Paintings Department at Sotheby's, responsible for worldwide auctions of Chinese paintings and calligraphy. C. C. was a consultant to the department. Together we helped to build the market for Chinese paintings in New York and Hong Kong. In this capacity we were able to view paintings together on a regular basis. C. C. did not compartmentalize his overlapping roles as connoisseur, collector, and creative artist, which, for him—like Chinese scholar-artists of the past—existed in a symbiotic relationship with one another. You learned to paint in order to better understand and appreciate paintings by past artists. Conversely, by understanding the work of great artists of the past, you could become a better painter.

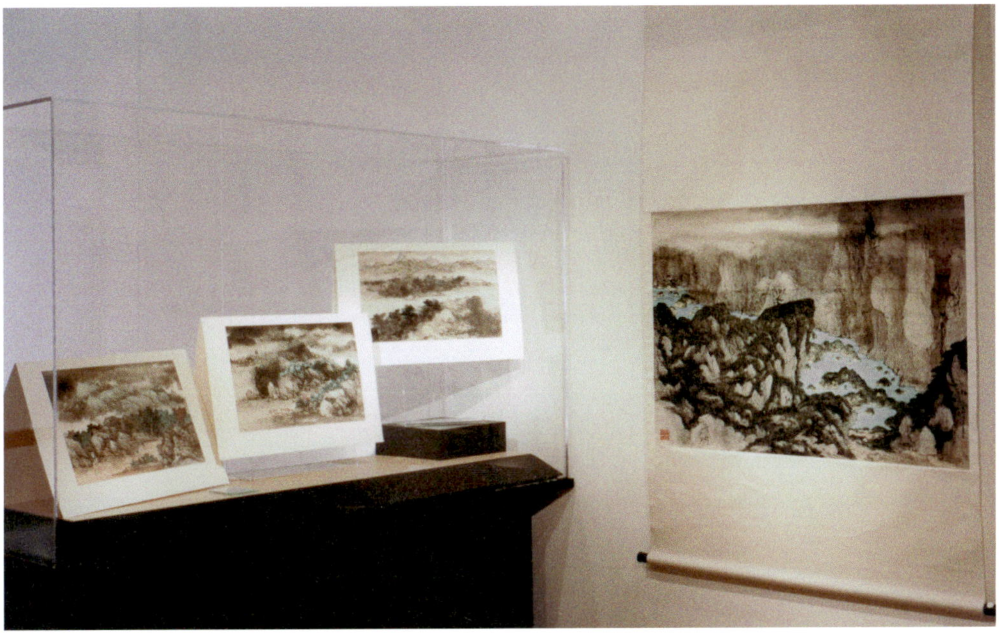

Fig. 4 (far left). Dong Qichang. *Landscape after Wang Meng*, from the series *Landscapes in the Manner of Old Masters*, 1621–24. Album leaf; ink and color on paper, 22 × 13 ¾ inches (55.9 × 34.9 cm). The Nelson-Atkins Museum of Art, Kansas City, Missouri. Purchase: acquired through the generosity of the Hall Family Foundation and the exchange of other Trust properties, 86-3/3.

Fig. 5 (left). Arnold Chang. Copy of Dong Qichang, *Landscape after Wang Meng*. One leaf from the series *Landscapes in the Manner of Old Masters* (1621–24), ca. 1980. Ink and color on paper, 25 × 17 inches (63.5 × 43.1 cm). Courtesy the artist.

Fig. 6 (above). *C. C. Wang at Ninety—A Kaikodo Celebration*, exhibition at Kaikodo Gallery, New York, spring 1997.

If you had the means to collect masterworks, this would provide the opportunity to study paintings firsthand and improve your connoisseurship. Although not blessed with the means to become a great collector, I was able to benefit vicariously through my study of C. C.'s collection, my position at Sotheby's, and C. C.'s guidance. I looked at paintings almost every day.

As time went on, I spent less time painting in C. C.'s studio, but we continued to view paintings together in preparation for Sotheby's auctions. After leaving Sotheby's in 1993, I worked at the Kaikodo gallery in New York and organized several exhibitions of contemporary Chinese ink painting, including a major show of C. C.'s work in celebration of his ninetieth birthday (fig. 6). I never stopped painting, but instead of just making copies, I began to create my own landscape compositions, at first greatly indebted to the old masters but gradually developing something approaching a personal style. My painting is still a work-in-progress in a never-ending journey. I am eternally grateful for the valuable mentorship and deep friendship C. C. shared with me for so many years. He taught me to see more deeply, and encouraged me to look beyond the obvious elements of subject matter and narrative content, to savor the flavor of the brushwork and decode the underlying logic of compositional structure.

Every so often, I will be sitting alone in my studio and I will hear a voice in my head: "Zhang Hong, what would you like to paint today?" And then we continue our conversation from wherever we had left off.

BIBLIOGRAPHY

Alexander, Zeynep Çelik. *Kinaesthetic Knowing: Aesthetics, Epistemology, Modern Design*. Chicago: University of Chicago Press, 2017.

Andrews, Julia, and Kuiyi Shen. *The Art of Modern China*. Berkeley: University of California Press, 2012.

Ashton, Leigh. "Some Notes on the Chinese Exhibition." *Burlington Magazine for Connoisseurs* 68, no. 395 (1936): 86–91.

Barnhart, Richard. "Chinese Calligraphy: The Inner World of the Brush." *Metropolitan Museum of Art Bulletin* 30, no. 5 (April–May 1972): 230–41.

———. "The Song Experiment with Mimesis." In *Bridges to Heaven: Essays on East Asian Art in Honor of Professor Wen C. Fong*, edited by Jerome Silbergeld et al., 1:115–40. Princeton, NJ: P. Y. and Kinmay W. Tang Center for East Asian Art, Department of Art and Archaeology, Princeton University, 2011.

Cahill, James. "Albert Skira and Chinese Painting." Accessed September 30, 2022. http://jamescahill.info/the-writings-of-james-cahill/responses-a-reminiscences/143-21albert-skira-and-chinese-painting.

———. *C. C. Wang: Landscape Paintings*. Seattle: Xi An Tang, 1986.

———. *Chinese Painting*. Geneva: Skira, 1960.

———. "London 1935/36 Exhibition: 'Early' Paintings from China." Accessed September 21, 2022. https://jamescahill.info/the-writings-of-james-cahill/london-193536-exhibition-early-paintings-from-china.

———. "The Orthodox Movement in Early Ch'ing Painting." In *Artists and Traditions: Uses of the Past in Chinese Culture*, edited by Christian F. Murck, 168–81. Princeton, NJ: Princeton University Press, 1976.

———. "The Place of the National Palace Museum in My Scholarly Career." Originally published in *Gugong wenwu yuekan* 故宮文物月刊 (National Palace Museum Monthly) 23, no. 8 (November 2005): 93–99. Accessed February 21, 2022. https://jamescahill.info/the-writings-of-james-cahill/cahill-lectures-and-papers/81-clp-117-2005.

———. "2004 Brief Talk Given at New York Chinese Scholar's Garden Society," April 27, 2004. Accessed August 14, 2022. https://jamescahill.info/the-writings-of-james-cahill/cahill-lectures-and-papers/61-clp-61-2004.

Cao, Baolin. "Self-Expression versus Tradition: Calligraphy of the Song, Jin, and Yuan Dynasties." In *Chinese Calligraphy*, edited by Wang Youfen, 241–302. New Haven, CT: Yale University Press; Beijing: Foreign Languages Press, 2008.

Chang, Arnold. "C. C. Wang at Ninety: A Kaikodo Celebration." *Kaikodo Journal* 3 (Spring 1997): 10–17.

———. "New York Rhythms, Suzhou Rhymes." Fu Qiumeng Fine Art, January 14, 2022. Accessed February 15, 2023. https://fuqiumeng.com/news/54-article-new-york-rhythms-suzhou-rhymes-author-arnold-chang/.

Chung, Anita. *Chinese Art in an Age of Revolution: Fu Baoshi (1904–1965)*. Cleveland: Cleveland Museum of Art; New Haven, CT: Yale University Press, 2012.

Cho, Frank Fulai. "The Question of Brushwork (Bi-Mo) in Chinese Painting." *Chinese American Forum* 12, no. 2 (October 1996): 3–10.

———. "Reminiscences of Mi Chou: The First Chinese Gallery in America." *Chinese American Forum* 1, no. 3 (May 1985): 4–8.

Cooper, Martha, and Henry Chalfant. *Subway Art*. New York City: Owl Books, Henry Holt, 1984.

Edwards, Richard. *The Painting of Tao-Chi*. Ann Arbor: Museum of Art, University of Michigan, 1967.

Fan, Liya. "The 1935 London International Exhibition of Chinese Art: The China Critic Reacts." *China Heritage Quarterly*, no. 30–31 (September 2012): 1–8.

Ferguson, John C. "Reflections on the London Exhibition of Chinese Art." *T'ien-Hsia Monthly* 2, no. 5 (May 1936): 433–42.

Foster, Hal et al. *Art Since 1900: Modernism, Antimodernism, Postmodernism*. New York: Thames & Hudson, 2016.

Giuffrida, Noelle. "The Right Stuff: Chinese Art Treasures' Landing in Early 1960s America." In *The Reception of Chinese Art across Cultures*, edited by Michelle Ying Ling Huang, 201–28. Newcastle upon Tyne: Cambridge Scholars Publishing, 2014.

Greenberg, Clement. "Towards a Newer Laocoön" *Partisan Review* 7, no. 4 (July–August 1940), 296-310.

Harrist, Robert E., Jr. *The Embodied Image: Chinese Calligraphy from the John B. Elliott Collection*. Princeton, NJ: Art Museum, Princeton University; New York: Harry N. Abrams, 1999.

Hay, John. *Kernels of Energy, Bones of Earth: The Rock in Chinese Art*. New York: China House Gallery, 1985.

Ho, Wai-kam, and Dawn Ho Delbanco. "Tung Ch'i-chang's Transcendence of History and Art." In *The Century of Tung Ch'i-ch'ang, 1555–1636*, edited by Wai-kam Ho, 3–41. Kansas City: Nelson-Atkins Museum of Art, 1992.

Hsio-yen Shih, Reginald William Finlayson, and Henry Trubner. *Catalogue of the Exhibition of Individualists and Eccentrics: The Mr. and Mrs. R. W. Finlayson Collection of Chinese Paintings*. Toronto: University of Toronto Press, 1963.

Hua, Ming. "Bridging the Tradition to the Modern, the East to the West: C. C. Wang and His Life in Art." PhD diss., Arizona State University, 2014.

Ju, Jane. "Chinese Art, the National Palace Museum, and Cold War Politics." In *Partisan Canons*, edited by Anna Brzyski, 115–34. Durham, NC: Duke University Press, 2007.

Larsen, Ingrid. "'Don't Send Ming or Later Pictures': Charles Lang Freer and the First Major Collection of Chinese Painting in an American Museum." *Ars Orientalis* 40 (2011): 6–38.

Li Tung-keung 李東強. "Professor Wang Jiqian 王季遷老師." In *Department of Fine Arts at 50*, 33. Hong Kong: Department of Fine Arts, Chinese University of Hong Kong, 2007.

Metropolitan Museum of Art. "Metropolitan Museum Acquires Twenty-Five Important Chinese Paintings." Press release, July 13, 1973. Museum Archives.

Mountains of the Mind: The Landscapes of C. C. Wang. Washington, DC: A. M. Sackler Foundation, 1977.

Ouyang, Zhongshi. Introduction to *Chinese Calligraphy*, edited by Wang Youfen, 33–46. New Haven, CT: Yale University Press; Beijing: Foreign Languages Press, 2008.

Pacific Heritage Museum. *The Living Brush: Four Masters of Contemporary Chinese Calligraphy; C. C. Wang, Wang Fangyu, Tseng Yuho, Grace Tong*. Exh. cat. San Francisco: American Asian Cultural Exchange Pacific, 1997.

Pope, John Alexander, Aschwin Lippe, and James Cahill. *Chinese Art Treasures*. Exh. cat. Geneva: Skira, 1961.

Seitz, William C. *Abstract Expressionist Painting in America*. Cambridge, MA: Harvard University Press, 1983.

Shen, Fu, and Jan Stuart. C*hallenging the Past: The Paintings of Chang Dai-chien*. Washington, DC: Arthur M. Sackler Gallery, Smithsonian Institution; Seattle: University of Washington Press, 1991.

Siegel, Katy ed. *Abstract Expressionism*. London: Phaidon, 2011.

Silbergeld, Jerome. *Chinese Painting Style: Media, Methods, and Principles of Form*. Seattle: University of Washington Press, 1982.

———. *Mind Landscapes: The Paintings of C. C. Wang*. Seattle: Henry Art Gallery and University of Washington Press, 1987.

Smith, Judith G., and Wen Fong, eds. *Issues of Authenticity in Chinese Painting*. New York: Department of Asian Art, Metropolitan Museum of Art, 1999.

Stanley-Baker, Joan [Xu Xiaohu 徐小虎]. *Hua yu lu: Wang Jiqian jiao ni kan dong Zhongguo shu hua* 畫語錄：王季遷教你看懂中國書畫 (C. C. Wang reflects on painting). Taipei: Diancang yishu jiating gufen youxian gongsi, 2013.

———. “The Last Literatus.” *Asian Pacific Quarterly of Cultural and Social Affairs* 6 (1974): 1–15.

Steuber, Jason. “The Exhibition of Chinese Art at Burlington House, London, 1935–36.” *Burlington Magazine* 148, no. 1241 (August 2006): 528–36.

Stuart, Jan. “C. C. Wang: Singing Brush and Dancing Ink.” *Arts of Asia* 32, no. 3 (May 2002): 44–52.

von Spee, Clarissa. “Victoria Contag: Pioneer, Scholar and Collector of Chinese Paintings.” In *Modern Chinese Painting and Europe: New Perceptions, Artists* [sic] *Encounters, and the Formation of Collections*, edited by Michaela Pejčochová and Clarissa von Spee, 61–80. Berlin: Reimer, 2017.

———. *Wu Hufan: A Twentieth Century Art Connoisseur in Shanghai*. Berlin: Reimer, 2008.

———. “Wu Hufan, Victoria Contag, and C. C. Wang—A Passion for Paintings and a Lifelong Friendship.” Lecture recorded April 27, 2019. Accessed February 10, 2022. https://www.youtube.com/watch?v=Dmc8z7nJ3y0.

Wang, Cheng-hua. “New Printing Technology and Heritage Preservation: Collotype Reproduction of Antiquities in Modern China, circa 1908–1917.” In *The Role of Japan in Modern Chinese Art*, edited by Joshua Fogel, 273–308, 363–72. Berkeley: University of California Press, 2013.

Wang, Chi-ch'ien. “The Importance of Brushwork in Chinese Painting.” *Kaikodo Journal* 21 (Autumn 2001): 27–39.

———. “Ni Yunlin shengping ji shiwen 倪雲林生平及詩文 (The life and writing of Ni Tsan).” *Gugong jikan* 故宮季刊 1, no. 2 (October 1966): 29–42.

———. “Ni Yunlin zhi hua 倪雲林之畫” (Paintings by Ni Tsan). *Gugong jikan* 故宮季刊 2, no. 1 (April 1967): 53–54.

———. “Notes on Calligraphy and Painting,” August 1999. Accessed November 16, 2022. http://www.echinaart.com/Advisor/adv_ccwang_landscape.htm.

———. “Rare Rocks Are God's Creations.” In *The Spirit of Gongshi: Chinese Scholar's Rocks*, edited by Keming Hu, 16. Newton, MA: L. H., 1999.

———. *Recent Works*. New York: EastWest Studios, 1993.

———. *Wang Jiqian shu hua guo yan lu* 王季迁书画过眼录 (Works of painting and calligraphy seen by C. C. Wang). Shanghai: Shanghai shuhua chubanshe, 2021.

———, and Victoria Contag. *Ming-Qing huajia yinjian* 明清畫家印鑑 / *Maler-und sammler-stempel aus der Ming-und Ch'ing-zeit*. Shanghai: Shangwu, 1940.

———. *Seals of Chinese Painters and Collectors of the Ming and Qing Periods*. Rev. ed. Hong Kong: Hong Kong University Press, 1966.

Wang, David Der-wei. “In the Name of the Real.” In *Chinese Art: Modern Expressions*, edited by Maxwell K. Hearn, 28–59. New York: Metropolitan Museum of Art, 2001.

Wang, Youfen ed. *Chinese Calligraphy*. New Haven, CT: Yale University Press; Beijing: Foreign Languages Press, 2008.

Weatherby, Meredith, ed. *Mountains of the Mind: The Landscape Painting of Wang Chi-ch'ien*. New York: Weatherhill, 1970.

Whitfield, Roderick. *In Pursuit of Antiquity: Chinese Paintings of the Ming and Ch'ing Dynasties from the Collection of Mr. and Mrs. Earl Morse*. Princeton, NJ: Art Museum, Princeton University, 1969.

Yang, Kathleen, ed. *Through A Chinese Connoisseur's Eye: Private Notes of C. C. Wang*. Beijing: Zhonghua shuju, 2010.

________. Wang Jiqian Duhua Biji 王季遷讀畫筆記 (Through a Chinese connoisseur's eye: private notes of C. C. Wang) Beijing: Zhonghua shuju, 2010.

Yee, Chiang. *Chinese Calligraphy: An Introduction to Its Aesthetic and Technique*. Cambridge, MA: Harvard University Press, 1938.

Yeung, Mei Lan. “A New Traditionalist: C. C. Wang the Artist.” Master's thesis, Ohio State University, 2006.

Young, Martie W., et. al. *The Eccentric Painters of China*. Ithaca, NY: Andrew Dickson White Museum of Art, Cornell University, 1965.

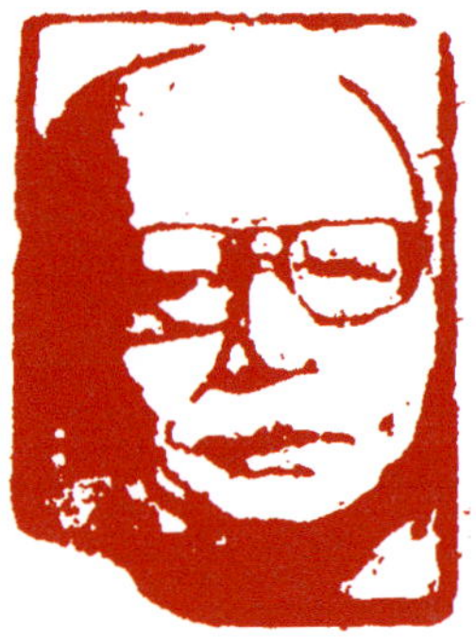

ACKNOWLEDGMENTS

C. C. Wang: Lines of Abstraction is the outcome of a year-long curatorial seminar at Hunter College and a semester-long seminar at the University of Minnesota. To understand Wang's multifaceted commitment to artistic practice, we have made invaluable connections with an extraordinary community of artists, scholars, and collectors in New York City, especially in and around the Upper East Side, where Wang lived and worked for most of his life, sometimes within a stone's throw from Hunter's Leubsdorf Gallery on 68th Street. We are deeply grateful to our lenders and acknowledge the extended community in which C. C. Wang's artistic legacy continues to live.

We are indebted to the MA students who provided support and who participated in the curatorial seminar that shaped *Lines of Abstraction*: Thais Bignardi-Engstrom, Carolyn Bishop, Rawls Bolton, Jeremy Gloster, Sophie Kaufman, Emerald Lucas, Lindsey Poremba, Jennie Tang, Mia Ye, and especially Margaret Liu Clinton, Hofmann Graduate Curatorial Fellow, who infused every aspect of our collective scholarship with her passion for brushwork and activism.

A project anchored on the art of C. C. Wang could not be accomplished without a rethinking of the history and historiography of Chinese painting as well as the local histories of Shanghai, New York, and many other cities where C. C. lived and worked. To this end, we relied on the insights, critiques, and memories of C. C. Wang's family and former students as well as those of colleagues and scholars. We are especially grateful to Yien-koo King, Ray King, Arnold Chang, Kathleen Yang, Freda Murck, Jerome Silbergeld, Wang Shaofang, Pao Yung Chao, and Fu Qiumeng for their unwavering support on all fronts; Joan Stanley-Baker, Patricia Berger, Ellen Huang, David Sensabaugh, Joseph Scheier-Dolberg, Liz Hammer, Jennifer Perry, Margaret Tao, Martie Young, Michele Matteini, and Rosaline Kyo, and Julia White for providing invaluable sources and perspectives; and Sarah Cahill, Carol Conover, Joan Cummins, Cary Liu, Stephanie Cassidy, Ling-en Lu, Diana Edkins, Tellie Simpson, and Ming Hua for access to collections, photographs, and archival materials. We are equally indebted to our colleagues at Hunter, especially Lynda Klich and Tara Zanardi, for feedback on the introductory essay; and Nebahat Avcioglu, Emily Braun, Cynthia Hahn, Michael

Left: C. C. Wang began to use this portrait seal in the late 1980s on his experimental and abstract works. Seals inscribed with a name or official title have long been understood as the veritable identification of their owner. The seal's impression marks the presence of an artist or collector directly on the artwork. Wang's self-portrait brings a modern, cheeky physicality to this practice—looking out from the surface of his art to watch the viewer engage with his work.

Lobel, Harper Montgomery, Antonella Pelizzari, and Howard Singerman for their guidance on the curatorial practicum and exhibition planning.

Lines of Abstraction could not have been realized without the generous support of the Wolf Kahn Foundation and Emily Mason and the Alice Trumbull Mason Foundation on behalf of the artists Emily Mason and Wolf Kahn, the James Howell Foundation, the Renate, Hans, and Maria Hofmann Trust, and the Leubsdorf Fund. Furthermore, this publication would not be possible without the partnership of the University of Minnesota, Twin Cities and the Weisman Art Museum.

The catalogue owes its thoughtful and creative design to Natalie Wedeking. Mary Cason provided swift and thorough copyediting; Kunhua Liu rendered precise translation of seals and inscriptions; and Stan Narten comprehensively photographed the works in this publication.

At the Hunter College Art Galleries, Sarah Watson, Chief Curator and Director of Administration, expertly shepherded the exhibition and publication from beginning to end; Anna Lee, Exhibitions and Programs Coordinator, went above and beyond to facilitate loans and documentation of artworks from our lenders. We would also like to acknowledge the following individuals whose energy and commitment have been integral to the success of *C. C. Wang: Lines of Abstraction*: Howard Singerman, Phyllis and Joseph Caroff Chair of the Department of Art and Art History and Executive Director of the Hunter College Art Galleries; Joachim Pissarro, Bershad Professor and Director; Tara Ohanian, Gallery Manager; Harper Montgomery, Director of the Advanced Certificate for Curatorial Studies; and the installation team of Head Preparator Phi Nguyen and art handlers Joe Gannon and George Simonds. Finally, we express our gratitude to Hunter College President Jennifer J. Raab and Dean Andrew J. Polsky for their ongoing support of the Advanced Certificate for Curatorial Studies and the Hunter College Art Galleries.

Wen-shing Chou

Associate Professor of Art History
Hunter College and the Graduate Center, The City University of New York

Daniel M. Greenberg

Assistant Professor of Art History
University of Minnesota, Twin Cities

Published in association with the exhibition
C. C. Wang: Lines of Abstraction
The Bertha and Karl Leubsdorf Gallery
February 2–April 29, 2023
Curated by Wen-shing Chou and Daniel M. Greenberg with Hofmann Graduate Curatorial Fellow Margaret Liu Clinton

C. C. Wang: Lines of Abstraction was developed through a two-semester curatorial seminar at Hunter College led by Professor Wen-shing Chou with MA Art History students Thais Bignardi-Engstrom, Carolyn Bishop, Rawls Bolton, Jeremy Gloster, Sophie Kaufman, Margaret Liu Clinton, Emerald Lucas, Lindsey Poremba, and Mia Ye.

C. C. Wang Lines of Abstraction is published in collaboration with the Weisman Art Museum at the University of Minnesota and is made possible by the Wolf Kahn Foundation and Emily Mason and Alice Trumbull Mason Foundation on behalf of artists Emily Mason and Wolf Kahn.

HUNTER COLLEGE
ART GALLERIES

WAM
UNIVERSITY OF MINNESOTA

WOLF KAHN
FOUNDATION

EMILY MASON
ALICE TRUMBULL MASON

Published by:
Hirmer Verlag GmbH
Bayerstra.e 57-59
80335 Munich
Germany

Edited by:
Wen-shing Chou and Daniel M. Greenberg

Authors:
Thais Bignardi-Engstrom
Carolyn Bishop
Arnold Chang
Wen-shing Chou
Margaret Liu Clinton
Jeremy Gloster
Daniel M. Greenberg
Jordan Homstad
Lindsey Poremba
Joseph Scheier-Dolberg
Mia Ye

Editorial Management, Hunter College Art Galleries: Sarah Watson and Anna Lee

Design and visual editing: Natalie Wedeking

Senior Editor, Hirmer Publishers:
Elisabeth Rochau-Shalem

Project Manager, Hirmer Publishers: Rainer Arnold

Copyediting and proofreading: Mary Cason

Translating: Kunhua Liu, with additional translations provided by Kathleen Yang

Pre-press: Reproline Mediateam, Munich

Printed and bound: Grafisches Centrum Cuno, Calbe

This book is typeset in Minion Pro and Adobe Fangsong R

The paper is Primaset 150 g/sqm

Printed in Germany

ISBN 978-3-7774-4103-0

Bibliographic information published by the Deutsche Nationalbibliothek
The Deutsche Nationalbibliothek lists this publication in the Deutsche Nationalbibliografie; detailed bibliographic data is available on the Internet at http://www.dnb.de.

www.huntercollegeartgalleries.org
www.hirmerpublishers.com

The Bertha and Karl Leubsdorf Gallery
Hunter West Building
132 E. 68th Street
New York, New York 10065
www.leubsdorfgallery.org

Owing to the artist's personal preferences, there are works for which titles were clearly identified, and other works for which they were assigned by an exhibitor. With a fidelity to the artist's practice, as well as each work's exhibition history, several works appear in this publication without titles but may include descriptors set within parentheses.

Photo Credits
All works by C. C. Wang are © the Estate of C. C. Wang. All other works reproduced are © the artist(s) or their estates. Every effort has been made to trace rights holders and obtain permissions for the use of copyrighted material. If there are errors or omissions, please contact Hunter College Art Galleries. Photos by Stan Narten unless stated otherwise below.

Page 12: image courtesy National Palace Museum, Taipei. K2A000967N000000000PA; 14: image courtesy The Metropolitan Museum of Art, New York; 15: (left) image courtesy The Palace Museum, Beijing, (right) image courtesy The Art Institute of Chicago / Art Resource, New York; 17: image courtesy The Archives of the Art Students League of New York; 18: image courtesy Princeton University Art Museum. Photo: Bruce M. White; 20: (left) image courtesy The Harvard Art Museums / Arthur M. Sackler Museum. Copyright © The Liu Kuo-sung Archives. Photo © President and Fellows of Harvard College, 2013.159; 22, 23 (left): image courtesy National Palace Museum, Taipei, K2A000826N000000000PAA; 26, 76, 110, 114, 115: image courtesy Private Collection and Fu Qiumeng Fine Art, New York. Photo: Yunqian Lin; 52: image courtesy Private Collection; 95, 100: image courtesy Yien-koo King; 96, 129–30, 132, 134 (right), 135: image courtesy Arnold Chang; 101: image courtesy Freer Gallery of Art and the Arthur M. Sackler Gallery Archives. Photo: Ming Hua, PhD; 102, 106: image courtesy UC Berkeley, Berkeley Art Museum and Pacific Film Archive; 103: image courtesy Center for Creative Photography, University of Arizona. Photo © 1991 Hans Namuth Estate; 104: photo: Joseph Scheier-Dolberg; 105: image courtesy © Whitney Museum of American Art / Licensed by Scala, Florence / Art Resource, NY. © 2023 Mark Tobey / Seattle Art Museum, Artists Rights Society (ARS), New York; 111: image courtesy National Archives & Records Administration, photo no. 553823; 114: image courtesy The Richard C. Carpenter Collection; New York Transit Museum, New York. Photo: New York Transit Museum, New York; 121: image courtesy Sarah Cahill; 123–24: image courtesy The Metropolitan Museum of Art; 134 (left): image courtesy The Nelson-Atkins Museum of Art, Kansas City, Missouri. Photo: Nelson-Atkins Media Services.

Cover
Detail of no title (Abstract Work with Blue and Green), 1998, pl. 16.